THE DOCTRINE OF PRIVITY IN NEGLIGENCE

This book traces the path of the doctrine of privity in negligence, from inception to its famous ousting in *Donoghue v Stevenson* in 1932.

It begins with the origins of negligence's privity rule in the Industrial Revolution, before considering pressure points for change in the early 20th century, including rising consumerism and the array of issues faced by married women when suing on a contract. This book challenges the orthodox story that products-based claims in tort were a rarity in English law prior to *Donoghue* because of the privity bar. Viewed within this narrative, Mrs Donoghue's claim is a tipping point rather than a revolution.

Volume 61 in the series Hart Studies in Private Law

Hart Studies in Private Law

This monograph series brings together in one place two types of book: works which examine in-depth the fundamental doctrines and principles of private law, and works which engage with the theoretical underpinnings of private law. The series thus aims to contribute to ever-evolving debates about the nature of private law such as problems of classification and taxonomy, remedies, the relationship with public law and the boundaries of private law generally.

The series includes, but is not confined to, works on contract, tort, unjust enrichment, equity, property and the conflict of laws, welcoming work which intersects with other fields of study to enable a deeper understanding of private law theory and practice.

The Doctrine of Privity in Negligence

Understanding the Path to Donoghue v Stevenson

Emily Gordon

•HART•
OXFORD • LONDON • NEW YORK • NEW DELHI • SYDNEY

HART PUBLISHING

Bloomsbury Publishing Plc

Kemp House, Chawley Park, Cumnor Hill, Oxford, OX2 9PH, UK

1385 Broadway, New York, NY 10018, USA

Bloomsbury Publishing Ireland Limited, 29 Earlsfort Terrace, Dublin 2, D02 AY28, Ireland

HART PUBLISHING, the Hart/Stag logo, BLOOMSBURY and the Diana logo are trademarks of Bloomsbury Publishing Plc

First published in Great Britain 2026

A catalogue record for this book is available from the British Library.

A catalogue record for this book is available from the Library of Congress.

Library of Congress Control Number: 2026934313

ISBN: HB: 978-1-50998-764-1
ePDF: 978-1-50998-766-5
ePub: 978-1-50998-765-8

Typeset by Compuscript Ltd, Shannon

For product safety related questions contact productsafety@bloomsbury.com

To find out more about our authors and books visit www.hartpublishing.co.uk. Here you will find extracts, author information, details of forthcoming events and the option to sign up for our newsletters.

ACKNOWLEDGEMENTS

I owe a significant debt of gratitude to a number of people and institutions.

This book is based on a doctoral thesis I completed at the University of Cambridge. It would not have been possible to do this research without the generous financial support I was fortunate to receive in the form of the Maitland Studentship in Legal History from the FW Maitland Memorial Fund and the Hollond–Whittaker Research Studentship in Law from Trinity College. I am grateful to the Managers of the Maitland Fund and to Trinity College and its Fellows.

I would like to express my heartfelt thanks to my PhD supervisor, Professor David Ibbetson. It was a real privilege to be supervised by David. During my doctoral studies, and in the years afterwards, he has been unfailingly generous in offering his time and advice. His contribution to this book is very significant. He also welcomed me into his academic family, where I found friends for life.

I would like to thank my PhD examiners, Professor Paul Mitchell and Dr Colm McGrath, for their very helpful comments, advice and continued support over the years. I am also grateful to Professor Jonathan Morgan, Dr Joe Sampson and Dr Benjamin Spagnolo for their comments on earlier drafts of this work. I am also indebted to the other scholars who have provided helpful comments, or simply encouragement, at the forums at which I presented this work.

Thanks must go to the staff at the Squire Law Library for their help with scanning services during the periods of lockdown in the COVID pandemic. I am grateful also for the assistance provided by the archivists at the Aviva Group Archive in Norwich.

Finally, my wonderful family – Tom, Matilda, Felix, Mum and Dad – I dedicate this book to you. Thank you for your patience, support and encouragement.

CONTENTS

TABLE OF CASES

TABLE OF STATUTES

Introduction

Much has been written already about the famous case of *Donoghue v Stevenson*.[1] Accordingly, this book will, at first glance, appear to tread well-worn ground. However, the focus of this book is not the development of a generalised principle for liability in negligence. Rather, it is concerned with better understanding the other reason for which *Donoghue* is considered a landmark case: the abandonment, by the House of Lords, of the doctrine of privity in the law of negligence, and the recognition of a duty of care owed by manufacturers of goods to their ultimate consumers.

Liability for products during the nineteenth and early twentieth centuries has received some attention but there is still more to be learned. This is particularly true of the apparently 'silent' period between *Blacker v Lake and Elliot*[2] in 1912 and *Donoghue* in 1932, a period in which most treatments of this area suggest the law was relatively settled. The House of Lords in *Donoghue* certainly concentrated on English precedents before the mid-1910s, and referred to very few decided in the 20 years before *Donoghue*. The traditional narrative has been that in the United Kingdom 'there was no significant volume of tort-based product claims until the rejection of the privity bar, in 1932'.[3]

This book uncovers the path of privity in the law of negligence and reveals, in particular, why it was in 1932 that the doctrine was finally ousted by *Donoghue*. In so doing, it also provides an explanation of part of Lord Macmillan's speech in *Donoghue* and thereby helps us better to understand this key case. In setting out some 'preliminary observations',[4] Lord Macmillan said:

> Where, as in cases like the present, so much depends upon the avenue of approach to the question, it is very easy to take the wrong turning. If you begin with the sale by the manufacturer to the retail dealer, then the consumer who purchases from the retailer is at once seen to be a stranger to the contract between the retailer and the manufacturer and so disentitled to sue upon it. There is no contractual relation between the manufacturer and the consumer; and thus *the plaintiff, if he is to succeed, is driven to try to bring himself within one or other of the exceptional cases where the strictness of the rule that none but a party to a contract can found on a breach of that contract has been mitigated in the public interest, as it has been in the case of a person who issues a*

[1] *Donoghue v Stevenson* [1932] AC 562. See, for recent examples in celebration of the 90th anniversary of the case, 'Donoghue v Stevenson – The Immortal Snail – 90th Anniversary Conference Papers' (The Continuing Legal Education Society of British Columbia, Vancouver, 2022).

[2] *Blacker v Lake and Elliot* (1912) 106 LT 533.

[3] J Stapleton, *Product Liability* (Butterworths, 1994) 20.

[4] *Donoghue* (n 1) 612.

> *chattel which is inherently dangerous or which he knows to be in a dangerous condition.* If, on the other hand, you disregard the fact that the circumstances of the case at one stage include the existence of a contract of sale between the manufacturer and the retailer, and approach the question by asking whether there is evidence of carelessness on the part of the manufacturer, and whether he owed a duty to be careful … the circumstance that the injured party was not a party to the incidental contract of sale becomes irrelevant, and his title to sue the manufacturer is unaffected by that circumstance (emphasis added).[5]

This book reveals a story sitting behind these words, filling a gap in our understanding of *Donoghue*. Contrary to the traditional narrative, there was a significant body of tort-based product claims before English courts prior to 1932 – moreover, these frequently met with success. The decision in *Donoghue*, though often described as a landmark case in which an innovative and bold majority unshackled the law of negligence from the constraints of privity, may be seen as occupying, to an extent, a formalising role in bringing doctrine into line with existing practice.

The Approach Adopted in this Study

Two cases serve as bookends for this study: *Winterbottom v Wright*[6] in 1842, and *Donoghue* in 1932. Though not the first to apply privity to the question of tortious duties,[7] it was *Winterbottom* that brought privity into prominence in the law of tort. It will, however, at times be necessary to go a little outside these defined markers, if only to clarify what is happening in the time between them.

Legal development often is, and justifiably can be, studied on its own, without looking at the social, political or economic context in which it occurs.[8] However, as Ibbetson notes, there are merits to looking outside a legal system as well:

> [The] wholly justifiable purely internal foci when we are describing legal change can lead seductively to a theorisation of legal history which is entirely internal, separate from anything that is happening in other places and governed entirely by its own internal logic; and this is not something that can be accepted uncritically (or, indeed, at all), any more than can a theorisation of legal history in which law is seen as a crude mechanistic response to changes in social or economic configurations.[9]

[5] ibid 611.

[6] *Winterbottom v Wright* (1842) 10 M & W 109, 11 LJ Ex 415, 152 ER 402.

[7] See, eg, *Tollit v Sherstone* (1839) 5 M & W 283, 151 ER 120, discussed in V Palmer, 'Why Privity Entered Tort – An Historical Re-Examination of Winterbottom v Wright' (1983) 27 *American Journal of Legal History* 85, 86. In *Winterbottom*, counsel also made reference to a pleading from the late-eighteenth century, '8 Wentworth 397', in which the issue of a third party action arose: see J Wentworth, *A Complete System of Pleading* (vol 8, 1799) 397. The issues in *Winterbottom* may therefore go back to the eighteenth century.

[8] DJ Ibbetson, 'Comparative legal history: A methodology' in A Musson and C Stebbings (eds), *Making Legal History* (Cambridge University Press, 2012) 131. See also discussion in R Cotterrell, *The Sociology of the Law*, 2nd edn (Butterworths, 1992) 2, 17.

[9] Ibbetson, 'Comparative legal history' (n 8) 132 (references omitted).

This is an idea that would be rejected by many modern private lawyers, who prefer an understanding of legal development and decision-making based on internal factors and notions of corrective justice.[10] Indeed, even Milsom might be understood as having adopted an approach to legal history focused on factors internal to the legal system.[11] Central arguments advanced in this book reject any 'closed system' view of the law. It will be argued that, as early as the 1830s, judges were reaching decisions based upon consideration of the *consequences* of extensions of liability. It will also be suggested that factors external, as well as internal, were important in bringing about a change in 1932 to the legal rules concerning suits in negligence.

This book adopts a framework that examines privity in the law of negligence by approaching the law at two levels: it considers both the formal law, the law 'in the books' – legal doctrine as accepted in treatises and authoritative appellate cases; and, the law 'in practice' – the legal outcomes reached before the lower courts.[12] At this second level, it is interesting to examine not just the decisions of courts, but also the outcomes negotiated by the parties in expectation of the result.[13] These are the focus of chapter four and chapter five. The approach adopted in this book is, in part, akin to that which Milsom suggested would be fruitful in relation to much earlier time periods, namely looking to the way lawyers choose to frame their clients' claims:

> Lawyers have always been preoccupied with today's details, and have worked with their eyes down. The historian, if he is lucky, can see why a rule came into existence, what change left it working injustice, how it came to be evaded, how the evasion produced a new rule, and sometimes how that new rule in its turn came to be overtaken by change. But he misunderstands it all if he endows the lawyers who took part with vision on any comparable scale, or attributes to them any intention beyond getting today's client out of his difficulty.[14]

Behind the apparently static formal words of the law may lie practices that are slowly changing or developing new principles.

There is, then, a third factor of which legal historians need to be aware: context, both inside and outside the law.[15] Certain legal and extra-legal developments can either apply pressure on the legal system to change or remove the pressure for change by creating alternative routes for resolving disputes.[16] These factors may

[10] See, eg, A Beever, *Rediscovering the Law of Negligence* (Hart Publishing, 2007); EJ Weinrib, *Corrective Justice* (Oxford University Press, 2012).

[11] See SFC Milsom, *A Natural History of the Common Law* (Columbia University Press, 2003). See also Ibbetson, 'Comparative legal history' (n 8) 132.

[12] See J Bell and D Ibbetson, *European Level Development: The Case of Tort* (Cambridge University Press, 2012) 45; Ibbetson, 'Comparative legal history' (n 8) 135–36.

[13] Bell and Ibbetson (n 12) 45.

[14] SFC Milsom, *Historical Foundations of the Common* Law, 2nd edn (Oxford University Press, 2009) 7.

[15] Bell and Ibbetson (n 12) 46, 49.

[16] See ibid, 49; Ibbetson, 'Comparative legal history' (n 8) 142–43.

give us a good indication of why a legal change occurred but not necessarily *when* – for this, we need to identify what Ibbetson describes as the 'tipping point, the straw that breaks the camel's back'.[17]

It may be impossible to describe with absolute certainty the reasons for a particular legal change at a particular time. What this book seeks to achieve using the approach just described is not to discover mechanical causality but instead to identify certain social, economic and political factors which, together with developments within the law, contributed to a climate in which that 'final straw' resulted in the removal of privity from negligence.

Extensive use will be made in this study of material reported in newspapers.[18] Newspapers are particularly useful for a study of this period as law reporting in the early twentieth century was incomplete. Outside what is recorded in newspapers and journals, there are scant records of pleadings and the majority of decisions made by courts went unreported. The coverage of cases in newspapers, even if sometimes light on technical legal detail, enables us to identify and appreciate patterns of claims on a large scale, rather than only through the highly selective lens of cases chosen for publication in the law reports. For the same reason, case reports and contemporary commentary reported in the *Solicitors' Journal* will also be relied upon in this study. This periodical was first published in 1857, the first edition declaring that its purpose was to represent solicitors, 'reflecting their opinions, watching over their interests and reputation, and urging upon the legislature and the nation their just and reasonable demands'.[19] It was created and written by solicitors, to be read by solicitors,[20] its contents including opinion pieces, excerpts of statutory instruments, and summaries of noteworthy decisions. It thus enables the legal historian to appreciate the legal principles and issues discussed by, and known to, the majority of those actually advising clients in the formulation of their claims. Drawing on this material, chapter four uncovers product liability cases from the 1910s and 1920s that were hidden as a result of the selective reporting. This evidence, together with the arguments advanced in chapter five to explain it, forms a significant new contribution to our knowledge of the law during this period in history and our understanding of the role and significance of *Donoghue*.

The focus of this book is the English law of negligence. However, *Donoghue* was, of course, a Scottish case. Scottish case law is explored in this book to a limited extent, and for the purpose of understanding how, in the late 1920s and early 1930s, the tipping point developed. The idea, accepted in *Donoghue*, that English and Scottish law were the same[21] is not without problems, but this is beyond the scope

[17] Ibbetson, 'Comparative legal history' (n 8) 140.

[18] This is sourced principally from the digitised collections of British newspapers available in the British Newspaper Archive (*British Newspaper Archive*: British Library, www.britishnewspaperarchive.co.uk/) and *The Times* Digital Archive (*The Times Digital Archive, 1785–2014*, Gale Cengage).

[19] 'The Solicitors' Journal' (1857) 1 *Solicitors' Journal and Reporter* 1.

[20] ibid.

[21] *Donoghue* (n 1) 566, 602–03, 618, 621.

of this work. It might be thought that if there were any major current of Scottish law contrary to English law, we could expect Lord Macmillan in *Donoghue*, as well as Rodger[22] and McBryde,[23] to have examined its significance in detail.[24]

Occasional reference will also be made to American case law. However, this will be done only to the extent that it advances our understanding of English developments. It is well known that American case law was influential in the developing law of negligence.[25] As the privity rule was removed from American negligence law earlier[26] in the twentieth century than it was from English law, a comparative analysis of the fortunes of privity may be an interesting and fruitful exercise for the future. However, such an exercise is beyond the scope of the present enquiry.

Outline

Chapter one provides an overview of the legal landscape and key case law from the introduction of the privity rule in the mid-nineteenth century through to *Donoghue* in 1932. Chapter two explains the decision in *Winterbottom* and adds value to the current literature on the orthodox story by developing our understanding of the treatment, in subsequent case law, of *Winterbottom* and the privity rule. It is argued that a close reading of *Winterbottom* and later cases reveals a shift, over time, from policy, or consequence-based, reasoning to doctrinal thinking. The doctrine of privity was introduced into the developing law by a court primarily concerned to limit the scope of negligence liability and to protect manufacturers, but towards the end of the nineteenth century, a strict privity rule had formed. The consequence-based arguments which had been persuasive in favour of the rule's imposition in 1842 had weakened in the new century and a tension developed, in the time before *Donoghue*, between doctrine and policy. Though chapter two discusses the use of consequence-based reasoning by courts concerned with the scope of a burgeoning area of tort law, the primary focus is not upon the particular backgrounds, preferences or political persuasions of individual judges involved in key cases. There is valuable knowledge to be gained

[22] A Rodger, 'Lord Macmillan's speech in Donoghue v Stevenson' (1992) 108 *Law Quarterly Review* 236.

[23] See, eg, WW McBryde, 'Donoghue v Stevenson: The Story of the 'Snail in the Bottle' Case' in AJ Gamble (ed), *Obligations in Context: Essays in Honour of Professor DM Walker* (Edinburgh W Green, 1990).

[24] Though see, on this, and more recently, J Brown, 'The Mouse and the Snail: Reappraising the Significance of *Donoghue v Stevenson*: Part One – A Case Worth Celebrating?' (2022) 35 *Scots Law Times* 229, and subsequent parts.

[25] DJ Ibbetson, 'The Tort of Negligence in the Common Law in the Nineteenth and Twentieth Centuries' in E Schrage (ed), *Negligence: The Comparative Legal History of the Law of Torts* (Duncker & Humblot, 2001) 229.

[26] *MacPherson v Buick Motor Company* (1916) 217 NY 382, 111 NE 1050.

through such enquiries.[27] However, the focus in chapter two is on a close reading of nineteenth-century and early twentieth-century cases.

Chapter three provides reasons why there was this tension between doctrine and policy discernible in early twentieth-century case law and commentary, connecting previously unconnected facts to better understand how the ground was prepared for *Donoghue*. This chapter identifies legal and extra-legal factors that may be said to have created a state of affairs supportive of the ousting of privity. It is argued that the continued challenges faced by married women (and perhaps also children) in suing on a contract, as well as the rise of an increasingly consumerist society in which goods were available and in demand as never before, the increased availability of liability insurance suddenly in the decade before *Donoghue*, and a changing conception of the nature of negligence, are all contemporaneous developments that are likely to have increased the pressure for change in the law, or, at least, not to have supported the status quo. Several of these factors also assist with understanding the new cases revealed and surveyed in chapter four.

Practices within the legal system are likely to have contributed to the pressure for change. It is argued in chapter four and chapter five that, behind the formal rules, an alternative legal pathway, or mechanism, was being utilised by lawyers and their clients in the 1910s and 1920s to successfully sue, in tort, the vendors and manufacturers of harmful products. Uncovering case law reported in regional newspapers of the 1910s and 1920s, chapter four demonstrates that, despite the outcomes one might expect given the formal privity rule, many plaintiffs were successfully suing for personal injury arising from the use of defective products. Chapter five seeks to explain this evidence and suggests that it may be attributed plausibly to the emergence, at the turn of the century, of a line of argument within the orthodox law based on the law concerning the supply of 'dangerous things'. Results similar to that in *Donoghue* were being reached, prior to 1932, without any change to the formal legal rules. In the words of Milsom, the injured plaintiffs' lawyers simply 'evaded' the obstacle of the doctrine of privity in the way they framed the claims. This practice contributed to a climate in which it was more likely that the privity doctrine would be ousted from the law of negligence.

Taken together, these several strands of development, occurring both within and outside the law, created a climate in which one further problem could be the tipping point for change. That tipping point came with the snail in a bottle. Drawing on a variety of sources which have not previously been brought together, this book demonstrates that, by 1930, everything was in place for a difficulty with

[27] Much has been learned by such an exercise in, eg, AWB Simpson, *Leading Cases on the Common Law* (Oxford University Press, 1996); PS Atiyah, *The Rise and Fall of Freedom of Contract* (Oxford University Press, 1979); RVF Heuston, 'Judicial Prosopography' (1986) 102 *Law Quarterly Review* 90. Indeed, for particular figures during this period (Baron Bramwell, for instance) it is difficult to resist certain inferences about the influence of their politics on their judicial decision-making: see, eg, Atiyah, ibid, 374–80; RA Epstein, 'For a Bramwell Revival' (1994) 38 *American Journal of Legal History* 246; D Abraham, 'Liberty and Property: Lord Bramwell and the Political Economy of Liberal Jurisprudence Individualism, Freedom, and Utility (1994) 38 *American Journal of Legal History* 288.

establishing a Scottish ginger beer manufacturer's liability to a woman in Paisley to provide the final straw to break the camel's long-resisting back.

This book shows *Donoghue* in a new light. Although it certainly remains an important case, it is perhaps not quite the cataclysmic event it has sometimes been understood to be. It was, in fact, the final, confirmatory (albeit necessary) step in a longer process, influenced by developments both inside and outside the law, which had been under way for some time before the Law Lords reached for their pens.

1

Privity in Negligence Law: The Orthodox Story

I. The Legal Landscape

Of particular interest for this chapter and the next is the question of how privity, as a doctrine concerning title to sue in contract, came to be applied in negligence law. Before turning to consider the principal case law from the doctrine's introduction to ousting, it is useful to consider, briefly, the background against which these cases were decided. The story of privity in negligence begins in the nineteenth century. This was a period of major change in the law of contract and in the law of tort. The discussion which follows does not attempt to cover the field; there are excellent works dealing in detail with the history of the law of contract and the law of negligence in the nineteenth and early twentieth centuries.[1] The focus in this part is developments centrally relevant to this book.

A. The Law of Contract

The late eighteenth and nineteenth centuries saw the development of an English 'law of contract', in the sense of a theorised body of principles concerning contractual liability.[2] It was during this period that many of the rules and principles still

[1] See, eg, D Ibbetson, *A Historical Introduction to the Law of Obligations* (Oxford University Press, 1999); P Mitchell, *A History of Tort Law, 1900–1950* (Cambridge University Press, 2015); M Lobban, 'Part Two: Contract' in WR Cornish et al (eds), *The Oxford History of the Laws of England, Vol XII: 1820–1914 Private Law* (Oxford University Press, 2010); and 'Part Four: Tort', *The Oxford History of the Laws of England, Vol XII: 1820–1914*; D Ibbetson, 'The tort of negligence in England' in N Jansen (ed), *The Development and Making of Legal Doctrine* (Cambridge University Press, 2010); DJ Ibbetson, '"The Law of Business Rome": Foundations of the Anglo-American Tort of Negligence' (1999) 52 *Current Legal Problems* 74, 77–78; DJ Ibbetson, 'The Tort of Negligence in the Common Law in the Nineteenth and Twentieth Centuries' in E Schrage (ed), *Negligence: The Comparative Legal History of the Law of Torts* (Duncker & Humblot, 2001) (hereafter: 'Negligence'); MJ Prichard, 'Scott v Shepherd (1773) and the Emergence of the Tort of Negligence' in *The Selden Society Lectures, 1952–2001* (Hein, 2003); J Plunkett, *The Duty of Care in Negligence* (Hart Publishing, 2018) 7–34.

[2] See, eg, DJ Ibbetson and W Swain, 'Third Party Beneficiaries in English Law: From *Dutton v Poole* to *Tweddle v Atkinson*' in EJH Schrage (ed), *Ius Quaesitum Tertio* (Duncker & Humblot, 2008) 191; Ibbetson, *Historical Introduction to the Law of Obligations* (n 1) 202–03, 220–28.

in use today, such as those concerning offer and acceptance and mistake, were clearly articulated.[3] Contractual arrangements before this had come before courts in numerous forms of action, including assumpsit and debt.[4] One reason that has been suggested for this articulation of detailed rules and of a coherent framework for contractual liability is that judges were increasingly deciding cases themselves and considering detailed questions of law, leaving less in the hands of juries.[5] There was also a proliferation of treatises on the law of contract at this time:[6] Powell (1790),[7] Chitty (1826),[8] Addison (1847),[9] Leake (1867),[10] Pollock (1876)[11] and Anson (1879),[12] to name just some. It seems that, certainly by the second half of the nineteenth century, jurists were thinking and writing more in terms of general principles.[13]

It has been a widely held view that the early nineteenth century saw the emergence of a conception of contract law based upon the voluntariness of the obligation created and the idea of freedom to choose, a 'will theory'.[14] As Manchester describes it, if '[i]ndividual liberty was the watchword … contract was its legal spearhead'.[15] Historians do not agree upon the reason for this new approach.[16] On one view, most associated with the ideas of Atiyah,[17] the shift came about because judges and contemporary commentators responded to changing political and economic theories.[18] The suggestion is that courts of the eighteenth century were mainly concerned with ensuring fairness in transactions; the principal theory of contract, if a coherent theory existed,[19] was based on the idea that the obligation was created by acceptance of benefits or by reliance.[20] By the nineteenth century, a theory championing freedom of contract was well-suited to the new industrial,

[3] See Ibbetson, *Historical Introduction to the Law of Obligations* (n 1) 220–28.

[4] See, eg, Ibbetson and Swain (n 2) 191.

[5] See, eg, Ibbetson, *Historical Introduction to the Law of Obligations* (n 1) 220; J Baker, *Introduction to English Legal History*, 5th edn (Oxford University Press, 2019) 373.

[6] See, eg, Ibbetson, *Historical Introduction to the Law of Obligations* (n 1) 220; PS Atiyah, *The Rise and Fall of Freedom of Contract* (Oxford University Press, 1979) 399.

[7] JJ Powell, *Essay upon the Law of Contracts and Agreements* (1790).

[8] J Chitty, *Practical Treatise on the Law of Contracts, not under Seal* (S Sweet, 1826).

[9] CG Addison, *Treatise on the Law of Contracts and Liabilities ex Contractu* (W Benning & Co, 1847).

[10] SM Leake, *The Elements of the Law of Contracts* (Stevens and Sons, 1867).

[11] F Pollock, *Principles of Contract at Law and in Equity* (Stevens and Sons, 1876).

[12] WR Anson, *Principles of the English Law of Contract* (Macmillan and Co, 1879).

[13] M Lobban, 'Introduction' in WR Cornish et al (eds), *The Oxford History of the Laws of England, Vol XII: 1820–1914 Private Law* (Oxford University Press, 2010) 306–07. However, Lobban argues that the development of contract doctrine in the nineteenth century was not driven by theory, and that contract writers by the close of the nineteenth century and at the beginning of the twentieth century were pragmatic when it came to theory; they 'did not strive to create logical and coherent systems of law': 313.

[14] See Ibbetson, *Historical Introduction to the Law of Obligations* (n 1) 221; M Lobban, 'Contractual Fraud in Law and Equity c1750–c1850' (1997) 17 *Oxford Journal of Legal Studies* 441, 441; Lobban, 'Introduction' (n 13) 297.

[15] AH Manchester, *Modern Legal History* (Butterworths, 1980) 267.

[16] See discussion in Lobban, 'Introduction' (n 13) 297–98.

[17] Atiyah (n 6). See also discussion in Lobban, 'Introduction' (n 13) 297.

[18] Lobban, 'Introduction' (n 13) 297.

[19] See Ibbetson, *Historical Introduction to the Law of Obligations* (n 1) 221.

[20] Atiyah (n 6) 419. See also discussion in Lobban, 'Introduction' (n 13) 297.

commercial society where commercial enterprise and free market individualism were prominent ideas.[21] However, Atiyah's ideas are not without critics.[22] Other reasons have been suggested, including the borrowing of ideas from the natural law writers.[23] Some suggest that the difference between the eighteenth and nineteenth centuries was not, in fact, so great. Defining contracts in terms of agreement was not a novel concept in the nineteenth century.[24] It has been argued that the orthodox view overestimates eighteenth-century courts' commitment to fairness and paternalistic practices, and underestimates nineteenth-century judges' concern with fairness.[25]

From the 1880s, it seems that confidence in this theoretical approach to contract law began to be eroded.[26] Much of the theory was ill-suited to the realities of commercial practice in a developed industrial society.[27] As Ibbetson has observed, the 'general principle that liability stemmed from a meeting of the minds was hard to defend in the light of the growth of standard-form contracts that, especially in non-commercial contexts, one (or all too commonly both) of the parties would never have read'.[28] Even so, Atiyah suggests that serious disquiet probably only emerged towards the middle of the twentieth century. The main doctrines connected with the 'will theory' survived – including offer and acceptance, and mistake – albeit amended with new principles and rules concerned with justice and fairness.[29]

[21] See Atiyah (n 6) 420; Lobban, 'Introduction' (n 13) 297–98.

[22] See discussion in Lobban, 'Introduction' (n 13) 298–302.

[23] See, eg, AWB Simpson, *Legal Theory and Legal History* (The Hambledon Press, 1987) 171–202; Ibbetson, *Historical Introduction to the Law of Obligations* (n 1) 220–21; J Gordley, *Philosophical Origins of Modern Contract Doctrine* (Oxford University Press, 1991) 175–80. See also discussion in Lobban, 'Introduction' (n 13) 300–02.

[24] See discussion in Lobban, 'Introduction' (n 13) 302; Ibbetson, *Historical Introduction to the Law of Obligations* (n 1) 222.

[25] Lobban, 'Contractual Fraud' (n 14) 441 ff. See also JH Baker, 'Reviews: The Rise and Fall of Freedom of Contract. By P.S. Atiyah' (1980) 43 *Modern Law Review* 467; JL Barton, 'The Enforcement of Hard Bargains' (1987) 103 *Law Quarterly Review* 118; and AWB Simpson, 'The Horwitz Thesis and the History of Contracts' (1979) 46 *University of Chicago Law Review* 533, also published in Simpson, *Legal Theory and Legal History* (n 23) 203–71. In the latter, Simpson responded to an argument advanced by Professor Horwitz in MJ Horwitz, *The Transformation of American Law, 1780–1860* (Oxford University Press, 1992) 160–210 (originally published by Harvard University Press in 1977), to the effect that private law of the eighteenth century reflected the pre-market economy and was concerned principally with imposing fairness and a just order upon society, which was then replaced, in the nineteenth century, by a law better suited to the market economy. The argument suggests that eighteenth-century courts sometimes refused to enforce obligations where there was underlying unfairness, but this gradually gave way to an idea of contract in which the source of obligation was the convergence of parties' wills and courts, in a manner more friendly to commercial ventures, would uphold the bargain struck. Simpson argues that Horwitz's thesis is oversimplified and suggests that there was, in fact, much more continuity between these two periods than Horwitz' thesis might suggest.

[26] See, eg, Manchester (n 15) 264; Ibbetson, *Historical Introduction to the Law of Obligations* (n 1) 245–61; Lobban, 'Introduction' (n 13) 299.

[27] Ibbetson, *Historical Introduction to the Law of Obligations* (n 1) 246–47.

[28] ibid 246.

[29] ibid 245–46. The principle that there must be an intention to create legal relations was a later arrival: see Ibbetson, *Historical Introduction to the Law of Obligations* (n 1) 222–33.

It is unnecessary, for present purposes, to determine exactly when, and to what extent, attitudes changed one way and then the other. It is sufficient to note that, during the nineteenth century, respect for the bargain struck by individuals exercising free choice became increasingly prominent, even if not totally dominant. It was agreement between parties that came to be seen as the basis for the existence of a contract; parties' intentions, rather than their actions, became the source of contractual obligations.[30]

i. *Consideration and Privity*

The doctrine of privity is central to this book; the doctrine of consideration is closely linked to privity. There is disagreement as to whether the consideration rule and the privity rule are really separate rules, or merely different ways of saying the same thing.[31] However, this disagreement is beyond our current focus. It is enough, at present, to note that the two doctrines are closely linked, historically and conceptually.

During the medieval period, there was no clear parties-only principle in relation to informal contracts (those outside the arena of agreements recorded in sealed deeds).[32] Ibbetson and Swain have suggested that there was a 'weak parties-only rule' in place at the end of the sixteenth century in the action of assumpsit but that, by the second half of this century, a stronger consideration rule had emerged: informal promises, made without a deed, were only enforceable if made for consideration.[33] Though early modern case law was unsettled and confused,[34] what came to be seen as the main rule applicable to informal promises was that consideration had to come from the party seeking to bring the action of assumpsit.[35] With respect to sealed deeds, the parties-only rule continued to operate.[36]

[30] See, eg, Ibbetson, *Historical Introduction to the Law of Obligations* (n 1) 221; Lobban, 'Introduction' (n 13) 297.

[31] See discussion in R Flannigan, 'Privity – the End of an Era (Error)' (1987) 103 *Law Quarterly Review* 564, 568, and sources there cited; M Furmston and GJ Tolhurst, *Privity of Contract* (Oxford University Press, 2015) 2; VV Palmer, 'The History of Privity: The Formative Period (1500–1680)' (1989) 33 *American Journal of Legal History* 3, 3; G Samuels, 'Contracts for the Benefit of Third Parties' (1967–68) 8 *University of Western Australia Law Review* 378.

[32] DJ Ibbetson and EJH Schrage, 'Ius quaesitum tertio: A Comparative and Historical Introduction to the Concept of Third Party Contracts' in EJH Schrage (ed), *Ius Quaesitum Tertio* (Duncker & Humblot, 2008) 26–27. However, the authors also note that one must not put too much weight on this, as the idea of a 'contract' during this time lacked clarity: 26.

[33] Ibbetson and Swain (n 2) 196. See, eg, *Bourne v Mason* (1668) 1 Vent 6, 86 ER 5; *Dutton v Poole* (1677) 3 Keb 786, 2 Lev 210, 83 ER 523.

[34] See M Lobban, 'Consideration' in WR Cornish et al (eds), *The Oxford History of the Laws of England, Vol XII: 1820–1914 Private Law* (Oxford University Press, 2010) 388, and sources there cited; Ibbetson and Schrage (n 32) 27; SP De Cruz, 'Assumpsit, Consideration and Third Party Rights' (1986) 7 *Journal of Legal History* 53. Though see also Flannigan (n 31) 564–65.

[35] Ibbetson and Swain (n 2) 198–99; *Dutton* (n 33). Except in a situation analogous to that in *Dutton* where a close family member had provided the consideration for the party bringing the action, it was also treated as essential that the promise had been made to the person bringing the action: see Ibbetson and Swain, ibid, 206. Baker suggests that privity continued to play a part, and that privity to the promise or to the consideration were each sufficient to bring assumpsit: Baker, *Introduction to English Legal History* (n 5) 377–78.

[36] Ibbetson and Swain (n 2) 205–06.

However, in the first part of the nineteenth century, the parties-only rule would be revived for non-deed contractual arrangements.[37] Ibbetson has suggested that the transition to parties-only was 'well under way' by 1833 in *Price v Easton*,[38] where the two rules are considered alongside each other.[39]

The decision in *Tweddle v Atkinson*[40] in 1861 was to become the leading case.[41] It concerned a marriage agreement between two fathers, and an attempt by the groom to sue upon that agreement. As Ibbetson and Swain note, the reports of the decision vary in content, and there is significant ambiguity as to whether or not the decision was based principally on consideration or privity reasoning.[42] The case ultimately came to be seen as authority for the parties-only rule,[43] which, after *Tweddle*, became the dominant rule.[44] Consideration, however, still had to move from the party entitled to sue on the contract. What became impossible, then, was suit by someone to whom a promise had not been made but who was providing consideration.[45] Ibbetson and Swain have suggested that the change came not from a single case so much as from a reorientation of the law: a move beginning in the mid-eighteenth century towards understanding the law in terms of substantive doctrines and a unified 'law of contracts' rather than the old forms of action.[46] The authors suggest that the parties-only rule was, through this new conception, allowed to 'seep' across from the realm of formal contracts.

B. The Law of Tort

The decision in *Winterbottom v Wright*[47] was decided against the backdrop of the industrial revolution in England. Historians disagree as to the extent to which there was a revolutionary change in the century before 1850, some stressing longer trends and greater complexity in economic and social changes than earlier generations of historians had suggested.[48] Nevertheless, even if not all would call the

[37] See DJ Ibbetson, 'English Law before 1900' in J Hallebeek and H Dondorp (eds), *Contracts for a Third-Party Beneficiary: A Historical and Comparative Account* (Brill, 2008) 111; Ibbetson and Swain (n 2) 192. See also Flannigan (n 31) 566.

[38] *Price v Easton* (1833) 4 B & Ad 433, 110 ER 518.

[39] Ibbetson, 'English Law before 1900' (n 37) 111.

[40] *Tweddle v Atkinson* (1861) 30 LJQB 265, 4 LT 468, 9 WR 781, 1 B&S 393, 121 ER 762.

[41] Ibbetson and Swain (n 2) 210.

[42] ibid 210–13.

[43] See, eg, Ibbetson and Swain (n 2) 213; and Lobban, 'Consideration' (n 34) 390, and sources there cited.

[44] See Ibbetson, 'English Law before 1900' (n 37) 112–13, and sources there cited.

[45] Lobban, 'Consideration' (n 34) 390.

[46] Ibbetson and Swain (n 2) 192, 208.

[47] *Winterbottom v Wright* (1842) 10 M & W 109, 152 ER 402.

[48] See, eg, PK O'Brien, 'Introduction: Modern Conceptions of the Industrial Revolution' in P O'Brien and R Quinault (eds), *The Industrial Revolution and British Society* (Cambridge University Press, 1993); J Stevenson, 'Social Aspects of the Industrial Revolution' in P O'Brien and R Quinault (eds), *The Industrial Revolution and British Society* (Cambridge University Press, 1993); RV Jackson, 'Rates of industrial growth during the industrial revolution' (1992) 45 *Economic History Review* 1; M Berg and

period truly 'revolutionary', significant changes undoubtedly took place in British industry, agriculture and society.[49] From 1750 to 1900, a mainly rural society transformed into one in which the majority lived in urban areas, and the population grew to five times the size it had been in 1750.[50] It is well known that urban centres became dirtier, noisier and more crowded than ever before. Industrialisation and economic growth increased exponentially the level of risks in society, new forms and patterns of transport[51] and new machinery in factories[52] offering perhaps the most visible examples of increased risk of accidents.

Tort law played an important role in balancing the needs of economic activity against other social needs. The courts increasingly were forced to consider how far society should permit risky or intrusive activity before legal intervention, and perhaps compensation, was necessary.[53] This question was, of course, central in the law of nuisance: problems of smoke, pollution and noise existed before the nineteenth century, but were intensified substantially by rapid industrialisation and the expansion of city living.[54] The well-known 1865 nuisance case of *St Helen's Smelting Company v Tipping*[55] is a good example of the courts' conducting this balancing exercise between permitting commercial activity to proceed without undue restraint and protecting property rights. In *St Helen's Smelting Company*, damages and an injunction were granted with respect to the emission of smoke from copper-smelting works. This was so despite the fact that the Lord Chancellor said, in that case, that

> [i]f a man lives in a town, it is necessary that he should subject himself to the consequences of those operations of trade which may be carried on in his immediate locality, which are actually necessary for trade and commerce, and … for the benefit of the inhabitants of the town and of the public at large.[56]

A property owner could not complain of businesses carried on 'in a fair and reasonable way'.[57] Only where such operations caused a 'material injury' to his property might he complain and bring the law to his aid.[58]

P Hudson, 'Rehabilitating the Industrial Revolution' (1992) 45 *Economic History Review* 24. See also discussion in W Cornish et al, *Law and Society in England, 1750–1950*, 2nd edn (Hart Publishing, 2019) 6 and sources there cited.

[49] See Cornish et al, *Law and Society in England, 1750–1950* (n 48) 6–7.

[50] See, eg, Cornish et al, *Law and Society in England, 1750–1950* (n 48) 1–2, 74 and sources there cited.

[51] ibid 457–58.

[52] ibid 459–60.

[53] M Lobban, 'The Development of Tort Law' in WR Cornish et al (eds), *The Oxford History of the Laws of England, Vol XII: 1820–1914 Private Law* (Oxford University Press, 2010) 885.

[54] For a useful discussion about the law of nuisance in the nineteenth century, see JF Brenner, 'Nuisance Law and the Industrial Revolution' (1974) 3 *Journal of Legal Studies* 403. See also M Lobban, 'Nuisance' in WR Cornish et al (eds), *The Oxford History of the Laws of England, Vol XII: 1820–1914 Private Law* (Oxford University Press, 2010).

[55] *St Helen's Smelting Company v Tipping* (1865) 11 HLC 642, 11 ER 1483.

[56] ibid 650; 1486.

[57] ibid.

[58] ibid. See, on the difficulties involved in bringing an action (and therefore lack of nuisance litigation), Brenner (n 54) 408–31.

The developing law of negligence would also have to grapple with the limits of curial intervention in individual freedoms and in industrial and commercial processes. There was a dramatic increase in the number of negligence claims at the beginning of the nineteenth century, possibly attributable to new machinery and methods of transport.[59] Constantly facing new issues, judges could not simply rely on established rules; they were forced into the role of policy-makers.[60] It will be suggested in chapter two that this was the case in *Winterbottom*, leading to the introduction of the privity rule. However, it will also be suggested that, as the century progressed and the law of negligence became increasingly well-defined, there was perhaps greater scope and reason for rigid adherence to existing rules, as opposed to consequence-based reasoning.

i. Negligence

It is generally agreed that, during the period from the mid-1800s to the 1930s, negligence emerged as a significant and independent tort.[61] Ibbetson describes it as a 'creation of the nineteenth century, though its tendrils reach back into the eighteenth century and before'.[62]

The concept of the duty of care emerged in the early nineteenth century, as plaintiffs wishing to bring an action in tort rather than contract claimed that a duty existed beyond contract.[63] It was a time in which highway accidents were producing a significant amount of litigation.[64] Certain commercial relationships already gave rise to a recognised duty of care, particularly those exercising 'common callings', like innkeepers and carriers.[65] Prichard has argued that it was plaintiffs who first used the language of 'duty' to extend this concept to other situations.[66]

Where a wrong had occurred and the parties involved were linked by an agreement, there emerged the problem whether the claim should properly be understood as contractual or tortious.[67] The difference had substantive and procedural implications; it was not possible to join a claim in contract with one in tort, and all contracting parties had to be sued together in contract.[68] It was therefore

[59] See, eg, Plunkett (n 1) 13; Baker, *Introduction to English Legal History* (n 5) 439; PH Winfield, 'The History of Negligence in the Law of Torts' (1926) 42 *Law Quarterly Review* 184, 195.

[60] Lobban, 'The Development of Tort Law' (n 53) 886.

[61] For discussion of the development of the law see, eg, Ibbetson, *Historical Introduction to the Law of Obligations* (n 1) 169–201; M Lobban, 'Negligence' in WR Cornish et al (eds), *The Oxford History of the Laws of England, Vol XII: 1820–1914 Private Law* (Oxford University Press, 2010); Ibbetson, '"The Law of Business Rome"' (n 1) 77–78; Plunkett (n 1); Winfield, 'The History of Negligence in the Law of Torts' (n 59).

[62] Ibbetson, 'Negligence' (n 1) 229.

[63] See Prichard (n 1) 28–31.

[64] See discussion in Cornish et al, *Law and Society in England, 1750–1950* (n 48) 460–61.

[65] ibid. See also Prichard (n 1) 440–443.

[66] ibid 444–447.

[67] See discussion in Plunkett (n 1) 11.

[68] See Ibbetson, 'Negligence' (n 1) 237 and sources there cited.

often preferable to be able to sue in tort. The 1821 case of *Bretherton v Wood*,[69] which concerned an action against stagecoach proprietors by an injured passenger, offered guidance. Prichard describes the test reached there as follows:

> [P]rovided the plaintiff could formulate his cause of action without reliance on any contract, he could not be defeated by the joinder of too many or too few defendants – the action lay purely in tort – but if he could not maintain his action without referring to a contract, then the contractual rules of joinder applied.[70]

The question was then which *kinds* of contractual relationships could exist but would nevertheless allow an injured plaintiff to sue purely in tort without reference to the contract.[71]

By the 1830s, defendants and judges, as well as plaintiffs, began to use the language and concept of 'duty'.[72] Importantly, as Ibbetson has noted, the concept of duty of care was 'of primary importance in practice since it constituted the principal judicial tool … to regulate the scope of the tort'.[73] The existence (or not) of a duty was a legal question for judges; whether or not this duty had been breached was one of fact for the jury.[74] Judges could use this division to reduce the range of tortious liability by removing cases from juries where there was no duty.[75] During the nineteenth century, courts and litigants alike were thus increasingly concerned about the boundary between tort and contract.[76] Whether or not this issue is behind the reasoning in *Winterbottom* will be considered further below.

By the mid-nineteenth century, judges were concerned to control the scope of the growing tort of negligence.[77] Rather than developing an open-ended tort and a general principle to cover new scenarios, a practice emerged of courts' identifying specific duties of care that would give rise to liability.[78] Liability in negligence came to be linked to duties already recognised at common law.[79] For example, there emerged a duty owed by railway companies to ensure passenger safety, analogous to the contractual duties owed between a railway company and its paying passengers.[80] This liability also arose from their status as common carriers.[81] This

[69] *Bretherton v Wood* (1821) 9 Price 408, 147 ER 134.
[70] Prichard (n 1) 442.
[71] ibid.
[72] See Plunkett (n 1) 14.
[73] Ibbetson, 'The tort of negligence in England' (n 1).
[74] Ibbetson, 'The tort of negligence in England' (n 1) 59; Ibbetson, '"The Law of Business Rome"' (n 1) 89–90.
[75] ibid.
[76] This was exacerbated by the County Courts Act 1846, which forced the separate classification of actions in tort and actions in contract; an action could not be both: see PH Winfield, *The Province of the Law of Tort* (Cambridge University Press, 1931) 76–78.
[77] Lobban, 'Negligence' (n 61) 922.
[78] See, eg, Lobban, 'Negligence' (n 61) 923; Manchester (n 15) 285. See also DJ Ibbetson, 'George v Skivington (1869)' in C Mitchell and P Mitchell (eds), *Landmark Cases in the Law of Tort* (Hart Publishing, 2010) 81–83.
[79] Lobban, 'Negligence' (n 61) 923.
[80] ibid 923, 959.
[81] ibid 959.

duty did not depend on a passenger having made a contract.[82] In *Foulkes v The Metropolitan District Railway Company*,[83] it was unclear whether or not the injured passenger had a contract with the defendant company or another company, as both operated over a particular stretch of rail and issued tickets from the same booth. He was injured while being carried by the defendant. It was held that, even if the contract was exclusively with the other railway company, this did not exempt the defendant company from liability: they were 'liable in respect of the wrongful act which led to the plaintiff's injuries, by virtue of their actual reception of him in their carriage on his return journey'.[84]

The carriage of passengers was, therefore, one area of liability in which a duty in tort was recognised and in which the existence of a contract did not interfere with its recognition. The treatment by courts of injured railway passengers has been considered in detail by Kostal.[85] There were large numbers of passengers and workers injured by this expanding mode of transport, though Kostal's work shows that courts took a more generous approach to injured passengers than to injured workers.[86]

Outside transport, it was established early in the nineteenth century that certain professional men might owe duties to people other than the person with whom they had contracted to provide services.[87] Medical practitioners were one such group. While actions for negligently administered medical treatment have a long history,[88] it was really in the early nineteenth century that these came to be tied clearly to the action on the case, and therefore with the developing tort of negligence.[89] In *Pippin v Sheppard*,[90] it was held by the Court of Common Pleas that a surgeon might be liable for the injuries sustained by his patient owing to his treatment of her, even when there was no contract between them. It was held that the duty was not founded on contract but upon the undertaking to treat the patient. The reasoning of Garrow B was clearly grounded in concern for the

[82] See, eg, *Austin v The Great Western Railway Co* (1867) LR 2 QB 442, 446; *Marshall v The York, Newcastle, and Berwick Railway Company* (1851) 11 CB 655, 662–65; 138 ER 632, 635–36.

[83] *Foulkes v The Metropolitan District Railway Company* (1879) 4 CPD 267, affirmed on appeal (1880) 5 CPD 157.

[84] *Foulkes v The Metropolitan District Railway Company* (1880) 5 CPD 157, 167–68.

[85] See RW Kostal, *Law and English Railway Capitalism 1825–1875* (Clarendon Press, 1994) ch 7.

[86] The 'doctrine of common employment' was confirmed as a principle in English law in *Hutchinson v York, Newcastle and Berwick Railway* (1850) 5 Ex 343, 155 ER 150. *Hutchinson* decided that, as the employee Mr Hutchinson was not compelled to accept employment with the defendant, he had bargained and therefore accepted the risk of injury by any other employee: (1850) 5 Ex 343, 349–52; 155 ER 150, 153–54. See Kostal (n 85) 270–71.

[87] See, eg, Ibbetson, 'George v Skivington (1869)' (n 78) 81.

[88] See, eg, PH Winfield, 'Duty in Tortious Negligence' (1934) 34 *Columbia Law Review* 41, 45.

[89] See discussion in MA Stein, CP Guzelian and KM Guzelian, 'Expert Testimony in Nineteenth Century Malapraxis Actions' (2015) 55 *American Journal of Legal History* 194, 195, and cases there cited. It was clearly established that medical practitioners owed a duty of care in the law of negligence by the early twentieth century: see, eg, AS Taylor and FJ Smith, *The Principles and Practice of Medical Jurisprudence* (J & A Churchill, 1905) 80–90.

[90] *Pippin v Sheppard* (1822) 11 Price 400, 147 ER 512.

consequences that would follow if no action were allowed independently of a contract of retainer:

> It would be of most mischievous consequence if this declaration could not be sustained. In the practice of surgery particularly, the public are exposed to great risks from the number of ignorant persons professing a knowledge of the art, without the least pretensions to the necessary qualifications, and they often inflict very serious injury on those who are so unfortunate as to fall into their hands. To hold the contrary, would be to leave such persons in a remedyless state.[91]

Gladwell v Steggall[92] is another case where the liability of persons holding themselves out to be medical practitioners was held to extend beyond the boundaries of contract. The mistreated patient in *Gladwell* was a child, and her father had engaged the surgeon (described as being one who, 'though a clergyman, practised also as a medical man') to treat his daughter. One of the members of the court, Bosanquet J, confirmed that 'this action … is neither brought on a contract nor founded on one: it is brought by a person who has sustained bodily injury, and by the only person who could sue for it'.[93]

By 1851, this position appears settled. It was recognised by Parke B, citing *Pippin* and *Gladwell*, as established law that:

> There are other cases … in which a third person, though not a party to the contract, may sue for the damage sustained, if it be broken … As for example, if an apothecary administered improper medicines to his patient, or a surgeon unskilfully treated him, and thereby injured his health, he would be liable to the patient, even where the father or friend of the patient may have been the contracting party with the apothecary or surgeon …: *Pippin v. Sheppard … Gladwell v. Steggall.*[94]

Although the word 'surgeon' is used in these cases, it does not seem that the principle applied only to those performing what we might now call 'surgery'. Rather, it seems that the principle applied broadly to those holding themselves out to be skilled professionals in the provision of medical treatment. The surgeon in *Gladwell* was described as being 'in the profession and business of a surgeon and apothecary';[95] it is not clear from the reports exactly what was done in the way of treatment.

Whether or not the duty owed by medical practitioners, independently and irrespective of contract, was extended to those claiming professional skills more generally is unclear. The writings of Charles Addison, for instance, might suggest so. He included a wide principle in his 1864 edition of *Wrongs and their Remedies*:

> Every person who exercises an employment is bound … to take especial care to do his work so as not to injure another by the negligent performance of that work, whether what he does is merely to please himself, or by virtue of a contract made with another.[96]

[91] ibid 409; 515.
[92] *Gladwell v Steggall* (1839) 5 Bing NC 733, 132 ER 1283.
[93] ibid 736; 1284.
[94] *Longmeid v Holliday* (1851) 6 Ex 761, 767, 155 ER 752, 755.
[95] *Gladwell* (n 92) 733; 1283.
[96] CG Addison, *Wrongs and their Remedies*, 2nd edn (Stevens, Sons, and Haynes, 1864) 813. See also discussion in Ibbetson, 'George v Skivington (1869)' (n 78) 82.

He also explained:

> Clockmakers, jewellers, opticians, and all kinds of skilled workmen, and all persons belonging to the learned professions,[97] are responsible in damages if they profess to accomplish more than they are able to perform, and undertake works of skill without being possessed of sufficient skill, or apply less than the occasion requires.[98]

However, the extent to which this was widely accepted, and whether or not there was a recognised duty imposed on professionals generally in the exercise of their calling, is not clear. In *Langridge v Levy*,[99] a rule nisi for arresting judgment was obtained on the ground that there could be no duty arising out of private contract, as the defendant was 'clothed with *no official or professional character* out of which a known duty could arise' (emphasis added).[100] *George v Skivington*[101] may also provide clues. Counsel for the defendant had sought to distinguish between a professional and the maker of harmful hairwash: he argued that 'a common ordinary tradesman does not hold himself out to be skilful'.[102] Although this limitation was rejected by the court,[103] the general lack of enthusiasm for the decision in *George* until *Donoghue* makes it difficult to draw any firm conclusions on this point.

Labatt, writing in the *Law Quarterly Review* in 1900, commented that the reason courts took the view that surgeons and apothecaries could be sued by a patient without any contractual relationship was that 'under any other doctrine, the defendant would virtually evade all liability, since, in the nature of the case, only the patient could prove actual damage'.[104] Labatt was apparently in favour of a more expansive approach to the law of negligence and commented that this reasoning was interesting, as it 'dimly' suggested the existence of a general principle which would 'aid us greatly in putting the limits of responsibility upon a more rational basis'.[105] He concluded by commenting that, if not for the fact that inconsistencies were so common in English law, one might be surprised that a doctor could be held liable to a person not privy to the contract while 'in other cases of professional services … the immunity of the defendant being equally inevitable unless the stranger to the contract … is permitted to sue, this consideration is not only not allowed the same weight, but … has not even been discussed'.[106] The exception for medical men appears, therefore, to have been drawn narrowly.

Occupiers of property also were recognised as owing a duty to a person coming onto their property, though the content of the duty varied according to the nature

[97] Later editions contain the note that this does not apply to barristers: see, eg, CG Addison, *Wrongs and their Remedies*, 4th edn (Stevens and Sons, 1873) 403.
[98] Addison, *Wrongs and their Remedies*, 2nd edn (1864) (n 96) 335.
[99] *Langridge v Levy* (1837) 2 M & W 519, 521; 150 ER 863, 864.
[100] ibid 521; 864.
[101] See *George v Skivington* (1869) LR 5 Ex 1; see also discussion in Ibbetson, 'George v Skivington (1869)' (n 78) 82.
[102] *George v Skivington* (1869) 21 LT 495, 496.
[103] See also (1869) 39 LJ Ex 8, 9, and discussion below.
[104] CB Labatt, 'Negligence in Relation to Privity of Contract' (1900) 16 *Law Quarterly Review* 168, 173–74.
[105] ibid 174.
[106] ibid.

of the person's presence on the property. Occupiers owed the most stringent duties to people who had been invited to be there.[107] Invitees were 'entitled to expect that the occupier shall on his part use reasonable care to prevent damage from unusual danger, which he knows or ought to know'.[108] A mere licensee (for example, a servant) was owed a less taxing duty; it required only that the occupier did not hide traps and did not take positive steps to place them in danger.[109]

Negligence law for the majority of the nineteenth century was therefore characterised by pockets of liability, governed by recognised categories of duty.[110] Courts were wary of imposing too widely the burdensome duty to take care.[111] As Manchester suggests, judges who were concerned with the consequences of the 'unlimited duty' did, on occasion, 'seek refuge in contract'.[112] It will be suggested in the next chapter that the *Winterbottom* court did just this.

Nevertheless, attitudes began to change in the last quarter of the nineteenth century. A more expansive view of the law of negligence was championed by some influential judges and jurists.[113] Expansion and the formulation of a general principle for the imposition of a duty of care was attempted by Brett MR in *Heaven v Pender*.[114] Frederick Pollock was also a champion of a more open law of negligence, governed by a general principle rather than categories of case in which a duty was recognised. He was influenced by the writings of Oliver Wendell Holmes, the first common law jurist to advocate a theory of tort.[115] Holmes argued that liability followed only harms that were foreseeable and over which the tortfeasor had control, and that questions of fault were to be determined objectively.[116] Pollock, in turn, advocated a general duty to 'to observe … an appropriate measure of prudence to avoid harm' to others.[117] This echoes Pufendorf, a natural lawyer whose work was particularly influential in England as negligence law developed an independent existence.[118]

[107] See Cornish et al, *Law and Society in England, 1750–1950* (n 48) 478–79; M Lobban, 'Personal Injuries' in WR Cornish et al (eds), *The Oxford History of the Laws of England, Vol XII: 1820–1914 Private Law* (Oxford University Press, 2010) 977–79.

[108] *Indermaur v Dames* (1866) LR 1 CP 274, 288 (Willes J), affirmed in (1867) LR 2 CP 311.

[109] See Cornish et al, *Law and Society in England, 1750–1950* (n 48) 479; Lobban, 'Personal Injuries' (n 107) 979.

[110] See, on the idea of 'pockets' of liability for negligence in the nineteenth and into the twentieth century, J Stapleton, 'Duty of care and economic loss: a wider agenda' (1991) 107 *Law Quarterly Review* 249.

[111] Manchester (n 15) 285. See also Ibbetson, *Historical Introduction to the Law of Obligations* (n 1) 174. See, for example, *Langridge* (n 99) 530; 868. Further examples of judicial concern for the potential reach of negligence liability will be considered below.

[112] Manchester (n 15) 285.

[113] Lobban, 'The Development of Tort Law' (n 53) 889–94.

[114] *Heaven v Pender* (1883) 11 QBD 503. Brett MR's reasoning in *Heaven* is discussed below.

[115] Lobban, 'Negligence' (n 61) 941–42. See OW Holmes, *The Common Law* (Little, Brown and Company, 1881).

[116] Holmes (n 115) 96, 108.

[117] See, eg, F Pollock, *The Law of Torts* (Stevens and Sons, 1887) 22.

[118] See discussion in Ibbetson, *Historical Introduction to the Law of Obligations* (n 1) 165–68, 170–71.

Other treatise writers of the nineteenth century were less convinced by arguments for a general principle. Salmond doubted that there was a general principle, preferring the 'catalogue' approach proscribing specific wrongs and certain kinds of harmful activity (leaving 'the residue outside the sphere of legal responsibility').[119] Beven also appeared unconvinced by Brett MR's formulation, finding it to be too broad.[120]

The law continued to follow the 'catalogue' approach until *Donoghue*, and probably afterwards too. *Donoghue* is, in the wider law of negligence, somewhat a symbolic turning point; indeed, until at least the 1960s, the courts' approach to negligence generally looked similar to the pre-*Donoghue* position.[121] However, for product liability, *Donoghue* paved the way for consumers to bring their action in negligence against the makers and suppliers of defective products, in circumstances where there was no opportunity for intermediate inspection.

C. Defective and Damaging Goods

Donoghue was, of course, a case concerning liability for a defectively-manufactured product. It is therefore necessary to consider, specifically, the law concerning defective or damaging products in the nineteenth and early twentieth centuries.

In contractual perspective, product liability developed significantly in the second part of the nineteenth century.[122] *Caveat emptor* was the starting point.[123] Benjamin's 1868 work, *A Treatise on the Law of Sale of Personal Property*, explained:

> [N]o warranty of the *quality* of a chattel is implied from the mere fact of sale. The rule in such cases is caveat emptor, by which is meant that when the buyer has required no warranty, he takes the risk of quality upon himself, and has no remedy if he chose to rely on the bare representation of the vendor, unless indeed he can show that representation to be fraudulent (original emphasis).[124]

However, certain exceptions to this general principle existed to protect the buyer, including, for example, an implied condition precedent that goods sold would conform to the description given by the vendor[125] and an implied warranty that goods were of a saleable or merchantable quality (where not inspected by the

[119] See JW Salmond, *The Law of Torts*, 2nd edn (Stevens and Haynes, 1910) 8–9.

[120] See T Beven, *Principles of the Law of Negligence* (Stevens and Haynes, 1889) 5, 54, 60–65. See also Lobban, 'Negligence' (n 61) 948.

[121] See discussion in Ibbetson, *Historical Introduction to the Law of Obligations* (n 1) 190–92; Ibbetson, 'The tort of negligence in England' (n 1) 64. On Stapleton's analysis, this was still the approach in some areas into the 1980s: see Stapleton (n 110).

[122] See discussion in S Whittaker, *The Development of Product Liability* (Cambridge University Press, 2010) 61.

[123] ibid 61.

[124] JP Benjamin, *A Treatise on the Law of Sale of Personal Property* (H Sweet, 1868) 453.

[125] See, eg, *Josling v Kingsford* (1863) 12 CBNS 447, 143 ER 177. For a more comprehensive discussion of these exceptions, see Whittaker (n 122) 62–64.

buyer).[126] In 1893, the Sale of Goods Act was enacted, with the intention of reproducing the existing rules relating to the sale of goods.[127] Even if it did not achieve this,[128] Whittaker suggests that the clarity with which the provisions governing implied terms were set out 'helped to establish their importance in practice'.[129] The effect of these exceptions, now in statute, was therefore that parties to a contract of sale could rely on the protection of certain implied terms.[130] These could, of course, be excluded or modified by express terms.

The position with regard to manufacturers' and sellers' liability in tort was, however, far more restricted until *Donoghue*. The question of liability would only arise if a contractual action was not available. Development of the law, thus, was slow, but, with the growth of commercial enterprise around this time, it became increasingly likely that manufacturers of products would not sell directly to the consumer.[131]

The issue of liability for the handing over of dangerous goods was considered by courts in actions against carriers.[132] In 1856, it was decided in *Brass v Maitland*[133] that it was an implied term in a shipping contract that notice was required to be given when loading onto a ship cargo of a dangerous nature. This duty to give notice was then extended to parties beyond those strictly party to a contract for carriage in *Farrant v Barnes*.[134] In *Farrant* it was held that, where one party asks another party to carry dangerous goods that require additional caution in handling, and are likely to cause injury if not properly handled, the first party has a duty to inform the second about the nature of the goods. In question was a container of nitric acid (a glass bottle in a wicker basket) that the defendant required to be conveyed to Croydon. Unfortunately, the employee of the railway carrier asked to transport the container was unable to convey it by railway in time to meet the defendant's requirements. As such, the employee asked the plaintiff, an employee of a Croydon carrier, to take it. The plaintiff was told it contained acid, but no more. When offloading the container, the contents escaped and burned him badly. When sued by the plaintiff, the defendant submitted that there was no case to answer, because there was no privity of contract between them. This argument

[126] See, eg, Benjamin (n 124) 484–88. Though see also P Mitchell, 'The development of quality obligations in sale of goods' (2001) 117 *Law Quarterly Review* 645. There was some uncertainty as to the exact parameters of the rule.

[127] Whittaker (n 122) 65, citing Memorandum, Sale of Goods Bill 1893, 1.

[128] See Mitchell, 'The development of quality obligations in sale of goods' (n 128). Mitchell argues that although the aim of the Act was to codify existing law, it, in fact, removed a concept central to the common law before its enactment.

[129] Whittaker (n 122) 65. Sections 13, 14 and 15 were the central provisions.

[130] See, generally, discussion in M Lobban, 'Contractual Terms and their Performance' in WR Cornish et al (eds), *The Oxford History of the Laws of England, Vol XII: 1820–1914 Private Law* (Oxford University Press, 2010) 479–85.

[131] Cornish et al, *Law and Society in England, 1750–1950* (n 48) 480. See also ch 3.

[132] Lobban, 'Personal Injuries' (n 107) 986–87.

[133] *Brass v Maitland* (1856) 6 El & Bl 470, 119 ER 940.

[134] *Farrant v Barnes* (1862) 11 CBNS 553, 142 ER 912.

was not accepted, and the plaintiff succeeded. Lack of privity did not, in such a case, preclude a duty from being recognised.

However, courts seemed more reluctant to recognise liability in cases of goods supplied or sold. Though it remained something of a vexed question into the twentieth century,[135] the orthodox position seemed to be that in only two types of case was a duty recognised in relation to the supply of goods to persons not party to the contract: first, where a supplier knew an item to be unsafe and fraudulently represented that it was not so;[136] and second, in the supply of things dangerous in themselves, or not inherently dangerous but *known* to be dangerous by the supplier because of some quality or defect.[137]

i. Liability in Tort Beyond the Contract: Fraud

Langridge v Levy[138] concerned the sale of a gun to the plaintiff's father, where the defendant gave a fraudulent warranty that the gun was made by a certain respected gun-maker and was safe to use. In fact, the gun was made by an inferior maker and unsafe, causing injury to the plaintiff. There was no possibility of suing on the contract, as the father was the contracting party and was therefore the only party able to sue on that contract. Between the son and defendant there was no privity.[139] The plaintiff was ultimately successful, despite the lack of privity, because of the fraudulent warranty or representation.[140] Parke B, delivering the judgment of the court, said:

> If the instrument in question, which is not of itself dangerous, but which requires an act to be done, that is, to be loaded, in order to make it so, had been simply delivered by the defendant, without any contract or representation on his part, to the plaintiff, no action would have been maintainable for any subsequent damage which the plaintiff might have sustained by the use of it. But if it had been delivered by the defendant to the plaintiff, for the purpose of being so used by him, with an accompanying representation to him that he might safely so use it, and that representation had been false to the defendant's knowledge, and the plaintiff had acted upon the faith of its being true, and had received damage thereby, then there is no question but that an action would have

[135] Lobban, 'Personal Injuries' (n 107) 988–990. See also discussion in ch 5, below. *George v Skivington* (1869) LR 5 Ex 1 was one of the few cases in which a manufacturer had been held liable to the ultimate consumer, and as will be discussed below, the decision was not generally accepted as good law until 1932.

[136] This is the case in *Langridge* (n 99) outlined below.

[137] See, eg, *Clarke v Army and Navy Co-operative Society* [1903] 1 KB 155; Robert FV Heuston, 'Donoghue v Stevenson in Retrospect' (1957) 20 *Modern Law Review* 1, 11.

[138] *Langridge* (n 99).

[139] ibid 529; 867.

[140] Though, for a slightly different interpretation, see JL Barton, 'Liability for Things in the Nineteenth Century' in JA Guy and HG Beale (eds), *Law and Social Change in British History* (Royal Historical Society, 1984) 150: Barton suggests that the plaintiff in *Langridge* could be understood to succeed because the defendant was aware that the gun was bought for *his* use – this was, the argument goes, also the basis for reliance on the *Langridge* case in *George*.

> lain, upon the principle of a numerous class of cases, of which the leading one is that of *Pasley v Freeman* (3 TR 51)[141] … There is a false representation made by the defendant, with a view that the plaintiff should use the instrument in a dangerous way, and, unless the representation had been made, the dangerous act would never have been done.[142]

Parke B concluded 'that as there is fraud, and damage, the result of that fraud, not from an act remote and consequential, but one contemplated by the defendant at the time as one of its results, the party guilty of the fraud is responsible to the party injured'.[143] This was, however, qualified: the court did not, he specified, decide whether this action would have succeeded if the plaintiff had not known of, and acted upon, the representation, 'nor whether the defendant would have been responsible to a person not within the defendant's contemplation at the time of the sale, to whom the gun might have been sold or handed over'.[144] The result was thus confined within tightly drawn parameters.

Longmeid v Holliday[145] was decided several years later. It was alleged for the plaintiffs, Mr and Mrs Longmeid, that Mr Longmeid had purchased from Mr Holliday a 'Holliday Lamp' to be used by the plaintiffs in their shop. Unfortunately, when Mrs Longmeid was lighting the lamp, it exploded, and she was seriously burned. The plaintiffs said it was cracked and leaky. It was said that Mr Holliday had fraudulently warranted that the lamp was fit for purpose. Mr Holliday was the vendor, but not manufacturer, of the lamp. At the trial, evidence had been brought that the lamp was defective in its construction but there was no evidence that Mr Holliday had known of the defect – the lamp had been put together by others, seemingly at Mr Holliday's instruction, and made of parts purchased from third parties. The jury found no fraud or deceit here but in other respects accepted the facts put forward by the plaintiffs.

Counsel for the plaintiffs argued that the case fell within the principle in *Langridge*. It was said that there was a general duty on every shopkeeper who sells articles that are or may become dangerous to take care that they are fit for use. The defendant here knew of the purpose for which the lamp was purchased. If the vendor was not the manufacturer and therefore unaware that the article was unsafe, he ought to inform the purchaser; if he sold it as secure and it was not, he was 'guilty of a breach of duty, which renders him responsible to everyone who is in consequence injured'.[146]

[141] *Pasley v Freeman* (1789) 3 TR 51 was a case of deceit.
[142] *Langridge* (n 99) 530–31; 868.
[143] ibid 532; 868.
[144] ibid 532; 868–69.
[145] *Longmeid* (n 94).
[146] ibid 764; 754.

Counsel for the defendant maintained that, because fraud was not found, there could be no action founded on breach of duty but only an action arising out of the contract. For that reason, the husband alone had an action. It was argued that any analogy drawn with surgeons' duties was of no assistance:

> [A surgeon's] liability arises from the common law obligation to use due care and skill towards his patient, by whomsoever employed. In like manner, a stage-coach proprietor is bound to exercise due caution in driving, and, if he neglects to do so, he is liable to any person who is thereby injured. But no duty is imposed on a tradesman to furnish articles fit for the purpose of every individual into whose hands they may come. Such a doctrine would be productive of the greatest injustice. For instance, if an accident occurred to an omnibus or a steam boat in consequence of some latent defect in the construction, could every passenger injured maintain an action against the respective builders? *Winterbottom v. Wright* is an express authority to the contrary.[147]

The Court of Exchequer found for the defendant. Unlike in *Langridge*, there was a lack of knowledge here as to the defect in the lamp and so the defendant could not be said to have acted fraudulently. Without fraud, no action was available to Mrs Longmeid.

Langridge and *Longmeid*, though different in outcome, established the principle that a defendant would be held liable in tort if he *knowingly* made a false statement. However, if knowledge was absent, the defendant's conduct could not be said to be fraudulent and there would be no liability.

ii. 'Dangerous Things'

As already identified, beyond instances of fraudulent representation there was a further exception to the privity rule when it came to product liability in tort: a duty would be owed, outside of contract, in the supply of things *inherently dangerous* or *known to be dangerous* by the supplier because of some quality or defect.

The early case of *Parry v Smith*[148] merits mention. The plaintiff was a housekeeper. The defendant gas-fitter had been employed by the plaintiff's master to repair the gas meter in a cellar in the house in which the plaintiff was employed. The defendant had, for purposes of repairing the gas meter, taken it away and replaced it with a temporary installation. After the defendant had left, the plaintiff went into the cellar to light the gas but, when he opened the cellar door, an explosion took place. The temporary installation had not been made safe.

In the resulting action before the Common Pleas Divisional Court, it was submitted for the defendant gas-fitter that there was, in fact, no case for the jury. It was argued that there was no cause of action unless there was privity of contract

[147] ibid 765; 754.
[148] *Parry v Smith* (1879) 4 CPD 325.

between the plaintiff and the defendant, or unless what had been done was a public nuisance, or unless there had been fraud, misrepresentation or concealment by the defendant.[149] In response, it was argued by counsel for the plaintiff that the action would lie because the defendant knew he was dealing with gas, 'a thing highly dangerous in itself unless great care and caution were used in its management'.[150] This, it was said, meant that the plaintiff's right of action was founded not on contract, but on the duty attaching to the use or dealing with a dangerous thing.

The plaintiff's argument was accepted by Lopes J, who said:

> I think the plaintiff's right of action is founded on a duty which I believe attaches in every case where a person is using or is dealing with a *highly dangerous thing*, which, unless managed with the greatest care, is calculated to cause injury to by-standers. To support such a right of action, *there need be no privity between the party injured and him by whose breach of duty the injury is caused, nor any fraud, misrepresentation, or concealment; nor need what is done by the defendant amount to a public nuisance. It is a misfeasance independent of contract* (emphasis added).[151]

He noted that it was strange there was no direct authority on the point, but pointed to discussion in several other cases where, he said, actions like the present had been contemplated.

More significant[152] is the 1903 Court of Appeal decision in *Clarke v Army and Navy Co-operative Society*,[153] which concerned the sale of a tin of disinfectant powder. Mr Clarke was a ticketholder at a set of co-operative stores, and the defendants were the owners of the stores. His wife went to a branch of the co-operative and, on the recommendation of a shop assistant, purchased a tin of chlorinated lime for disinfecting purposes.[154] No warning was given of any danger in relation to the tin. When Mrs Clarke went to open the tin by prising the lid up with a spoon, it was alleged that a kind of explosion occurred. Certainly, some of the powder flew up and went into her eyes, causing injury. This was the basis for the action brought by Mr and Mrs Clarke. The cause of action was either breach of warranty, or breach of a duty 'arising under the circumstances to warn a purchaser of the explosive or otherwise dangerous character of the article sold'.[155] The jury found that there was no explosion but that the tins were badly constructed and so dangerous.[156] The jury also found that the defendants were negligent in not taking further steps, and gave a verdict for the plaintiffs.[157]

In the Court of Appeal, the plaintiffs were again successful. The central question, according to Collins MR, was whether or not the tin with its contents

[149] ibid 327.
[150] ibid.
[151] ibid.
[152] See discussion in ch 5.
[153] [1903] 1 KB 155.
[154] ibid 161.
[155] ibid 155.
[156] ibid 160.
[157] ibid.

was, to the knowledge of the defendants, dangerous.[158] The defendants here knew the tins to be potentially dangerous to open and therefore owed a duty to take care to prevent injury to purchasers.[159] Romer LJ and Mathew LJ were of the same opinion, delivering brief separate judgments to similar effect.

Within two years of *Clarke*, a second decision was set down by the Court of Appeal involving duties arising from the supply of a harm-causing item: *Earl v Lubbock*.[160] In *Earl*, the defendant was a wheelwright, who had contracted to keep in repair several vans owned by a firm. The plaintiff was a driver employed by the firm. He was injured when a wheel came off the van he was driving, after that wheel, supposedly, had been repaired by the defendant's employees. Collins MR held that the principle in *Winterbottom* was conclusive.[161] Stirling and Mathew LLJ were of the same opinion. The circumstances in which the principle was laid down in *Winterbottom* were said to be 'indistinguishable' from the present case.[162] Collins MR noted that this was not a case of delivery of a dangerous thing, which was one of the circumstances that could give rise to an action by a non-party to the contract.[163]

As will be discussed in further detail in chapter five, in order to succeed a would-be litigant would have to bring their case against the manufacturer or seller of an injury-inducing product within these exceptional categories.

II. Key Case Law: *Winterbottom* to *Donoghue*

Apart from those considered already, there are several key decisions on the road to *Donoghue*. It is necessary to examine the detail of these cases, familiar though they may be: they provide crucial background to arguments advanced in the chapters to follow.

A. *Winterbottom v Wright* (1842)

In 1842, the Court of Exchequer in *Winterbottom* was asked to consider whether or not a coach-driver, employed to drive a carriage containing mail, could sustain an action against the defendant coach-supplier for injuries caused by the break-down of a coach. The supplier of the coach had, under contract, provided the coach to the Postmaster-General and had agreed to keep the coach in good condition. It was held that no such action could be brought. The Court appeared to be

[158] ibid 164.
[159] ibid.
[160] *Earl v Lubbock* [1905] 1 KB 253.
[161] ibid 256.
[162] ibid 255.
[163] ibid 256–57.

persuaded by arguments made by the defendant's counsel, Byles, who is reported to have said:

> Now it is a general rule, that wherever a wrong arises merely out of the breach of a contract, which is the case on the face of this declaration, whether the form in which the action is conceived be ex contractu or ex delicto, the party who made the contract alone can sue … If the rule were otherwise, and privity of contract were not requisite, there would be no limit to such actions. If the plaintiff may, as in this case, run through the length of three contracts, he may run through any number or series of them; and the most alarming consequences would follow the adoption of such a principle. For example, every one of the sufferers by such an accident as that which recently happened on the Versailles railway, might have his action against the manufacturer of the defective axle. So, if the chain-cable of an East Indiaman were to break, and the vessel went aground, every person affected, either in person or property, by the accident, might have an action against the manufacturer, and perhaps against every seller also of the iron.[164]

The Versailles railway accident, to which counsel referred, had taken place in the same year, and was the most catastrophic in the world around this time. Many people were injured and more than 50 people died horribly in the inferno.[165] It seems to have loomed large as a warning about the potential extent of liabilities in the modern world.

Counsel for the plaintiff, Peacock, sought to rely on the decision in *Langridge*. He argued that here the defendant entered into a contract with a public officer to supply a thing which, if it were to be imperfectly constructed, would be dangerous. It was also a thing which, 'from its nature and the use for which it was destined', was going to be driven by a coachman.[166] This was, he said, sufficient to bring this case within the principle on which *Langridge* was decided. He argued that there was nothing in *Langridge* to suggest that the defendant was aware of the particular son who was injured. Here, while the specific coachman could not be identified, the coach was, of course, to have a driver.

On this point, Byles said simply that *Langridge* was a case expressly decided on the basis that the defendant had knowledge of the party who was to use the item. There was no allegation that the defendant supplier knew that it was to be driven by the plaintiff. There was also no fraud alleged. He further distinguished *Langridge* from the case at hand in that the former concerned a weapon that was dangerous through a defect, and the defendant was alleged to have had notice of this defect. Nothing of this sort, he said, was alleged in this case. In response to a comment from the bench that *Langridge* turned on knowledge and fraud by the defendant, it seems that counsel for the plaintiff, Peacock, argued that there was indeed fraud in this case: the defendant represented, he said, the coach to be in a

164 *Winterbottom* (n 47) 110–11; 403.

165 See, eg, 'Dreadful Railroad Accident Near Paris: Immense Loss of Life' *The Times* (11 May 1842); 'The Late Railroad Accident Near Paris' *The Times* (12 May 1842); 'The Accident on the Versailles Railway' *The Times* (9 December 1842).

166 *Winterbottom* (n 47) 112; 404.

proper state, and 'whether he represented that which was false within his knowledge, or a fact as true which he did not know to be so, it was equally a fraud'.[167]

Lord Abinger CB delivered a judgment strongly in favour of the defendant. He urged that the court 'ought not to permit a doubt to rest upon this subject', or it might be the means of allowing 'an infinity of actions'.[168] He noted that he was unwilling to extend the principle in *Langridge*, which he said had failed as an authority in favour of the current action. He suggested that, in *Langridge*, the son had been the party 'really and substantially … contracting' but could not make the bargain himself.[169] Here, the plaintiff was simply a third party to the contractual arrangement. Lord Abinger went on:

> There is no privity of contract between these parties; and if the plaintiff can sue, every passenger, or even any person passing along the road, who was injured … might bring a similar action. Unless we confine the operation of such contracts as this to the parties who entered into them, the most absurd and outrageous consequences, to which I can see no limit, would ensue.[170]

Alderson B's reasoning was in similar terms:

> If we were to hold that the plaintiff could sue in such a case, there is no point at which such actions would stop. The only safe rule is to confine the right to recover to those who enter into the contract: if we go one step beyond that, there is no reason why we should not go fifty.[171]

He was not prepared to find any allegation of misrepresentation or fraud in the declaration, which meant that *Langridge* was of no assistance. There is a sense, in his reasoning, of commitment to the idea of upholding the bargain that had been freely struck: '[t]he only real argument in favour of the action is, that this is a case of hardship; but that might have been obviated, if the plaintiff had made himself a party to the contract'.[172] One cannot help but think that it would be an odd sort of supply contract that included, as parties, the employees of the public officer purchasing the item.

Gurney B simply concurred. Rolfe B was the final member of the Court to provide reasons. The duty, he said, had arisen solely from the contract. He went on:

> [T]he fallacy consists in the use of that word 'duty'. If a duty to the Postmaster-General be meant, that is true; but if a duty to the plaintiff be intended (and in that sense the word is evidently used), there was none.[173]

[167] ibid 113; 404.
[168] ibid.
[169] ibid 114; 404.
[170] ibid. See also VV Palmer, 'Why Privity Entered Tort' – An Historical Re-Examination of Winterbottom v Wright' (1983) 27 *American Journal of Legal History* 85, 92. Note: the substance of this article also appears as a chapter in VV Palmer, *The Paths to Privity: A History of Third Party Beneficiary Contracts at English Law* (Austin & Winfield, 1994). For expediency, reference will be made to the article only.
[171] *Winterbottom* (n 47) 115; 405.
[172] ibid.
[173] ibid 116; 405.

This reasoning appears to be grounded on the idea that no duty could have arisen towards the plaintiff out of the contract between the other parties.

The treatment of *Winterbottom* in subsequent case law will be the focus of chapter two. For now, it suffices to say that this case became the principal authority for the rule enduring until *Donoghue* that, if there were a contract between A and B, then C, if injured by the acts of B but not a party to that contract, could have no action in tort.

B. *George v Skivington* (1869)

There were challenges to this restrictive approach during the later nineteenth century. In *George v Skivington*,[174] the defendant chemist was found liable, having sold hairwash that had caused serious injury to Mrs George. The claim had been brought in the Court of Exchequer, and Mr and Mrs George were the plaintiffs. The pleadings alleged that Mr George had bought the bottle of hairwash, which was to be used, as the defendant knew, by Mrs George. When Mrs George used the hairwash, she had been injured and her hair destroyed.[175]

The problems for the Court stemmed from the fact that Mrs George was a married woman (rather than single, or a man). It was, by 1869, already settled that the purchaser could sue in either contract or tort. However, as a married woman, she may not have provided the consideration (we might call this the 'consideration problem'), and independently of that, may not have been the contracting party to the sale (the 'privity problem').[176] In 1869, a married woman's wealth vested in her husband,[177] and so any money possessed by Mrs George would have belonged to Mr George. Concerning the privity problem, a married woman was often considered the agent of her husband – even if she were the person handing over payment and taking the item from the seller, her husband may still be considered in law to be the true party.[178] This would, following *Tweddle* and therefore after 1861, preclude her from bringing an action on the contract.[179] A contractual action in this case would likely have failed. Of course, Mr George could have brought an action, but damages would have been modest as the injury had been suffered by Mrs George. The remaining option was tort.

[174] *George v Skivington* (1869) LR 5 Ex 1. See also [1869] WN 231 (1869) 21 LT 495, 39 LJ Ex 8, 18 WR 118, and 'Court of Exchequer, Nov. 15' *The Times* (16 November 1869) (noted as *George v Skeffington*).

[175] For a detailed discussion of this case and its background, see Ibbetson, 'George v Skivington (1869)' (n 78).

[176] Ibbetson, 'George v Skivington (1869)' (n 78) 71–72.

[177] See, eg, Law Revision Committee, *Fourth Interim Report* (Cmd 4770, December 1934) 4. This is discussed further in ch 3.

[178] See discussion in ch 3.

[179] See discussion in Ibbetson, 'George v Skivington (1869)' (n 78) 72.

There are five different reports of the case.[180] The content of the reasoning varies from report to report, a point that has been explored by Ibbetson in detail that is beyond the scope of this discussion.[181] The focus here is on the general features of the case and the Court's reasoning.

In one report, Kelly CB is recorded as saying:

> I think that, quite apart from any question of warranty, express or implied, there was a duty on the defendant, the vendor, to use ordinary care in compounding this wash for the hair … there was such a duty towards the purchaser, and it extends, in my judgment, to the person for whose use the vendor knew the compound was purchased.[182]

The warranty point – namely, that the defendant had not fraudulently warranted that the item was safe – was not important. For Kelly CB, what was important was the negligent manufacture, rather than any representation.[183]

Pigott B was also prepared to find the defendant liable, and on similar grounds to Kelly CB. He could see no reason why the duty ought not to extend to the wife of the purchaser: 'She cannot contract for herself alone, but that is no reason why the defendant's duty should stop short of her'.[184] The report in the *Law Journal* is perhaps yet more explicit on this point:

> And then comes the question whether, when the goods had been purchased by a husband *for his wife*, to the knowledge of the defendant, the duty to the wife is imposed on the defendant – whether that duty, in fact, extends to a person who could not contract for herself, who could not purchase these articles, and make a contract for them on her own account, and must do it through her husband? I cannot see how it can be reasonably suggested, that the duty stops with the husband, and does not extend to the wife in the circumstances (emphasis original).[185]

Cleasby B relied on warranty in his reasoning.[186] He saw similarities between *Langridge* and the present case, and thought the situation in *George* to be covered by the authority of *Langridge*: '[s]ubstitute the word "negligence" for "fraud"', he said, 'and the analogy between *Langridge* … and this case is complete'.[187] Unsurprisingly, then, he appeared to place importance on the fact that it was alleged that Skivington had 'held [the hair-wash] out and professed it to be of a certain quality, and it was not of that quality; and that he knew it was purchased for the purpose of being used by the female plaintiff'.[188] There is an apparent lack of recognition in this judgment of the difference between fraud and negligence – unlike

[180] (1869) LR 5 Ex 1, 21 LT 495, 39 LJ Ex 8, 18 WR 118, [1869] WN 231, and see also 'Court of Exchequer, Nov. 15' (n 174) (noted as *George v Skeffington*).
[181] Ibbetson, 'George v Skivington (1869)' (n 78) 84–85.
[182] (1869) LR 5 Ex 1, 3–4.
[183] Ibbetson, 'George v Skivington (1869)' (n 78) 82–84.
[184] (1869) LR 5 Ex 1, 4.
[185] 39 LJ Ex 8, 10.
[186] Ibbetson, 'George v Skivington (1869)' (n 78) 79.
[187] (1869) LR 5 Ex 1, 5.
[188] ibid.

in *Longmeid*, the lack of knowledge on the part of Skivington did not preclude a successful claim.[189]

Ibbetson has suggested that the impression one gets in reading the decision is that the court does not appear to have thought overly long about this case.[190] Indeed, it is not difficult to see why: '[n]o sensible legal system would allow damages to be awarded for injuries to men and single women and refuse them if exactly the same injury occurred to a married woman'.[191] Parliament had also made moves, around this time, to improve the legal status and legal rights of married women.[192]

This decision clearly had the potential for expansion. Perhaps for this reason, it became a case so widely criticised that it caused Lord Buckmaster in *Donoghue* to comment that few cases 'have lived so dangerously and lived so long',[193] and vindicated only when it received approval more than 60 years later in *Donoghue*. Chapter five returns to the criticism levelled against *George*. For now, it is sufficient to note that it was understood in some quarters as threatening the privity rule: without being a party to the contract and even in the absence of fraud, the female plaintiff was able to bring an action against the defendant chemist. The *Solicitors' Journal* reported that it had 'extended the principle of *Langridge v. Levy* most materially'.[194] The report goes on:

> As no fraud was alleged in the declaration this decision goes far beyond that of *Langridge v. Levy*, and it is the first decision where such an extension of the principle of *Langridge v. Levy* has been permitted. The principle of *George v. Skivington* is that if one person undertakes a duty towards another, the latter may have a right of action against the former for negligence in the performance of that duty although the duty arose originally entirely from a contract between the first and some third person. This principle is not a new one although it has never until now been applied to such cases as that of *George v. Skivington*. For instance, if A. employs a doctor to attend to B., and the doctor is negligent in his treatment, B. has a right of action against the doctor for the consequences of such negligence, although no party to, and ignorant of, the contract between A. and B. This is a well-known liability and one which has been long recognised. (*Pippin v Sheppard …; Gladwell v Steggall …*). The fact that the hair-wash in *George v. Skivington* was bought for the use of the female plaintiff was held to create a sufficient privity between her and the defendant to support the right of action by her, although there was no fraud by the defendant.[195]

The author of this report in the *Solicitors' Journal* seemed generally in favour of the decision, noting that, if the action were not allowed there would be no means of obtaining substantial damages for this wrong. Nevertheless, the understanding put forward is that this case marked a radical step and an extension of a principle that had 'hitherto been very carefully restricted'.[196]

[189] See discussion in Ibbetson, 'George v Skivington (1869)' (n 78) 79 on this point.
[190] Ibbetson, 'George v Skivington (1869)' (n 78) 75.
[191] ibid.
[192] See discussion in ch 3.
[193] *Donoghue v Stevenson* [1932] AC 562, 570.
[194] 'Right of Action – Privity – Negligence: *George and Wife v Skivington*' (1870) 14 *Solicitors' Journal and Reporter* 309, 314.
[195] ibid 315.
[196] ibid.

C. *Heaven v Pender* (1883)

Along with *George*, *Heaven v Pender*[197] is another case in which a restrictive approach to finding tortious duties alongside contractual liability was challenged, though by only one of the three members of the Court of Appeal.

The defendant was the owner of a dry dock used for painting ships and supplied staging for that purpose. The plaintiff was the employee of a master painter, engaged by the owner of a vessel in the defendant's dock. The plaintiff was injured when a rope in the staging gave way and he fell into the dock. There was evidence that the ropes were scorched, and therefore not fit for use. The county court judge had given judgment for the plaintiff but a rule nisi obtained by the defendant was upheld in the Queen's Bench Divisional Court.[198] The plaintiff appealed, and was successful before Brett MR, Cotton LJ and Bowen LJ.

Brett MR considered it unnecessary for the Court to consider the question of fraudulent misrepresentation here, which he acknowledged was a well-recognised head of law.[199] Instead, he identified the question for the Court as whether or not the defendant owed to the plaintiff a duty to take care to prevent injury, outside of contract and aside from fraud. He found there to be such a duty in this case. His reasoning may be understood to advocate a general principle that a duty of care should exist towards all those foreseeably harmed by negligence:[200]

> [W]henever one person is by circumstances placed in such a position with regard to another that every one of ordinary sense who did think would at once recognise that if he did not use ordinary care and skill in his own conduct with regard to those circumstances he would cause danger of injury to the person or property of the other, a duty arises to use ordinary care and skill to avoid such danger.[201]

This principle, he said, included all the cases of recognised liability (such as *Langridge*).[202] Brett MR clearly saw *George* as an instance of this wide principle:

> [T]he article was, to the knowledge of the defendant, supplied for the use of the wife and for her immediate use … if he or anyone in his position had thought at all, it must have

[197] (1883) 11 QBD 503.
[198] (1882) 9 QBD 302.
[199] *Heaven* (n 114) 507.
[200] See Lobban, 'Personal Injuries' (n 107) 988.
[201] *Heaven* (n 114) 509.
[202] Brett MR was highly critical of *Langridge* and deemed it unsatisfactory to act on as an authority. He said it could not be accurately reported, pointing out the apparent inconsistency in the grounds for the motion and on which the decision was based. Nevertheless, he said: 'taking the case to be decided on the ground of a fraudulent misrepresentation made hypothetically to the son, and acted upon by him, such a decision upon such a ground, in no way negatives the proposition that the action might have been supported on the ground of negligence without fraud. It seems to be a case which is within the proposition enunciated in this judgment, and in which the action might have been supported without proof of actual fraud. And this seems to be the meaning of Cleasby, B., in the observations he made on *Langridge v. Levy* … in the case of *George v. Skivington*': 511–12. See also Barton, 'Liability for Things in the Nineteenth Century' (n 140).

> been obvious that a want of ordinary care or skill in preparing the prescription sold, would endanger the personal safety of the wife.[203]

As to *Winterbottom*, he said that the declaration did not seem to demonstrate that the defendant, if he had thought about it, must have known, or ought to have known, that the coach would be necessarily or probably driven by the plaintiff. The declaration 'relied too much on contracts entered into with other persons than the plaintiff', and that the 'facts alleged did not bring the case within the proposition herein enunciated'.[204] He appeared to think that counsel for the plaintiff was proposing a principle more extensive than the principle he himself was advocating in the present case: 'it was an attempt to establish a duty towards all the world … the case was decided on the ground of remoteness'.[205]

The rest of the Court (Cotton LJ, Bowen LJ concurring) did not agree with Brett MR's approach but found for the plaintiff on different grounds. It was said that those working on the ship must be considered as having been *invited* by the dock owner to use all appliances. The dock owner benefited from the workers' presence, receiving payment for the use of the dock. To such people the dock owner owed a duty to take reasonable care that the appliances provided were fit for use.[206] As to *George*, Cotton LJ referred only to the judgment of Cleasby B. While acknowledging that *George* might seem to support the general principle advocated by Brett MR, he did not support such a principle. *George* was thus apparently cast as standing for a wider principle than one might have anticipated, which, Ibbetson has suggested, would prove to be detrimental to its reputation for the next 50 years.[207]

D. *Blacker v Lake and Elliot* (1912)

Blacker v Lake and Elliot[208] demonstrates the strength of the privity rule understood to come from *Winterbottom*: any wider principle that might be put forward by *George*, it was said, could not stand as it would be inconsistent with *Winterbottom*.

In *Blacker*, the plaintiff was a bicycle-maker, who had been seriously burned when a brazing lamp exploded; a joint in the lamp broke and caused ignited paraffin oil to spill out. He had purchased the lamp not from the defendants, the makers

[203] *Heaven* (n 114) 512.
[204] ibid 513.
[205] ibid.
[206] ibid 514–17.
[207] Ibbetson argues that the 'treatment meted out to [*George*] in *Heaven* … had weakened it seriously'. It was increasingly marginalised in the early twentieth century: see Ibbetson, 'George v Skivington (1869)' (n 78) 91.
[208] *Blacker v Lake and Elliot* (1912) 106 LT 533.

of the lamp, but from a firm selling various articles required in bicycle-making. There was therefore no privity of contract between the injured party and the defendants. The nature of the lamp was such that it was a portable instrument that could supply a 'powerful and easily directed flame' – that is to say, a blowtorch.[209] The plaintiff was successful in the county court but unsuccessful before Hamilton and Lush JJ in the King's Bench Divisional Court.

The plaintiff's case was that the lamp was a 'dangerous thing', and that the maker owed a duty of care and skill which extended 'not only to the employment of skill in the manufacture and the avoidance of a possible case of misfeasance, but even to an obligation … to provide themselves with the best knowledge in existence at the time'.[210] The respondents, on the other hand, relied upon comments made in *Langridge* to the effect that care should be taken before a precedent was created for an action against the vendors, even regarding articles dangerous in themselves, at the suit of *any* person who might be injured.[211] Similarly cautious comments in *Longmeid* were also brought to the attention of the bench.[212]

Hamilton J took the view that the lamp was not a 'dangerous thing'. The lamp had worked safely for almost a year. Citing *Winterbottom*, *Earl* and *Cavalier*, Hamilton J went on to note that it was established that a breach of the defendant's contract with A, due to a lack of skill and care in manufacture or repair, will not itself give rise to any claim being available to B if B is injured by the defective article.[213] Hamilton J then proceeded to an extensive discussion of *George*, noting its unsettled reception: it had perhaps been followed, but not expressly affirmed and had been expressly doubted.[214] Reviewing several subsequent decisions, he confirmed his inability 'to see in these judgments any dissent from the discredit cast on the decision in *George*'.[215] Ultimately, Hamilton J concluded that *George* was not a case that he felt able to follow, being in conflict with *Winterbottom*.

Lush J asserted the law following *Earl* and *Cavalier* to be that, where an ordinary chattel – that is, not one that is 'dangerous' – is manufactured negligently, negligence 'cannot be made the foundation of an action by a person towards whom there was no contractual duty'.[216] The privity rule and the authority of *Winterbottom* was empathically confirmed; the only option for an injured consumer was to bring

[209] ibid 534.
[210] ibid 536.
[211] ibid 537; *Langridge* (n 99) 530; 868.
[212] *Blacker* (n 208) 537. Parke B suggested in *Longmeid* that 'it would be going much too far to say, that so much care is required in the ordinary intercourse of life between one individual and another, that, if a machine not in its nature dangerous, – a carriage for instance, – but which might become so by a latent defect entirely unknown, although discoverable by the exercise of ordinary care, should be lent or given by one person, even by the person who manufactured it, to another, the former should be answerable to the latter for a subsequent damage accruing by the use of it': 768; 755.
[213] *Blacker* (n 208) 536.
[214] ibid.
[215] ibid 539.
[216] ibid 540.

their case within one of the established exceptions. To maintain an action for a defective chattel, a stranger to a contract had to demonstrate one of three classes of case: fraud or misrepresentation as to safety; chattels dangerous in themselves; or the supply of things constituting a public nuisance.[217] Lush J also dealt unfavourably with *George*. He said that, although the case had never been overruled, it was often relied upon as establishing that a party who undertakes to do work under a contract is bound to use due care in doing the relevant work, and could be sued for the breach of that duty by somebody not a party to the contract if the defendant knew that the person was going to use the thing made.[218] This, he said, was inconsistent with *Winterbottom*, *Earl* and other authorities.[219] It was therefore 'quite impossible now, in view of these numerous authorities, to follow the decision in *George* … and it cannot … be regarded as good law in so far as it lays down the general proposition to which I have referred'.[220]

E. *Mullen v Barr* (1929)

The Scottish case of *Mullen v Barr*[221] is significant for its closeness, in time and in factual and legal content, to *Donoghue*. Despite this closeness, the plaintiffs in *Mullen* failed.

Two actions for damages were brought against a ginger beer manufacturer, Barr & Co, and concerned injuries allegedly sustained through consumption of a bottle of ginger beer containing a decaying mouse. The first action was brought by Francis Mullen on behalf of his two children. The evidence was that Mrs Mullen, the children's mother, had purchased the bottle and had given some to both children. The second was brought by Mrs M'Gowan, who alleged that her son had bought for her a bottle of ginger beer and that, after discovering the mouse, she had become ill. Both actions were brought in negligence.[222] In both cases, the defenders pleaded that the actions were irrelevant and sought their dismissal. In the Sheriff Court, the Mullen case was dismissed and the M'Gowan action was allowed to go to proof before answer. Appeals were lodged in both cases, and it was decided that both would go to proof before answer. In both cases, it was established that the pursuers had indeed consumed some of the contents of a dark glass bottle of the defenders' ginger beer containing the corpse of a mouse, resulting in temporary illness. The defenders led unchallenged evidence that their system for

[217] ibid 540–41.
[218] ibid 540.
[219] eg, *Malone v Laskey* [1907] 2 KB 141: this was another case of alleged negligence in repair work, this time by the servants of the defendant landlords. The plaintiff was injured when a bracket fixed under a water tank fell onto her. It was held that no duty was owed to the plaintiff.
[220] *Blacker* (n 208) 540.
[221] *Mullen v Barr* 1929 SC 461. The SLT report differs slightly and does not contain as much detail as to the arguments advanced: see *Mullen v Barr* 1929 SLT 341.
[222] In *Mullen*, the counsel for the pursuer expressly gave up, in argument, any argument based on implied warranty.

cleaning and inspection was the 'best known in the trade', and that for at least 35 years there had been no other instance of a mouse being found in the bottles.

The pursuers' legal team sought to establish that '[o]ut of the contracts between two parties a general duty might arise towards third parties', citing, amongst other authorities, *Foulkes*.[223] Beyond the two 'supply of dangerous things' exceptions to the rule that a manufacturer owes no duty to the ultimate consumer outside of contract, the pursuers asserted that another exception existed: where, if there was carelessness by the manufacturer, damage to the final user of the article would probably result.[224] They noted that *George* had never been overruled, and that it had been 'recognised that [*George*] could be supported on the ground that a person who sent out a dangerous compound, the dangerous character of which he did not know but would have known if he had used reasonable care, was in the same position as if he had known'.[225] The pursuers also sought to distinguish the facts at hand from those in *Winterbottom*, *Longmeid* and *Earl* on the basis that the defect in those earlier cases had been 'native to the product', rather than being a foreign substance.[226]

The defenders denied the existence of a duty of care and asserted that there were only two, not three, exceptions to the general rule against a duty's being owed by a manufacturer to a consumer: supplying an item not usually dangerous but known to be dangerous without disclosing such danger, and supplying an item dangerous in itself.[227] The defenders argued that *George* might be understood to follow *Langridge* and to be decided on the same grounds (misrepresenting the safety of a product) and, if not, it was unsound; for this, the reasoning of Hamilton J in *Blacker* was cited. If a duty did exist, they said, there was no proof of negligence: the system was sound.

Lord Ormidale and Lord Anderson decided in favour of the defenders. The Lord Justice-Clerk reserved his opinion on the duty question but dismissed the pursuers' claim on the basis that no negligence had been established. Lord Ormidale lamented the 'difficulty of determining … [the question of whether or not a duty was owed by the manufacturers of a product to the consumer] with either confidence or satisfaction', and said that 'were it not for the unbroken and consistent current of decisions beginning with *Winterbottom*', he would have been 'disposed to answer it in the affirmative'.[228] As to the two recognised exceptions, he said that ginger beer was not 'intrinsically dangerous', and it had not been alleged that the defenders *knew* of the deleterious matter contained in the bottles. He dismissed *George* as authority for a third exception or extension, saying that it was, as it had always been, 'regarded as of little, if any, authority'.[229] Other authorities

[223] *Mullen* (n 221) 464–65. See above (n 83).
[224] *Mullen* (n 221) 465.
[225] ibid.
[226] ibid.
[227] ibid 465–66.
[228] ibid 471.
[229] ibid.

relied upon by the pursuers – *Dominion Natural Gas Company v Collins*[230] and *Thomas v Winchester*[231] – were interpreted as instances of the supply of dangerous things, and thus within established categories in which a duty was owed. Lord Ormidale further found that, in any event, if a duty was owed, there had been no negligence in its performance.

Similarly, Lord Anderson thought the pursuers had failed to bring their cases under one of the recognised exceptions to the general rule that manufacturers owed no duty to final consumers of goods.[232] The Lord Justice-Clerk asserted that the position established by the authorities was that

> a man who puts a product manufactured by him on the market has no duty to anyone regarding it except to the person with whom he contracts, unless (a) he knows that the article which he sells is dangerous and conceals that knowledge from the buyer, in which case he is guilty of a fraud, or (b) he is a dealer in articles which are *per se* dangerous, e.g., explosives, and gives no warning to the buyer of the fact.[233]

He declared himself unable to 'discover any adequate authority for the third exception from the general rule'.[234] He asserted that *George*, on which the pursuer relied, had been treated with 'scant respect', and he took 'the liberty of doubting whether it is part of the law of England to-day'.[235] However, he ultimately avoided the duty issue (described as a 'thorny and difficult question of law') and based his final conclusion on the fact that the pursuer had failed to prove fault on behalf of the defenders.

In dissent, Lord Hunter was not satisfied that the classification put forward by the defenders – namely, the two exceptions to the general rule – was exhaustive.[236] He did not think that the relationship of duty was confined to cases of the supply of dangerous goods. He appeared to approve Brett MR's wide formulation in *Heaven* of when a duty might be owed, noting that 'in its practical application

[230] *Dominion Natural Gas Company v Collins* [1909] AC 640. *Dominion* concerned damage sustained when a gas leak caused an explosion. The plaintiffs were two injured workers employed by a railway company, who were not in a contractual relationship with the gas company. After being held liable for damages in the Court of Appeal in Canada, the gas company appealed to the Privy Council. However, it was unsuccessful; the Privy Council affirmed the decision of the Court of Appeal in favour of the workers. Lord Dunedin, delivering the judgment of the Committee, said, after noting that no contractual action would be available: 'There may be, however, in the case of any one performing an operation, or setting up and installing a machine, a relationship of duty. What that duty is will vary according to the subject-matter of the things involved. It has, however, again and again been held that in the case of articles dangerous in themselves, such as loaded firearms, poisons, explosives, and other things ejusdem generis, there is a peculiar duty to take precaution imposed upon those who send forth or install such articles when it is necessarily the case that other parties will come within their proximity': 646.

[231] *Thomas v Winchester* (1852) 6 NY 397, an American decision: a chemist was held liable when a third party became seriously ill after ingesting a medicine labelled 'extract of dandelion', but which contained deadly belladonna.

[232] *Mullen* (n 221) 480.

[233] ibid 469.

[234] ibid.

[235] ibid 469–70.

[236] ibid 475.

qualification of the terms … may be required', but suggesting that it nevertheless formed a 'useful guide'.[237] He referred to the outcome in *George* without noting any negative reception, or suggesting that it was not reliable authority. He appeared to draw a somewhat artificial distinction between the facts at hand and those in *Winterbottom*, *Earl*, *Bates* and *Blacker*, on the basis that in the latter cases there was 'not such a relationship established between the parties as, in the absence of contract, to create a duty on the defendant towards the plaintiff, and the claim of damages was too remote to be considered as the direct or natural result of the alleged negligence'.[238] We can see this as an attempt to move the law forward by side-stepping what his colleagues recognised as binding authority against this outcome.

F. *Donoghue v Stevenson* (1932)

The reign of privity in tort came to an end in 1932. *Donoghue*'s fame means that it requires only a short introduction. Mrs Donoghue claimed to have become seriously ill after discovering that her partially consumed ginger beer contained a decomposing snail. She had not purchased the ginger beer herself; her friend had purchased it for her consumption. Mrs Donoghue was party to no contract, which, on a strict application of the law as it stood, might have precluded her suit for the injuries sustained. It was argued for Mrs Donoghue, when her case reached the House of Lords:

> When a manufacturer puts upon a market an article intended for human consumption in a form which precludes the possibility of an examination of the article by the retailer or the consumer, he is liable to the consumer for not taking reasonable care to see that the article is not injurious to health. In the circumstances of this case the respondent owed a duty to the appellant to take care that the ginger-beer which he manufactured, bottled, labelled and sealed … and which he invited the appellant to buy, contained nothing which would cause her injury.

For this argument, counsel relied upon *George* (noting that, while it had not always been favourably commented on, it had not been overruled) and invited the court also to consider the decision of Brett MR in *Heaven*, among other authorities.[239] The case rested solely upon negligence, rather than any suggestion of fraud.

As in *Mullen*, counsel for the respondent sought to argue that there was no 'third' exception to the general rule that a manufacturer owed no duty to the final consumer, outside of contract. It was also asserted that Brett MR's statement of

[237] ibid 476.
[238] ibid 476–77.
[239] *Donoghue* (n 193) 564.

principle in *Heaven* had cast the principle too widely and had not been accepted in that case or subsequently. Both Hamilton and Lush JJ in *Blacker*, counsel said, had treated *George* as overruled and inconsistent with *Winterbottom*, insofar as it proceeded on a duty's being owed to the ultimate user of a product.[240]

It seems that it was agreed between the parties, and had not been queried in earlier proceedings or by the House of Lords, that 'the English and the Scots law on the subject are identical'.[241] Lord Atkin, Lord Macmillan and Lord Thankerton formed the majority in upholding Mrs Donoghue's claim, with Lord Buckmaster and Lord Tomlin dissenting. It was recognised that a manufacturer of products owed a duty to the ultimate consumer to take care in their manufacture, in circumstances where the article reached the consumer in the condition in which it left the manufacturer and there was no opportunity for intermediate examination.[242]

Lord Atkin's decision has become the most famous, particularly his discussion of the 'neighbour principle' and general approach to negligence.[243] He opened his speech by asserting the importance of the case at hand, stating dramatically:

> I do not think a more important problem has occupied your Lordships in your judicial capacity: important both because of its bearing on public health and because of the practical test which it applies to the system under which it arises.[244]

The neighbour principle aside, Lord Atkin's decision on the narrower question of whether or not a manufacturer owes a duty of care to the final consumer is based principally upon consequences. He came close to rejecting established authorities out of concern for the consequences for injured consumers if no duty were recognised. He stated:

> It is said that the law of England and Scotland is that the poisoned consumer has no remedy against the negligent manufacturer. If this were the result of the authorities, I should consider the result a grave defect in the law, and so contrary to principle that I should hesitate long before following any decision to that effect which had not the authority of this House.

In the end, he found that 'on examination … there is no case in which the circumstances have been such as I have just suggested where the liability has been negatived'[245] and found support in cases such as *George* and *Oliver v Saddler and Company*[246] – the latter being a case he had decided. Lord Thankerton delivered a relatively short speech stating his agreement with Lord Atkin.

[240] ibid 565–66.
[241] ibid 566 (Lord Buckmaster). See also, for example, 602–03 (Lord Thankerton) and 618, 621 (Lord Macmillan).
[242] *Donoghue* (n 193) 582, 595, 599 (Lord Atkin); 622 (Lord Macmillan).
[243] See *Donoghue* (n 193) 580.
[244] ibid 579.
[245] ibid 583.
[246] *Oliver v Saddler and Company* [1929] AC 584.

Lord Macmillan was, as Whittaker has suggested, perhaps the clearest in rejecting the notion that privity of contract operated to constrain the law of negligence.[247] He was unconvinced by the assertion that there was an 'unbroken' line of authority from *Winterbottom* to which Lord Ormidale had referred in *Mullen*.[248] He expressly sought to show, in his reasoning, that there was no such line of authority that would justify the suggestion that the law was irrevocably committed to a principle that was 'neither reasonable nor equitable'.[249] He did not think *George* had deserved to be severely handled (if it had been), and was prepared to accept Brett MR's *Heaven* principle as a sound guide.[250] However, he appeared not to support the kind of general approach to negligence advocated by Lord Atkin. Instead, his reasoning appears to advocate the continuance of the 'catalogue' approach, with a duty of care recognised in appropriate relationships:

> [T]he conception of legal responsibility may develop in adaptation to altering social conditions and standards. The criterion of judgment must adjust and adapt itself to the changing circumstances of life. The categories of negligence are never closed (emphasis added).[251]

As Rodger has uncovered, it seems that Lord Macmillan wrote two versions, both marked 'final' and 'confidential', but only delivered one.[252] In the earlier draft he focused on Scottish law and purported to decide the case on the basis of Scottish material. This differs markedly from the version delivered, which treats Scottish and English law as being sufficiently alike on this subject as to decide based on principles common to both. Rodger suggests that the most likely explanation for this change was the persuasion of Lord Atkin.[253] Rodger notes that *Donoghue* was the case for which many in the legal profession had been waiting: '*Donoghue* was that test case and Lord Atkin was clearly determined to settle the matter and to write himself into the history books'.[254]

Whether or not this is true, it is clear that the Law Lords were aware of the importance of this decision.

In dissent, Lord Buckmaster carefully went through the authorities relied upon by the appellant.[255] He quoted from Parke B's words of caution in *Langridge* about the scope of the precedent created and noted the narrow application

[247] Whittaker (n 122) 69.
[248] *Donoghue* (n 193) 608.
[249] ibid.
[250] ibid 614–15.
[251] ibid 619.
[252] See A Rodger, 'Lord Macmillan's speech in Donoghue v Stevenson' (1992) 108 *Law Quarterly Review* 236, 236–38 and generally. The earlier draft judgment is included in an appendix to the article.
[253] Rodger (n 236) 246. See also discussion in P Mitchell, 'The impact of institutions and professions on fault liability in England' in P Mitchell (ed), *The Impact of Institutions and Professions on Legal Development* (Cambridge University Press, 2012) 23–25.
[254] Rodger (n 236) 246.
[255] *Donoghue* (n 193) 567–78.

ascribed to that case in *Longmeid*. He went on to say that *Langridge* could thus be 'dismissed from consideration with the comment that it is rather surprising it has so often been cited for a proposition it cannot support'.[256] He noted that the general principle applicable to cases of manufactured goods was that laid down in *Blacker*, namely that there is generally no duty owed towards B arising through the breach of a defendant's contract with A to use care and skill in the manufacture of a product. To this, there were just two exceptions, both based on the dangerous nature of the article. He knew of no other modification of the general rule, other than *George*, and he did 'not propose to follow the fortunes of *George*'.[257] It was, he said, in conflict with *Winterbottom*. Any argument based on Brett MR's general principle in *Heaven* was also firmly rejected, Lord Buckmaster noting that the majority in that case was not in support of such a wide principle. *George* and *Heaven*, he said, 'should be buried so securely that their perturbed spirits shall no longer vex the law'.[258] The decisions coming out of the United States, *Thomas* and the more recent 1916 case of *MacPherson v Buick Motor Company*,[259] were treated as cases concerning dangerous articles.[260] He therefore found the authorities to be against Mrs Donoghue's contention and that the appeal ought to be dismissed.

Lord Tomlin delivered only a short speech, agreeing with Lord Buckmaster. He added that, if the appellant were to succeed, this would mean that every manufacturer was under a duty to everyone 'who may thereafter legitimately use the article'.[261] He also noted that *Winterbottom* was 'directly in point against the appellant'; it was clear, he said, that negligence had been alleged in that case and was the basis of the claim, and that the plaintiff had there contended for the wide proposition – that is, a duty owed by manufacturers to consumers. Both Lord Buckmaster and Lord Tomlin advanced the point that if the law was as the appellant said it was, then it was impossible to explain how the cases involving 'dangerous' things could have been treated as exceptions.

It has been suggested on several occasions by commentators and judges alike that it is likely that the facts in *Donoghue* were fabricated; that there was never any

[256] ibid 567.
[257] ibid 569–70.
[258] ibid 576.
[259] *MacPherson v Buick Motor Company* (1916) 217 NY 382, 111 NE 1050. See, on this point, F Bohlen, 'Liability of manufacturers to persons other than their immediate vendees' (1929) 45 *Law Quarterly Review* 343. Bohlen suggests that *MacPherson* had the effect, in several jurisdictions in the US, of 'stimulating the already existing tendency to extend the previously recognized exceptions to the manufacturer's immunity which imposed liability for negligence in the manufacture of "imminently dangerous" articles, for failure to disclose known defects in "non-dangerous articles". So widely have these exceptions, particularly the latter, been extended that in many American jurisdictions little or nothing is left of the original immunity': 361–62. Lord Atkin in *Donoghue* also treated *MacPherson* as a case supportive of the appellant's case, and the judgment of Cardozo J as one in which 'he states the principles of the law as I should desire to state them': 598.
[260] *Donoghue* (n 193) 577.
[261] ibid 599.

snail.[262] Indeed, this has even been suggested in the Court of Appeal.[263] Following the decision of the House of Lords the case was to go to proof. However, unfortunately Mr Stevenson passed away before the date set down. Thereafter, his estate settled the claim.[264] Heuston asserted confidently in 1957 that this 'persistent rumour' was false and that the 'truth is that the issue of fact was never decided: the defender died before proof and the pursuer in consequence compromised the action and received £100 in settlement of her claim'.[265] Geoffrey Lewis, who wrote a biography of Lord Atkin, notes that the 'no snail' story was traced by Lord Atkin through Lord Macmillan to something said by Stevenson's counsel.[266]

There are several factors that suggest a likely element of invention to the *Donoghue* case. Mr Leechman, Mrs Donoghue's solicitor, acted pro bono. At first glance, this may seem a charitable act. However, the situation becomes more curious when coupled with the knowledge that Mr Leechman had acted for the soft drink manufacturer in *Mullen*. A very short amount of time passed between the unsuccessful final outcome in the *Mullen* litigation and Mr Leechman's commencing the *Donoghue* claim: less than three weeks.[267] It is also curious that the case was commenced in the Court of Session, when it is likely that the local Sheriff Court had jurisdiction.[268] McBryde has also noted the following:

> Mrs. Donoghue's action cannot have appeared to have had good prospects. She probably had very little money. The defender was a businessman with a reputation to defend. On the point of law involved the highest civil court situated in Scotland had indicated that the defender would not be liable. How many practitioners today would tell a poor client with a belly upset to sue, and persist to the House of Lords, if necessary, although there were recent adverse decisions of an appeal court which involved intruding rodents rather than an intruding gastropod?[269]

How this case, ostensibly unlikely to succeed given the recent decision in *Mullen*, was *financed* is also curious. Mrs Donoghue did not litigate *in forma pauperis* until her case reached the House of Lords.[270] McBryde speculates that it may

[262] See, eg, Heuston (n 137) 2; G Lewis, *Lord Atkin* (Butterworths, 1983) 52; MR Taylor, 'Mrs Donoghue's Journey', *Donoghue v Stevenson: Resources*, Scottish Council of Law Reporting: www.scottishlawreports.org.uk/resources/dvs/mrs-donoghue-journey.html; James Edelman, 'Fundamental Errors in Donoghue v Stevenson?', Speech to the Friends of University of Western Australia, London, July 2014: www.supremecourt.wa.gov.au/_files/Fundamental%20Errors%20in%20Donoghue%20v%20Stevenson%20by%20Edelman%20J%20July%202014.pdf.

[263] See *Adler v Dickson* [1954] 1 WLR 1482, 1483 (Jenkins LJ).

[264] See, eg, D Ashton-Cross, 'Donoghue v Stevenson' (1955) 71 *Law Quarterly Review* 472, 472.

[265] Heuston (n 137) 2.

[266] Lewis, *Lord Atkin* (n 262) 52, discussed in Taylor (n 262).

[267] Taylor (n 262).

[268] See, eg, J Conn, 'Gingerlore: The Legends of Donoghue v Stevenson' (2013) 3 *Juridical Review* 265, 277–78.

[269] WW McBryde, 'Donoghue v Stevenson: The Story of the 'Snail in the Bottle' Case' in AJ Gamble (ed), *Obligations in Context: Essays in Honour of Professor DM Walker* (Edinburgh W Green, 1990) 22.

[270] ibid 49.

well have been a speculative action, with payment to her lawyers contingent on success.[271]

It seems likely that this was indeed, as Rodger has said, a test case. The proximity to *Mullen* is striking. We might speculate, without being able to confirm, that interested parties were financing the progress of the case before it reached the House of Lords. It is not necessary to explore this in depth; indeed, it is likely that the evidence is simply not available. It will suffice to say that it is likely that the *Donoghue* litigation was the chance for which many had been waiting. It was desirable that the law should 'move with the times'.

[271] ibid.

2

Winterbottom in the Courts: Consequences to Formalism

As noted in 1983 by Vernon Palmer, the rise of the privity doctrine in tort has been 'one of the most enigmatic, controversial, and misunderstood phenomena of 19th century law'.[1] In particular, there has been substantial disagreement as to the correct interpretation of the 1842 decision in *Winterbottom v Wright* and its impact upon the development of the law of negligence.[2]

This chapter is devoted to explaining the decision in *Winterbottom*, which was introduced in the previous chapter, and then to understanding its treatment in subsequent case law. It will be suggested that the most plausible explanation for the outcome is that the court in *Winterbottom* was motivated principally by concern for the consequences of imposing liability: a desire not to impose a potentially significant liability upon would-be defendants to a vastly increased pool of possible plaintiffs. In 1842, the *Winterbottom* court was concerned more with economic consequences than with doctrine. It is argued that this is the way the outcome in *Winterbottom* was understood and applied for many years. Then, in the lead up to *Donoghue v Stevenson*, there grew a tendency to formalism in the application of the privity rule; it became a rule often rigidly applied and treated as an insurmountable bar to recovery. A general shift is discernible, in the case law that makes up the orthodox story, from consequence-based (or policy) reasoning to doctrinal reasoning.

I. Understanding *Winterbottom*

A. *Winterbottom*: 'Privity Fallacy'

Some commentators have suggested that, in coming to its conclusion, the *Winterbottom* court fell for the 'privity of contract fallacy': believing that the existence of a contract between A and B prevented C from suing B in tort for carelessness in relation to those contractual obligations, unless C was also a party to

[1] VV Palmer, 'Why Privity Entered Tort – An Historical Re-Examination of Winterbottom v Wright' (1983) 27 *American Journal of Legal History* 85, 85.

[2] ibid 92.

the contract.[3] Parts of Lord Abinger's judgment could be understood in that way; for example:

> There is also a class of cases in which the law permits a contract to be turned into a tort; but unless there has been some public duty undertaken, or public nuisance committed, they are all cases in which an action might have been maintained upon the contract. Thus, a carrier may be sued either in assumpsit or case; but there is no instance in which a party, who was not privy to the contract entered into with him, can maintain any such action. The plaintiff in this case could not have brought an action on the contract.[4]

Others have argued that this interpretation is flawed. Atiyah does not support the notion that the judges actually fell for any fallacy 'which escaped the perspicuity of judges like Abinger CB … [and] was, of course, brilliantly exposed in the twentieth century in *Donoghue*'.[5] He goes so far as to label the story 'complete nonsense'.[6] Similarly, Palmer labels it a misconception to think that the *Winterbottom* court was deceived by the 'privity fallacy' and simply adopted the view that the tort action was unavailable because the plaintiff was not a party to the contract.[7] Instead, he argues that privity was part of a more complex analysis. In Palmer's view, the judicial reasoning process had three steps: first, the absence of any recognised duty; second, the perception that the tort action may be at odds with the normal rule against the concurrence of tortious and contractual remedies; and, third, the privity point.[8] Palmer argues that it is evident from the report that the court reached the conclusion that the plaintiff had no remedy, even without the privity point.[9] He points, amongst other things, to Lord Abinger's comment that the plaintiff was 'remediless':

> We ought not to attempt to extend the principle [in *Langridge v Levy*] … which, although it has been cited in support of this action, wholly fails as an authority in its favour … Here the action is brought simply because the defendant was a contractor with a third person; and it is contended that thereupon he became liable to every body who might use the carriage. If there had been any ground for such an action, there certainly would have been some precedent of it; but with the exception of actions against innkeepers, and some few other persons, no case of a similar nature has occurred in practice. That is a strong circumstance, and is of itself a great authority against its maintenance. It is however contended, that this contract being made on the behalf of the public by

[3] See, eg, PH Winfield, 'Duty in Tortious Negligence' (1934) 34 *Columbia Law Review* 41, 54–55; PH Winfield, *The Province of the Law of Tort* (Cambridge University Press, 1931) 74–75. Winfield points also to *Alton v Midland Railway* (1865) 19 CB NS 213,144 ER 768, in which, he suggests, the court had a 'hypnotic gaze' upon privity and saw it as precluding the recognition of a duty in tort. See also MJ Prichard, 'Scott v Shepherd (1773) and the Emergence of the Tort of Negligence' in *The Selden Society Lectures, 1952-2001* (Hein, 2003) 444; RFV Heuston, '*Donoghue v Stevenson* in Retrospect' (1957) 20 *Modern Law Review* 1, 10.

[4] *Winterbottom v Wright* (1842) 10 M & W 109, 115; 152 ER 402, 405.

[5] PS Atiyah, *The Rise and Fall of Freedom of Contract* (Oxford University Press, 1979) 502.

[6] ibid.

[7] Palmer (n 1) 93.

[8] ibid 93–94.

[9] ibid 94.

> the Postmaster-General, no action could be maintained against him, and therefore the plaintiff must have a remedy against the defendant. *But that is by no means a necessary consequence – he may be remediless altogether* (emphasis added).[10]

Palmer suggests that 'the "fallacy" argument must fall of its own weight if it is possible to show that the court truly reached a motivated conclusion that plaintiff was altogether remediless in tort quite apart from any privity considerations'.[11] He points to Lord Abinger's observations that *Langridge v Levy* was not to be extended further and that no 'public duty'[12] existed which would cover the facts at hand, which, says Palmer, was Lord Abinger's attempt to 'demonstrate the absence of an actionable tort'.[13]

However, when one considers more closely the context in which the 'remediless altogether' comment is made, it is clear that Lord Abinger is rebuffing the assertion that the court *must* find for the plaintiff, otherwise the plaintiff would suffer injustice as no other action is available.[14] The Postmaster-General was immune from suit,[15] so the plaintiff could indeed have been left, if the action pursued had failed, without a remedy. Lord Abinger is merely stating that the court is not *compelled* to find for the plaintiff; he may indeed be remediless. This understanding is supported by the final words of Rolfe B:

> This is one of those unfortunate cases in which there certainly has been damnum, but it is damnum absque injuria; it is, no doubt, a hardship upon the plaintiff to be without a remedy, but by that consideration we ought not to be influenced. Hard cases, it has been frequently observed, are apt to introduce bad law.[16]

The privity point was material to the conclusion that no action was available. Indeed, before the 'remediless' comment was made, Lord Abinger had already raised the subject of parties to the contract in distinguishing the case at hand from *Langridge*; he seemed to suggest that *Langridge* involved a situation *akin* to privity. Reliance on the notion of privity is apparent already in the first part of Lord Abinger's reasoning and not only as a third and additional point.

This is not to say that the *Winterbottom* court 'fell' for any privity fallacy; it was not lured into making any kind of category error. The second line of Lord Abinger's reasons provide a compelling indication of why the privity rule was relied upon by the court: '[w]e ought not to permit a doubt to rest upon this subject, for our doing so might be the means of letting in upon us an infinity of actions'.[17] As discussed

[10] *Winterbottom* (n 4) 114; 405–05.

[11] Palmer (n 1) 94.

[12] *Winterbottom* (n 4) 114; 405. See also *Langridge v Levy* (1837) 2 M & W 519, 150 ER 863.

[13] Palmer (n 1) 94.

[14] See *Winterbottom* (n 4) 114; 405.

[15] Possibly because of the role he occupied and the fact that the contract was made on behalf of the public (*Winterbottom* (n 4) 405) but also as a consequence of *Priestley v Fowler* (1837) 3 M & W 1, 150 ER 1030: see William Cornish et al, *Law and Society in England, 1750–1950*, 2nd edn (Hart Publishing, 2019) 480.

[16] *Winterbottom* (n 4) 116; 406.

[17] ibid 113; 404.

above, although it had been considered by the courts earlier in the century,[18] the parties-only rule really only gained in prominence after *Tweddle* in 1861. This point has been touched on briefly by Atiyah and by Swain.[19] It is thus unconvincing to suggest that the court would have believed its absence to be a doctrinal bar to liability in tort, when it was not yet firmly established as such in contract. Rather, it is suggested, the court perceived a need to limit the scope of liability and, in order to do so, drew upon the privity principle (which was certainly well known pre-*Tweddle*, at least in the form that consideration must move from the plaintiff). The necessity of using the privity rule to impose a 'limit to such actions' had been impressed upon the court by Byles in argument.[20]

B. *Winterbottom*: Mispleading/Technicalities

Other commentators have pointed to mispleading or technicalities concerning forms of action as the reason for the decision. On this view, it was the plaintiff's failure to allege negligence that led to the outcome. Indeed, in *Donoghue*, Lord Atkin noted in relation to *Winterbottom* that 'no duty was alleged other than the duty arising out of the contract' and concluded, in relation to the decision, that it appeared 'to have been manifestly right; no duty … arose out of the contract'.[21] In *The Law of Torts*, Pollock also appeared to support the 'mispleader' theory. He asserted that the decision was 'perfectly correct' in *Winterbottom* but may have had a different result if, amongst other suggestions, 'misfeasance by want of ordinary care' had been shown.[22] For this proposition he cited *George v Skivington*, although noted that it was 'not a very profitable case'. Clerk and Lindsell, in their first edition of *The Law of Torts* in 1889, appear also to have understood *Winterbottom* as a case of mispleading. The authors described the declaration in that case as 'an attempt to sue on [the] contract by a person who was a total stranger to it'.[23] Winfield, writing in the aftermath of *Donoghue*, apparently also saw technicalities as the problem. He asserted that it was 'hard to see how the court could have decided otherwise' when it had been held that the declaration was based on a contract to which the plaintiff was not a party.[24]

However, this mispleader/technicalities theory is not universally accepted. Atiyah gives it short shrift. He notes that the action was fully argued 'in tort by Byles, not a man to overlook a non-contractual argument'.[25] In *Donoghue*, Lord

[18] eg, in *Price v Easton* (1833) 4 B & Ad 433, 110 ER 518. See DJ Ibbetson, 'English Law before 1900' in J Hallebeek and H Dondorp (eds), *Contracts For a Third-Party Beneficiary: A Historical and Comparative Account* (Brill, 2008) 111.

[19] Atiyah (n 5) 502; W Swain, *The Law of Contract 1670–1870* (Cambridge University Press, 2015) 222.

[20] *Winterbottom* (n 4) 110–11; 403. See extract in ch 1, section II.A.

[21] *Donoghue v Stevenson* [1932] AC 562, 589. The same view was taken in RB Tucker and JC Kuhn, 'The Decline of the Privity Rule in Tort Liability' (1950) 11 *University of Pittsburgh Law Review* 236, 236.

[22] See, eg, F Pollock, *The Law of Torts* (London, Stevens and Sons, 1887) 449.

[23] JF Clerk and WHB Lindsell, *The Law of Torts* (Sweet and Maxwell, 1889) 370.

[24] Winfield, 'Duty in Tortious Negligence' (n 3) 54.

[25] Atiyah (n 5) 502.

Tomlin, unlike Lord Atkin, was in no doubt that the *Winterbottom* decision was not based on any mispleading, saying: 'The examination of the report makes it, I think, plain ... that negligence was alleged and was the basis of the claim'.[26] Perhaps the difference in approach is tied to the way each judge decided. Lord Atkin may have been keen to see *Winterbottom* as less of an obstacle to Mrs Donoghue's claim: if *Winterbottom* concerned a claim in contract, with the outcome based on inartful pleading, it laid down no principle that could stand in the way of Mrs Donoghue's success. Lord Tomlin, on the other hand, recognised the departure that would be required for the appellant to succeed.

Palmer's arguments that the court would have identified any technical or pleading objections,[27] and that the court was clearly aware that it was facing a potential negligence action, are highly persuasive. This very word was used explicitly to describe the action.[28] A thorough reading of the reports[29] reveals numerous references to 'negligent', 'case' and indeed 'tort'. Perhaps most telling are Lord Abinger's final words:

> By permitting this action, we should be working this injustice, that ... after all matters between them had been adjusted, and all accounts settled on the footing of their contract, we should subject them to be ripped open by this *action of tort* being brought against him (emphasis added).[30]

C. *Winterbottom*: A Doctrinal Explanation

Palmer suggests a doctrinal explanation instead: controlling concurrence between contractual and tortious duties.[31] He argues that the dominant focus of the period before the emergence of the tort of negligence was upon the problem of concurrence.[32] The common law was hostile to double or coexisting remedies.[33] Palmer notes that the most consistent policy discernible for reluctance to allow coexisting remedies was the perceived unfairness of increasing the defendant's liability if the plaintiff was able, unilaterally, to bring an action in tort.[34] There were advantages to an action in tort. Tort was thought to permit the recovery of more extensive damages and to

[26] *Donoghue* (n 21) 600.
[27] Palmer (n 1) 96.
[28] ibid 97.
[29] See *Winterbottom* (n 4); *Winterbottom v Wright* (1842) 11 LJ Ex 415.
[30] *Winterbottom* (n 4) 115; 405. The *Law Journal* report contains subtle but immaterial differences in wording: (1842) 11 LJ Ex 415, 418.
[31] Palmer (n 1) 85, 89.
[32] ibid 89.
[33] See, eg, DJ Ibbetson, 'Sixteenth Century Contract Law: *Slade's Case* in Context' (1984) 4 *Oxford Journal of Legal Studies* 295; JH Baker, 'New Light on *Slade's Case*' (1971) 29 *Cambridge Law Journal* 213. Palmer notes that the hostility towards double remedies existed long before *Slade's Case*, and may go back to the early medieval period: see Palmer (n 1) 89.
[34] Palmer (n 1) 89.

approach questions of causation more permissively.[35] There was also some scepticism surrounding tort, with tort actions sometimes seen to be 'naked attempts to bypass the protective rules of contract'.[36] Palmer points to cases such as *The Liverpool Adelphi Loan Association v Fairhurst*,[37] where the court was not prepared to allow an action in tort for fraudulent representation by a wife who lacked capacity to enter into a contract. There, Pollock CB opined that, while Mrs Fairhurst was 'undoubtedly responsible for all torts committed by her during coverture … when the fraud is directly connected with the contract, and is the means of effecting it, and parcel of the same transaction, the wife cannot be responsible'.[38] Palmer suggests that mutual exclusivity began to break down in the nineteenth century.[39] The broad view expressed by Tindal CJ in *Boorman v Brown*[40] – that contract created a duty the breach of which would ground an action in tort – was scaled down in subsequent decisions.[41] In *Courtenay v Earle*,[42] the court was not prepared to allow a joinder of certain counts in tort and assumpsit, and in so deciding Jervis CJ was expressly concerned to ensure that the court was not 'altogether destroying the well-known distinction between actions of contract and actions of tort'.[43] Thus, says Palmer, the danger of complete concurrence was reduced.[44]

Palmer sees concurrence as the predominant factor in the *Winterbottom* decision. He argues that Lord Abinger's contribution to the decision was 'to turn away from the traditional discourse that placed emphasis upon rule-oriented objections to concurrence', with his emphasis instead falling 'upon the higher ground that if a third person were entitled to convert a contract breach into a tort action, then the defendant would be burdened with a vast and limitless liability'.[45] Palmer acknowledges that Lord Abinger's reasoning could be seen to reflect 'the economic philosophy of a judge sharply inclined to place limits on enterprise liability'.[46] He then goes on to say that this point 'may be true, but it need not obscure, nor conflict with, the doctrinal point'.[47] Palmer contends that:

> The limitation was not being used here to explain why tort liability could not theoretically exist, but rather why tort duties should not be innovated merely as byproducts of contracts. The consequentialist arguments advanced by the court flowed from the fear

[35] ibid, citing *Addis v Gramophone Company Limited* [1909] AC 488, 492, and *Burrows v The March Gas and Coke Company* (1870) LR 5 Ex 67 respectively.

[36] Palmer (n 1) 89–90.

[37] *The Liverpool Adelphi Loan Association v Fairhurst* (1854) 9 Ex 422, 156 ER 180.

[38] ibid 429; 183.

[39] Palmer (n 1) 90.

[40] *Boorman v Brown* (1842) 3 QB 511, 526, see also *Boorman v Brown* (1844) 11 Cl & Fin 1, 8 ER 1003.

[41] See, eg, *Courtenay v Earle* (1850) 10 CB 73, 138 ER 30; *Woods v Finnis* (1852) 7 Ex 363, 155 ER 988, cited in Palmer (n 1) 91.

[42] *Courtenay* (n 41).

[43] ibid 83; 34.

[44] Palmer (n 1) 91.

[45] ibid 94–95.

[46] ibid 95.

[47] ibid.

> of a *self-generating* concurrence, which threatened to make every breach of contract into a wider liability in tort (emphasis original).[48]

However, it is not wholly clear in *Winterbottom* that the court there was concerned with the potential problems of coexisting remedies or that 'the entire field of contract [would be] made concurrent with tort'.[49] *Winterbottom* concerned a tort claim brought because there was no contractual duty. The court gives no clear indication that it was particularly concerned with the doctrinal boundaries between tort and contract, beyond the practical consequences for defendants in terms of potential liability. Certainly, there was no assertion like that of Jervis CJ in *Courtenay*. On balance, it seems the point taken up by the *Winterbottom* court was more practical than doctrinal. What is clear in the judgments is a desire to limit the scope of liability in negligence, not to impose too great a burden upon commercial parties in the conduct of their business. Arguably, privity offered a convenient mechanism for doing so.

D. *Winterbottom:* Concern for Consequences

Writing extra-judicially, Ipp has described the law of negligence as 'especially prone to influence by moral, social, economic and political values'; considerations that lie invisibly behind much judicial reasoning.[50] Whether or not all would agree with this, a close reading of *Winterbottom* indicates that the court was indeed influenced by such factors in finding for the defendant.

i. Factors Behind the Outcome in Winterbottom

Commentators have suggested various influences and concerns behind the outcome. Baker argues that the decision in *Winterbottom* was less concerned with logic than preserving the status quo and staving off excessive litigation.[51] He explains that the long-standing association of many forms of negligence with assumpsit, where one party was contractually bound to take care, and the fact that actions had not previously been brought for defective products except in assumpsit, meant that there was concern that any change might cause a flood of litigation.[52] It is unlikely that the courts, had they recognised such a duty, would have been faced with an unmanageable flood of litigation: while the industrialising nation and expansion of the law of tort was creating more work for courts, this was being dealt with by setting up smaller courts to operate alongside

[48] ibid.

[49] ibid 90.

[50] DA Ipp, 'Policy and the swing of the negligence pendulum' (2003) 77 *Australian Law Journal* 732, 734.

[51] J Baker, *Introduction to English Legal History*, 5th edn (Oxford University Press, 2019) 445.

[52] ibid.

existing courts.[53] Further, as discussed below, the courts of the nineteenth century appeared particularly concerned with the burden of potential liability on would-be defendants, not only the volume of cases. The courts' concerns appear in line with a policy consideration that Stapleton, in the modern context, regards as a sound factor weighing against imposition of a duty: indeterminacy of liability – the idea that a person ought to be able to know, and plan for, the extent of their obligations and what the law demands of them.[54] The cost of an activity ought to be able to be appreciated in advance. Indeed, Atiyah explains the case as based on two principal arguments: opening the door to vast potential lawsuits and upsetting the bargain struck, the 'manufacturer's expectations and calculations'.[55] Similarly, Morgan also understands the reasoning in *Winterbottom* to be reliant on policy, rather than '(fallacious) doctrinal "logic"' and links the court's prioritisation of manufacturers or suppliers' interests (over the injured consumer's) to an ideological commitment, in contract law, to respect for individual autonomy: if no promise had been made, '[o]nly the customer who paid for the goods should be entitled to sue the manufacturer in respect of defects'.[56]

Lobban sees the outcome in *Winterbottom* as largely attributable to Lord Abinger's 'anxiety about the scope of negligence [which] had already been evident in his judgment in *Priestley* [*v Fowler*[57]]'.[58] *Priestley* was decided in the same year as *Langridge*. While not expressly set out in this case, it was from the attitudes and judicial comments expressed in this case that the 'doctrine of common employment' was created, whereby an employer would not be liable where an employee was injured by the negligence of another employee.[59] Fowler was a butcher, and had ordered Priestley, his assistant, to convey some meat to London.[60] This was to be done by means of a cart, which was to be driven by another of Fowler's employees. Some employees inspected the cart and one expressed concern about the cart's being overloaded. Fowler brushed aside the worries.[61] During the journey, the cart

[53] P Polden, *A History of the County Court, 1846–1971* (Cambridge University Press, 1999) 5–37. Although it seems that the major changes took place after 1846: 37–73.

[54] See J Stapleton, 'Duty of Care Factors: A Selection from the Judicial Menu' in P Cane and J Stapleton (eds), *The Law of Obligations: Essays in Celebration of John Fleming* (Clarendon Press, 1998) 76.

[55] Atiyah (n 5) 502–03.

[56] J Morgan, 'Liability for independent contractors in contract and tort: duties to ensure that care is taken' (2015) 74 *Cambridge Law Journal* 109, 112.

[57] *Priestley* (n 15). See also AWB Simpson, *Leading Cases on the Common Law* (Oxford University Press, 1996) 100–34.

[58] M Lobban, 'Negligence' in WR Cornish et al (eds), *The Oxford History of the Laws of England, Vol XII: 1820–1914 Private Law* (Oxford University Press, 2010) 925.

[59] See Cornish et al, *Law and Society in England* (n 15) 470. See also P Bartrip, 'The impact of institutions and professions on compensation for occupational injury in England' in P Mitchell (ed), *The Impact of Institutions and Professions on Legal Development* (Cambridge University Press, 2012) 36–41.

[60] For a useful discussion of this case, see, eg, Simpson (n 57) 100–34; Cornish et al, *Law and Society in England* (n 15) 469–70; RW Kostal, *Law and English Railway Capitalism 1825–1875* (Clarendon Press, 1994) 259–70; RL Howells, '*Priestley v Fowler* and the Factory Acts' (1963) 26 *Modern Law Review* 367.

[61] Simpson (n 57) 100.

broke down, and Priestley was thrown from the cart and suffered a fractured leg. Priestley was initially successful in his action before Parke J at the Lincolnshire Summer Assizes. The matter then came before the Court of Exchequer.

The Court's judgment was delivered by Lord Abinger CB. It was acknowledged that there was no precedent for the action by a servant against his master, and so the case was to be decided upon general principles – the court being 'at liberty to look at the consequences of a decision the one way or the other'.[62] He noted that if the master were held liable to the servant in this action, a precedent would be established which might 'carry us to an alarming extent'; it would render masters responsible for the negligence of all 'inferior agents' and the principle could extend to many classes of case.[63] It was said that the 'inconvenience, not to say the absurdity of these consequences, afford[ed] a sufficient argument' against liability.[64] A master was, of course, under an obligation to provide for the safety of his servant while in the course of employment, to the best of his ability. However, the more significant burden to take care was on the servant: '[t]he servant is not bound to risk his safety in the service of his master … and may … decline any service'.[65] The many problems with this reasoning are obvious to modern audiences, not least because it fails to give sufficient weight to the power imbalance and possible vulnerability of the servant. It was said that, in most cases in which danger may arise, the servant was just as likely to be aware of the 'probability and extent' of the danger as the master might be – indeed, in this case, the plaintiff must have known the sufficiency and safety of the cart as well as the master, and 'probably better'.[66] Lord Abinger returned to consequences in concluding. To allow this sort of action to prevail would be to encourage the servant to 'omit that diligence and caution which he is in duty bound to exercise on behalf of his master'.[67] This was said to offer much better security against injury than recourse in the courts against the master.

Atiyah has also suggested that Lord Abinger's views on political economy may have influenced the outcome in both *Priestley* and *Winterbottom*.[68] In his political life, Lord Abinger had supported measures helpful to enterprise and industry, such as the free circulation of labour.[69] Indeed, Ibbetson argues that the court in *Winterbottom* was 'transparently concerned' not to allow an action that might place an unreasonable burden on manufacturers.[70] It is proposed here that a close reading of the reasoning in *Winterbottom* is consistent with this view. In the midst of the industrial revolution, the *Winterbottom* court prioritised the interests of

[62] *Priestley* (n 15) 5; 1032.
[63] ibid.
[64] ibid 6; 1032.
[65] ibid 6; 1032–33.
[66] ibid 7; 1033.
[67] ibid.
[68] Atiyah (n 5) 368.
[69] ibid, citing *Parliamentary Debates* (8 May 1821) vol V, col 579.
[70] D Ibbetson, *A Historical Introduction to the Law of Obligations* (Oxford University Press, 1999) 174. See also E Chamberlain, 'Lord Buckmaster: The reluctant villain in *Donoghue v Stevenson* (2013) 3 *Juridical Review* 245.

manufacturers or suppliers over injured consumers. Privity was the mechanism by which this could be done in a principled way.

ii. Prioritisation of Commercial Interests

The principal focus of the *Winterbottom* court appears to have been the (perceived undesirable) consequences, for commercial parties, of recognising any liability beyond the contract. Lord Abinger's concern for the potential proliferation of plaintiffs, 'even any person passing along the road', points clearly in this direction: '[u]nless we confine the operation of such contracts as this to the parties who entered into them, the most absurd and outrageous consequences, to which I can see no limit, would ensue'.[71] The spectre of indeterminate liability, even if the risk in this case seems overstated to modern eyes, loomed large for the *Winterbottom* court. How could commercial parties plan for, or anticipate, costs, if courts were to allow contractual arrangements to be 'ripped open' by the tort claim from one of a vast pool of potential plaintiffs? Alderson B worried that there would be 'no point at which such actions would stop' and thought the 'only safe rule' was to confine the right to recover to parties to the contract.[72]

We can return here to the argument advanced by Byles, as counsel for the defendant, which was noted in chapter one. The report in *The Times* of *Winterbottom* records the argument as follows:

> This, the learned gentleman contended, was not a state of things which conferred upon the plaintiff any right of action against the contractor. The proper remedy, if any, was against the Postmaster-General, with whom alone any privity existed, and not against the defendant … If this action, which was quite new, could be maintained, the contractors for the mails would be liable to all the passengers who might take seats therein, as well as the coachmen. The test of the matter, however, was to be found in the fact that if any such action were recognised by the law, then the real party to be sued would be not the contractor who furnished the coach, but the smith who supplied him with the axle, to the defect in which the accident was to be attributed.[73]

This reveals plainly the concern that the 'real party' to any negligence action, if permitted, would be the manufacturer at the end of the supply line, who would be faced by indeterminate potential plaintiffs. The report goes on to note that Lord Abinger believed it was a novel case for which there was no authority, except perhaps *Langridge*; but that the court in *Langridge* had gone a 'step beyond the established precedents, and the use of it to-day only showed the danger of doing so'.[74]

Writing in a different economic context by 1900, Labatt identified, and dismissed as 'doubtful', Lord Abinger's concerns in *Winterbottom* for the economic

[71] *Winterbottom* (n 4) 114; 405.
[72] ibid 115; 405.
[73] 'Court of Exchequer, Monday, June 6' *The Times* (7 June 1842).
[74] ibid.

consequences of an expanded pool of potential plaintiffs.[75] He explained what he perceived to be the nature of Lord Abinger's argument:

> The argument seems to amount, broadly speaking, to this: that to compel a negligent workman to indemnify each and every person who might be injured by his negligence would be inexpedient and unjust, for the reason that it would widen unduly the circle of liability, thus producing excessive intricacy of actions, and creating conditions of responsibility which would deter prudent men from engaging in certain occupations.[76]

Labatt argued that, in fact, the inconvenience to manufacturers and vendors in holding them liable to strangers was 'much less serious than the courts would have us suppose'.[77] A defective chattel, he explained, would likely exhaust its potential to do injury or mischief when it has caused the first injury. Nevertheless, that a commentator at the turn of the century found the fears to be unfounded and a poor basis for denying redress by manufacturers to ultimate consumers[78] does not mean that they were not the motivation for the introduction of the privity rule. Indeed, Labatt's very response suggests that this is how the mid-century court's reasons for deciding were understood at the turn of the century. Labatt comments that the inability by ultimate consumers to bring anyone to account for injuries sustained is a situation 'more "outrageous" than any of those which had suggested themselves to Lord Abinger'.[79] By 1900, the 1842 economic argument had weakened but a strict privity rule was in operation.

The economic context is important. Ibbetson warns that it would be wrong to be too quick to criticise the court for this decision, as the 'spectre of unlimited and indeterminate liability takes on a more substantial form in a world where loss-spreading is impracticable'.[80] Many nineteenth-century manufacturers were not large enough businesses to disperse losses amongst their customers and liability insurance was not yet available.[81] This is persuasive, and it will be argued in chapter three that the increased availability of liability insurance in the decade before *Donoghue* was crucial in creating the climate in which Mrs Donoghue's claim might form a tipping point for change.

We cannot conclude, from examples such as *Winterbottom* and *Priestley*, that the judges of this time were adopting a 'consistently pro-industrial policy'; for example, a tough approach was sometimes taken against railway companies.[82] This theme has also been explored by Kostal.[83] There are, indeed, numerous examples of decisions *against* the interests of industry and economic growth. Nevertheless, it is certainly

[75] CB Labatt, 'Negligence in Relation to Privity of Contract' (1900) 16 *Law Quarterly Review* 168, 188–90.
[76] ibid 188.
[77] ibid 188–89.
[78] ibid 189.
[79] ibid.
[80] DJ Ibbetson, 'The Tort of Negligence in the Common Law in the Nineteenth and Twentieth Centuries' in E Schrage (ed), *Negligence: The Comparative Legal History of the Law of Torts* (Duncker & Humblot, 2001) 254.
[81] ibid.
[82] Ibbetson, 'Negligence' (n 80) 257.
[83] See Kostal (n 60) especially ch 7. As noted above, Kostal's work shows that courts took a more generous approach to injured passengers than to injured workers.

plausible that the court was concerned, in the mid-1800s, not to burden to excess suppliers, manufacturers or other similar commercial parties with a wider pool of potential plaintiffs. The *Winterbottom* decision was made during the Industrial Revolution and following a period of substantial growth in trade and commerce, which may conceivably have had a significant bearing on attitudes towards protecting and encouraging commerce and enterprise. In surveying negligence cases as reported in *The Times* from the late 1700s to 1820, Oldham has argued that we can see cross-currents in the instructions given to juries by judges: judges had to balance fairness to the plaintiff and sympathy for those injured with concerns not to impede too much the public commercial benefits of common carriers and the like.[84] We see other examples of both courts and the legislature promoting industry and trade-friendly laws in the mid-nineteenth century. For example, railways enjoyed exclusion clauses in respect of damage to goods; Baker notes that courts were 'sympathetic to these clauses, because the invention of the railway had conferred new benefits on the public, and so the proprietors who exploited the invention were entitled to protect themselves against the unprecedented risks inherent in rail transport'.[85] Parliament intervened in 1854 and required that a court be satisfied that a particular exclusion or condition was 'just and reasonable'.[86] However, this concept proved difficult to apply and was not adopted in subsequent legislation, though courts generally began to construe such exclusion clauses narrowly.[87] Balance was necessary. Similar issues were no doubt at play for the *Winterbottom* court. A more plaintiff-friendly approach and a widening of the potential scope of liability in negligence during this period may perhaps have had, or have been seen as likely to create, a stifling effect on trade, entrepreneurial behaviour and investment.

The courts' primary concern, in *Winterbottom* and in some cases considered below, appears to be with the economic effects of liability upon defendants. Defendants, unless they were a particularly large commercial party with a large consumer base onto which costs might be passed, would not have been able to spread their losses. In 1842, a great many manufacturers and providers of services would still have been smaller-scale ventures, run by families and individuals.[88] A concern for the consequences of extending negligence liability beyond the constraining and predictable boundaries of contract is understandable.

II. *Winterbottom* in the Courts: Consequences to Formalism

In this section, case law preceding and following *Winterbottom* is considered to bolster the argument that of the four 'camps' outlined in the previous part, the most

[84] J Oldham, 'The Law of Negligence as Reported in *The Times*, 1785–1820' (2018) 36 *Law and History Review* 383.

[85] Baker, *Introduction to English Legal History* (n 51) 383–84. See also Carriers Act 1830.

[86] Railway and Canal Traffic Act 1854, s 7. See Baker, *Introduction to English Legal History* (n 51) 383–84.

[87] Baker, *Introduction to English Legal History* (n 51) 383–84.

[88] This is discussed in ch 3.

plausible explanation for the outcome in *Winterbottom* is that the court was motivated by a point of policy. While this argument has been advanced by others, the close reading of the contemporaneous case law developed here substantiates and adds weight to this viewpoint. Courts may be understood, at least in the mid-nineteenth century, to use privity as a convenient mechanism by which to prevent the perceived injustice and undesirable consequences of the imposition of liability: recognising liability could stifle commerce and individual endeavour. Privity provided a principled underpinning for this policy concern. However, it will also be argued that, as the nineteenth century drew to a close, *Winterbottom* began to be treated in a more formalistic way. Decisions appear to be based less on consequences, and more on doctrine. Courts began to apply the rule rigidly and treat the privity doctrine as a strict bar to recovery. Where the *Winterbottom* court was driven to rely upon the rule out of concern for the consequences of not doing so, later courts felt bound by the rule to ignore its consequences in their decision-making.

A. Privity in the Nineteenth Century: Underpinning Policy Concerns

In *Langridge*,[89] the facts of which were outlined in the previous chapter, the court had taken pains to place limits on future reliance on its decision that the supplier of a dangerous gun was liable:

> We are not prepared to rest the case upon one of the grounds on which the learned counsel for the plaintiff sought to support his right of action, namely, that wherever a duty is imposed on a person by contract or otherwise, and that duty is violated, any one who is injured by the violation of it may have a remedy against the wrong-doer: we think this action may be supported without laying down a principle which would lead to that indefinite extent of liability ... and we should pause before we made a precedent by our decision which would be an authority for an action against the vendors ... at the suit of any person whomsoever into whose hands they might happen to pass, and who should be injured thereby.[90]

The reluctance of the court to find a duty outside of fraudulent misrepresentation seems to be grounded in a concern not to place on potential defendants, and on vendors in particular, the burden of potentially vast numbers of claims and indefinite liability.

Policy considerations appear to have been at the forefront of the judges' minds in *Longmeid v Holliday*,[91] decided nine years after *Winterbottom*. As considered in the previous chapter, one of the principal arguments made by counsel for the

[89] *Langridge v Levy* (1837) 2 M & W 519, 150 ER 863.
[90] ibid 530; 868.
[91] *Longmeid v Holliday* (1851) 6 Ex 761, 155 ER 752.

defendant was based on the concern for too great an extension in the scope of liability. After acknowledging that a stagecoach proprietor had a duty in driving and might be liable to 'any person who is thereby injured', he argued:

> But no duty is imposed on a tradesman to furnish articles fit for the purpose of every individual into whose hands they may come. Such a doctrine would be productive of the greatest injustice. For instance, if an accident occurred to an omnibus or a steam boat in consequence of some latent defect in the construction, could every passenger injured maintain an action against the respective builders? *Winterbottom v Wright* is an express authority to the contrary.[92]

Parke B appears to have been sympathetic to this argument. While noting, as set out above, that there were indeed cases in which third parties could sue (surgeons, for example), he went on:

> But it would be going much too far to say, that so much care is required in the ordinary intercourse of life between one individual and another, that, if a machine not in its nature dangerous, – a carriage for instance, – but which might become so by a latent defect entirely unknown … should be lent or given by one person, even by the person who manufactured it, to another, the former should be answerable to the latter for a subsequent damage accruing by the use of it.[93]

From counsel's argument, and Parke B's reception of it, we see *Winterbottom* treated as authority for, or a warning about, the limits of tortious liability based on concerns about placing an unreasonable and unfair burden on individuals in their interactions. It seems likely that Parke B was indeed contemplating *Winterbottom* in his reference to 'a carriage for instance'.

Blakemore v The Bristol and Exeter Railway Company,[94] though not, perhaps, a 'key case', is nevertheless instructive of the way *Winterbottom* was understood and applied in the middle part of the nineteenth century. A railway company was sued by the administratrix of Mr Blakemore, who had been killed by an accident involving a crane kept at the station to facilitate the unloading of goods. The deceased had been asked to assist by the consignee but was a servant of neither the consignee nor the defendant. The deceased, therefore, was outside any contractual relationship. The court relied on *Winterbottom* and *Langridge* in deciding for the defendant and appears to have done so principally on the basis of concern that recognising such a duty might be unfairly burdensome. The court noted that, although one might say that the defendants must have known that help would be needed in the unloading of the goods, and therefore had the deceased person in mind, the same argument was unsuccessful in *Winterbottom*: merely knowing that a coach required a coach driver was not enough to found a duty towards the

[92] ibid 765; 754.
[93] ibid 768; 755.
[94] *Blakemore v The Bristol and Exeter Railway Company* (1858) 8 El & Bl 1035, 120 ER 385.

specific coach driver in question. The court appeared to suggest that it would be unfair to expect the defendant company to have known that more assistance would be necessary, and said:

> Upon the whole, therefore, we think we should be extending the law beyond any recognised principle, and in a way which might lead to very dangerous consequences, if we held that this action was maintainable. And therefore the rule will be discharged.[95]

Some treatments of *Winterbottom* in subsequent case law reveal a bench on which some judges reasoned by reference to consequences (and a consequence-based understanding of *Winterbottom*) while others were content to apply the privity rule without reference to the underlying policy. In another case involving a railway company from the middle of the century, albeit slightly later than *Blakemore*, the plaintiffs in *Alton v The Midland Railway Company*[96] were similarly unsuccessful. The plaintiffs were brewers suing for the loss of the services of an employee who had been injured while a passenger on the defendant's rail service. The plaintiffs argued that where a railway company allowed passengers onto the railway, the company became a common carrier and 'subject to all the responsibilities of a carrier according to the custom of the realm', and that this was a duty separate from any contract, which had been breached by the defendant.[97] Counsel for the defendant company argued that the custom of the realm applied to carriers of goods, not passengers, and that the duty to carry safely was one arising out of the contract between the parties and was thus owed only to parties to the contract.[98] The defendant relied on *Winterbottom*, drawing particular attention to Lord Abinger's comment that there was no privity between the parties, but also the risk of 'absurd and outrageous consequences', as well as Alderson B's warning that the only safe option was to 'confine the right to recover to those who enter into a contract'.[99] Counsel also set out Parke B's warning in *Langridge*. In finding for the defendant company, Erle CJ said as follows:

> I think there is very great weight in the observations of the learned judges in *Langridge* ... and *Winterbottom* ... as to the inconvenience of laying down a principle which would lead to an indefinite extent of liability. The liabilities of parties by reason of their contracts can be foreseen. As a general rule, they are under their own control. The liabilities arising out of them are bounded by the considerations affecting the two contracting parties. Upon that general view I found my opinion that ... the plaintiffs cannot sue.[100]

[95] ibid 1053–54; 392.
[96] *Alton* (n 3).
[97] ibid 215–30; 770–75.
[98] ibid 230; 775.
[99] ibid 232–33; 776.
[100] ibid 239; 779.

Erle CJ is clearly here concerned, as Lord Abinger was in *Winterbottom*, with indeterminate and unpredictable liabilities, with protecting the commercial arrangements agreed between parties – the agreed allocation of risk. Byles J, too, referred to 'alarming consequences'[101] if a stranger were able to sue in circumstances where a contract had been concluded between other parties. He said:

> It is plain … that there was no contract, express or implied, between the plaintiffs and the defendants … In most cases of this nature, no doubt, the plaintiff has his election to sue either upon the contract or for the tort: but, by changing the form of action, the right to sue cannot be extended to a stranger. It would lead to alarming consequences if it could. No man could sue for a breach of duty, unless for a breach of duty to himself. That was decided in *Winterbottom* … Suppose the case of a servant employing a surgeon to perform an operation, and sustaining an injury from the surgical-instrument maker having furnished the surgeon with an improper instrument, – would an action lie against the instrument-maker either at the suit of the servant or of his master? And yet the argument on the part of the plaintiffs must go to that length, if the law be as they contend it is. If we depart from the rule stated by my Lord and my Brother Willes, we open a way to a most inconvenient and dangerous extension of responsibility.[102]

Willes J was generally in agreement with the Chief Justice and concluded in strong terms: 'This is an action founded on a contract, and brought by persons who are no parties to the contract. There is no authority for the maintenance of such an action, and I cannot consent to be a party to its introduction'.[103] Montague Smith J noted at the beginning of his judgment that he was not present for all argument and was thus less familiar with the matter. He did say that there 'is no duty independent of contract: the whole foundation of it is the contract' and that 'the only persons who can sue for breach of a contract, or for the breach of any duty arising out of the contract, are the stipulating parties'.[104] It is difficult to know how much to read into this judgment, given its brevity and its stated limitations. Nevertheless, unlike Erle CJ, Montague Smith J did not explicitly deal with the *Winterbottom* authorities as based on policy concerns but confidently asserted the privity principle.

In *Collis v Selden*,[105] a chandelier put in place by the defendant had fallen on the plaintiff in a public house. Bovill CJ decided the case on the basis that it fell 'within the principle and the reasons given in *Winterbottom*'.[106] After determining that there was no duty of a public nature, the Chief Justice then said:

> Then, is there any contract or privity between the plaintiff and the defendant out of which a liability could arise? No contract is alleged, not even between the defendant

[101] ibid 244; 780.
[102] ibid 243–44; 780–81.
[103] ibid 243; 780.
[104] ibid 245; 781.
[105] *Collis v Selden* (1868) LR 3 CP 495.
[106] ibid 496.

> and the proprietor of the house. There is nothing to shew how any liability or duty to the plaintiff could arise.[107]

The lack of contract or privity was thus given as a reason against finding any kind of duty in negligence. Willes J, on the other hand, focused on the underlying rationale of *Winterbottom*. After noting that it was not alleged that this was a 'dangerous object', and so able to fall under that line of authorities, Willes J asserted:

> There would be no end of actions if we were to hold that a person having once done a piece of work carelessly, should, independently of honesty of purpose, be fixed with liability in this way by reason of bad materials or insufficient fastening. Take the case of a man building a house. His workpeople scamp the work: and five or six years afterwards a chimney-stack falls down through a high wind, and injures a person with whom he has no contract, to whom he owes no duty, and against whom he cannot have been guilty of any fraud. To hold him liable to an action … would be going far beyond anything which has been decided in our law.[108]

This is clearly consequence-based reasoning: the consequences of finding liability in such a case might be that individuals (and, by extension, their businesses) could not with accuracy predict their potential liabilities, the pool of potential plaintiffs being unclear but vast, and the risks involved in their enterprises very large.

The dispute in *Heaven v Pender*, it will be recalled, concerned defective staging around a ship, erected and supplied by the defendant. The decision of the Queen's Bench Divisional Court, finding liability in negligence, was reversed by the Court of Appeal.[109] Nevertheless, in what it reveals of contemporary understandings of *Winterbottom*, it remains helpful. The reasoning of Field J confirms the understanding of *Winterbottom* as a decision based on concern to avoid undesirable consequences:

> There the defendant, who supplied the coach, knew that it would certainly be used by some coachman. If ever the duty which is relied on here to create a liability existed, it was in that case, but the Court of Exchequer Chamber held that the public inconvenience caused by holding the defendant liable under such circumstances would be so great, that, in the absence of any principle compelling them so to hold, they gave judgment for the defendant. That decision has been followed in *Longmeid*.[110]

Field J went on to decide that the only doubt thrown upon this ruling had been in *George*, and that *Winterbottom* was to be followed over *George*. In the reference to 'public inconvenience', it is clear that Field J saw the outcome in *Winterbottom*, and thus the imposition of the privity rule, as based on concern

[107] ibid 497.
[108] ibid 497–98.
[109] See *Heaven v Pender* (1882) 9 QBD 302; reversed in (1883) 11 QBD 503.
[110] *Heaven v Pender* (1882) 307.

for the practical consequences of deciding one way or another, rather than any doctrinal point.

B. Privity in the Early Twentieth Century: The Rule Hardens

Towards the end of the nineteenth century and into the twentieth, courts appear to have become less inclined to consider and discuss the reasons for the introduction of the rule – the concern for the consequences of recognising a duty in a certain situation – and more inclined rigidly to apply the privity rule. This is perhaps unsurprising; it is, of course, to be expected that a legal rule will crystallise in hard form after consistent invocation over several decades. This crystallisation also had the effect of reducing the scope for extension of liability or recognising exceptions to the principle, even where there may have been competing and compelling policy rationales.

The Caledonian Railway Company v Warwick[111] was an appeal to the House of Lords from the Scottish Court of Session (Inner House). The respondent had brought an action against two railway companies following the death of her husband, when he was caught between two wagons filled with coal. The wagons belonged to the appellant, the Caledonian Railway Company (CRC), and were transported along the appellant's system, and delivered to another railway company, Glasgow and South Western Railway Company (GSW) at Dumfries station. GSW had a contract with the Gas Commissioners of Dumfries to move coal from the station to the gasworks. GSW provided the men and horses to haul the wagons, and so the appellants were not in direct control of the wagons from the time the wagons left the appellant's rail system. An incident occurred when the brakes of one of these wagons failed, and the respondent's husband – an employee of GSW – was killed. The question before the Court was whether there was a relevant case against the appellant, CRC. CRC, of course, knew how GSW was going to use the wagons. As such, it was alleged that it was bound to examine them when it handed them over to GSW, to see that they were in good working order. The House of Lords reversed the Court of Session's decision, holding that there was no duty owed by the appellant to anyone using the wagons on behalf of GSW to take care that the wagons were operating as they should, and in particular that the brakes were in good order, after the coal was delivered at Dumfries station.[112]

Lord Herschell appeared to find for the appellant principally on the basis that it would be unreasonable to find a duty here. He saw the situation as follows: 'The [appellant] carried certain coals to the Dumfries Station, and as

[111] *The Caledonian Railway Company v Warwick* [1898] AC 216.
[112] ibid 216.

soon as those coals arrived in the wagons at the Dumfries Station every obligation undertaken by the Caledonian Company in respect of them was at an end'.[113] Rather than taking delivery of the coals at Dumfries station, GSW, for their own purposes, hauled the wagons on to another destination. He saw the journey after Dumfries station as being a 'new journey along an entirely different railway' and said that 'with the incidents of that journey the Caledonian Railway Company were altogether unconnected'.[114] He felt it would be 'altogether unreasonable' to maintain that there was a duty on the part of the appellant to examine the wagons and to check the brakes, after they had fulfilled their existing contract.[115] He went on:

> I think, if we were to hold that … an obligation [to take care that the wagons were in a proper state, so as not to injure any workman of GSW] existed, some very strange consequences would ensue – consequences so unreasonable, it seems to me, as to shew that the duty cannot exist.[116]

He distinguished *Heaven* on somewhat slender grounds: in *Heaven*, the appliance was used at the invitation of the dock company, and it was one of the facilities by which it induced vessels to use their docks. There was nothing in the appellant's supply of the wagons, he said, that could be comparable to a trap into which they 'invited and led the deceased man to come'.[117]

Lord Macnaghten and Lord Morris agreed with Lord Herschell. Lord Shand, too, focused upon the separate journey and the 'separate undertaking between two different parties'.[118] He said:

> I can see no ground whatever for holding that having parted with the wagons at the station, and having nothing to do with the contract of carriage subsequently, which might have been for a long or a short journey, there was a duty upon the Caledonian Company, in a question with a stranger to them, to have their wagons either in a sound condition or examined with care. It may or may not be that the Caledonian Company had some duty towards the Glasgow and South Western Company – when I say 'some duty' I mean some obligation under a separate contract with them; but with that we have nothing to do here, because there is no such contract alleged in the first place, and, even if there were, I do not think that the husband of the plaintiff could have taken the benefit of it.[119]

However, Lord Shand's reasoning, in contrast to Lord Herschell's in the same case, appears purely formalistic: where the contract is at an end, no duty exists beyond that. His comment that the husband of the plaintiff could not have taken the benefit of the contract seems to be made in approval of the argument made by counsel

[113] ibid 224.
[114] ibid 226.
[115] ibid.
[116] ibid.
[117] ibid 227.
[118] ibid 229.
[119] ibid 231.

for the appellant company, citing *Winterbottom*, that, 'even if there had been … a contract, what is that to the respondent?'.[120] Lord Shand's final summary reveals quite plainly this formalism:

> My Lords, this being neither the case of a trap or an invitation to use a trap, nor a case of a noxious instrument, and there being no contract or obligation between the pursuer's husband and the Caledonian Railway Company in regard to the providing of these wagons, I am of opinion with your Lordships that the pursuer has failed to state a relevant ground upon which liability of the defenders can be founded.[121]

It should be noted here that, 32 years later, in *Oliver v Saddler and Company*,[122] we find a different outcome on similar facts. Both cases concerned an accident caused by the use of a defective item owned by one party and provided for the use of the other. In *Oliver*, a firm of stevedores, employed by the owner of a ship, and some porters, employed by the consignee of the cargo, were unloading a ship. The cargo was made up of bags of maize, and the stevedores allowed the porterage company to use some slings, free of charge, for transporting the bags to the quay. An employee of the stevedores was tasked with inspecting the slings. An accident occurred in which a sling broke while the bags were being transported to the quay, and an employee of the porterage company was killed. His dependents brought an action against the stevedores, which had been successful before the Lord Ordinary but then unsuccessful before the Inner House of the Court of Session.

In the House of Lords, Lord Buckmaster and Lord Atkin (on opposing sides in *Donoghue*, but united here) distinguished the case from *The Caledonian* on the basis that, here, the opportunity for examination was not equally open to both companies using the equipment: the immediate use of the sling by the porters meant that the stevedores were the only party who could carry out an inspection to ensure that they were in good working order.[123] Considering *The Caledonian*, Lord Atkin said that there was a 'gulf' between the case where a railway company handed over trucks *at rest* to another company for 'indefinite detention with ample opportunities' for inspection, and a case such as the present where the slings were handed over for 'immediate return for the first party's convenience'.[124] Viscount Dunedin was cautious. He disagreed with Lord Atkin's treatment of *The Caledonian*, finding instead that the one point of difference between the cases was that, in the present case, the use to which the item in question was being put was 'obviously dangerous', whereas in *The Caledonian* there was 'no obvious danger in allowing the wagon to be taken off

[120] Counsel continues: 'She is not entitled to found upon it, for her pleadings do not allege that any relation existed between her deceased husband and the appellants': *The Caledonian* (n 111) 223.

[121] *The Caledonian* (n 111) 232–33.

[122] *Oliver v Saddler and Company* [1929] AC 584.

[123] ibid 591, 596.

[124] ibid 597.

their own line on to another for transit into a siding'.[125] He concluded with the following remarks:

> I look on the case as *not only narrow but peculiarly dependent on its own circumstances*, and that must be my excuse for troubling your Lordships with these observations, which I have only added in case I should be thought to be *pushing the idea of the liability of the owner of the defective chattel far further than I think it ought to be pushed* (emphasis added).

The Caledonian was decided at the turn of the century; by 1929, the *Oliver* court appears more prepared to find a way to avoid the harsh effects of the (then rigid) privity rule.

Collins MR in *Earl v Lubbock*, a 1905 case considered in the previous chapter, quoted from the reasoning in *Winterbottom* in finding against the plaintiff, including Lord Abinger's comments about the danger of 'working [an] injustice' by permitting the action.[126] However, there was no engagement with the policy considerations, as with some earlier cases:

> [T]his case is concluded by the authority of *Winterbottom* ... the circumstances of which are indistinguishable from those of the present case, and that decision, since the year 1842 in which it was given, has stood the test of repeated discussion. Under these circumstances it would, in my opinion, be a waste of time to go through the numerous cases that have been cited, for the principles laid down by Lord Abinger CB in that case appear to me to be based upon sound reasoning, and to be conclusive in this case.[127]

He also noted that the case could not fall within the 'category of dangerous articles',[128] supply of which might give rise to a duty. The plaintiff's case was ultimately dismissed by Collins MR on the basis of rigid application of the privity rule. On the other hand, Mathew LJ emphasised that if suit were available to anybody injured as a result of the negligence, then it was 'difficult to see how ... trade could be carried on'.[129] No prudent man, he said, would enter into a contract to make or repair something if the employer intended to permit others to use it.

Cavalier v Pope[130] concerned an accident in rented accommodation. The owner of the house had agreed with his tenant that he would repair the flooring (after the tenant had threatened to leave) but failed to carry out the repairs. The tenant's wife fell through the flooring and was injured. The tenant's wife and the tenant brought an action against their landlord for damages and were successful at first instance. This was reversed by the Court of Appeal (Collins MR and Romer LJ, but Mathew LJ dissenting).[131] All five members of the House of Lords

[125] ibid 600.
[126] *Earl v Lubbock* [1905] 1 KB 253, 256.
[127] ibid 255–56.
[128] ibid 257.
[129] ibid 259.
[130] *Cavalier v Pope* [1906] AC 428 (*Cavalier* [1906]).
[131] *Cavalier v Pope* [1905] 2 KB 757.

upheld the Court of Appeal's decision. Lord Loreburn LC's reasons were short and pithy:

> I can find no right of action in the wife of the tenant against the landlord either for letting the premises in a dangerous state or for failing to repair them according to his promise. The husband has sued successfully for breach of contract, but the wife was not party to any contract.[132]

Lord Robertson agreed with Lord Loreburn's reasons. For Lords Atkinson and Macnaghten, too, lack of privity was an insurmountable problem. Lord James of Hereford also based his decision upon lack of privity: 'There was but one contract, and that was made with the husband. The wife cannot sue upon it'.[133] He expressed his regret, but noted that 'moral responsibility, however clearly established, is not identical with legal liability'.[134]

Formalism is particularly evident in *Blacker v Lake and Elliot*,[135] which may be seen as the high point of judicial formalism with respect to the doctrine of privity. As discussed in chapter one, the rule in *Winterbottom* was held to operate as a bar to any development of the law along the lines that might have been suggested in *George*: *George* was in conflict with the rule laid down in *Winterbottom*, and therefore could not be followed. There was no exploration of the reasons for the introduction of the rule in *Winterbottom*. The court's reasoning in *Blacker* was, instead, formalistic, and grounded on whether or not the plaintiff's case could be brought within one of the lines of authority (apart from the impermissible interpretation of *George*) in which it had been recognised that a duty exists.

There may have been reasons other than long use for this increasing formalism. It is possible that, with other significant developments in the English common law occurring during the later half of the nineteenth century, a practice emerged whereby courts were increasingly inflexible in their respect for the doctrine of precedent. As the law of negligence developed into more clearly defined principles, perhaps judges became less willing to be 'policy-makers'. Where established principles are available to draw upon, there is not only less scope for thinking through the consequences of deciding one way or another, but there is also merit in the consistency and predictability that comes from following established rules. It is also likely that there was an increasing commitment to the doctrine of precedent, and to judges' simply *applying existing* law, rather than making it. Baker explains that the 'duty of repeating errors is a modern innovation', and that any rigid adherence to precedent began later than the 1830s.[136] He suggests that it was likely a result of the implementation of a new, hierarchical

[132] *Cavalier* [1906] (n 130) 429–30.
[133] ibid 430.
[134] ibid 431.
[135] *Blacker v Lake and Elliot* (1912) 106 LT 533.
[136] Baker, *Introduction to English Legal History* (n 51) 211. See also J Evans, 'Precedent in the Nineteenth Century' in L Goldstein (ed), *Precedent in Law* (Clarendon Press, 1987) 35, 54, 64, pointing to, eg, *Veley v Burder* (1837) 1 Curt 372, 163 ER 127.

system of appellate courts in the Victorian period.[137] By the Judicature Acts of 1873-1875, the existing courts of common law, chancery, admiralty, probate and divorce were brought together as the Supreme Court of Judicature, consisting of the High Court (composed of various divisions) and, above that, a new Court of Appeal.[138]

It has also been suggested by Polden that after 1876 (and the passing of the Appellate Jurisdiction Act 1876),[139] there was a trend in the House of Lords of 'conducting a dignified retreat from any openly acknowledged law-making role'; boldness (and occasional dogmatism) was replaced with 'substantive formalism'.[140] He argues that judicial reticence to adopt explicitly a law-making role is probably also somewhat attributable to the fact that, after the Third Reform Act in 1884, there was concern over the legitimacy of unelected judges as law-makers.[141]

Drawing upon this literature, it is plausible that an unwillingness to question authorities laid down by superior courts, or an unwillingness to make law, may have encouraged judges rigidly to apply precedent even where they may have felt that the policy considerations behind the established rule did not apply with equal vigour to the case at hand. Disquiet with the consequences of application of the privity rule was brewing by 1882, when the *Solicitors' Journal*, in reporting *Heaven*, included the following:

> We cannot feel convinced that there is no duty whatever on the part of a person supplying an article towards any persons other than the person contracting for the supply of it
>
> …
>
> The argument that is relied on as a conclusive reason for the non-liability of the person supplying the article to third persons is that the liability thus created would be extensive and indefinite
>
> …
>
> We feel the force of this argument, but it seems to us doubtful whether the extensive nature of the consequences is necessarily a fatal argument against the existence of a cause of action. *The consequences of a breach of contract for which the consideration is but small may, in some cases, be very extensive. On the other hand, there are difficulties and monstrous consequences that seem to result from holding that no amount of negligence*

[137] Baker, *Introduction to English Legal History* (n 51) 211. See also TFT Plucknett, *A Concise History of the Common Law*, 5th edn (Butterworth & Co, 1956) 350.

[138] For a helpful overview of the changes made, see Cornish et al, *Law and Society in England* (n 15) 56–57.

[139] This Act, perhaps less well known, is that which provided for the reinstatement (after brief abolition) of appeals to the House of Lords: see JIH Jacob, *The Reform of Civil Procedural Law* (Sweet & Maxwell, 1982) 320.

[140] P Polden, 'The Judicial Roles of the House of Lords and Privy Council, 1820–1914' in WR Cornish et al (eds), *The Oxford History of the Laws of England, Vol XI: 1820–1914 English Legal System* (Oxford University Press, 2010) 545–46.

[141] ibid.

> *or recklessness gave rise a right of action against the person supplying an article to third parties* (emphasis added).[142]

It will be recalled that Labatt, writing in the *Law Quarterly Review* in 1900, thought the economic arguments in favour of the rule had little merit.[143] Speculation as to a perceived tension between doctrine and policy also rings true in *Mullen*. As we have already seen, in 1929 several members of the court in *Mullen* seemed to lament the state of the law that prevented them from finding for the plaintiffs. They felt constrained by what they saw as unsatisfactory precedent but were unwilling to depart from it. Lord Ormidale asserted that 'were it not for the unbroken and consistent current of decisions beginning with *Winterbottom*', he would have been disposed to find that a duty existed.[144] He appeared reluctant to follow the authorities, yet also reluctant to be seen to be taking the law in a new direction rather than following established principle:

> The evidence shows that the greatest care is taken by the manufacturers to ensure by tab and label that the ginger beer should pass, as it were, from the hand of the maker to the hand of the ultimate user uninterfered with by the retail dealer – who has little interest in, and no opportunity of, examining the contents of the containers. Accordingly, it would appear to be *reasonable and equitable to hold that, in the circumstances and apart altogether from contract, there exists a relationship of duty as between the maker and the consumer of the beer. Such considerations, however, as I read the authorities, have been held to be irrelevant in analogous circumstances* (emphasis added).[145]

Like Lord Ormidale, the Lord Justice-Clerk appeared reluctant to adopt any 'law-making' role. However, he expressly noted that he found the result unsatisfactory, even if this did not change the outcome: 'I may add that I am not satisfied that, in the result, the pursuer is left without a remedy. The mere fact that he may have none does not seem to me relevant to the decision of this case'.[146]

Lord Hunter, in dissent, would have found a duty in this case. He appeared to place weight on the inability of consumers to protect themselves from any negligence by the manufacturer (who was benefitting commercially):

> [T]he bottles are so dark in colour as to prevent the retail dealer or the consumer from detecting the presence of foreign or deleterious matter by any ordinarily careful examination of the bottle. The defenders invite the public by advertisement and by their labels to buy ginger beer manufactured by them. In these circumstances I am of opinion that there is such a relationship between the manufacturer and consumer as to impose a duty upon the former to exercise care that the latter does not suffer injury.[147]

142 'Damage to a third person caused by a defective article' (1882) 26 *Solicitors' Journal and Reporter* 665, 667.

143 Labatt (n 75) 188–89.

144 *Mullen v Barr* 1929 SC 461, 471; 1929 SLT 341.

145 ibid.

146 ibid 470.

147 ibid 477.

Lord Anderson seemed to recognise that *Winterbottom* was decided on the basis of concern for the consequences of deciding one way or another. He quoted Lord Abinger's warning as to the 'absurd and outrageous consequences' of failing to confine liability to those within the contract,[148] and went on:

> Lord Abinger gave no example of what he had in mind by this expression, but, in a case like the present, where the goods of the defenders are widely distributed throughout Scotland, it would seem little short of outrageous to make them responsible to members of the public for the condition of the contents of every bottle which issues from their works. It is obvious that, if such responsibility attached to the defenders, they might be called on to meet claims of damages which they could not possibly investigate or answer.[149]

His own reasoning thus also appeared to be based at least partially on concern for the consequences of recognising liability, namely that it would leave manufacturers open to potential claims from so many quarters that it would be unduly burdensome. These were the same concerns that influenced courts in the previous century. In this respect, Lord Anderson appears at odds with other members of the Court.

Despite the outcome of this case, Lord Ormidale, the Lord Justice-Clerk and Lord Hunter appear to be in favour of imposing liability upon manufacturers to the ultimate consumer. This case seems to reveal a majority which perceived itself to be bound by a precedent grounded on a policy that was no longer approved by all. Lord Anderson stands out in his concerns for manufacturers. The others appear concerned about the consequences, for the injured consumers, of not recognising a duty. Nevertheless, in the 1920s, it was apparently still difficult as a consumer to sue successfully.

III. Doctrine and Policy in *Donoghue*

The discussion above shows that, by the time we get to *Donoghue*, it might be said that tension had been building between the rigid doctrine, by this point held immovably to bar claims in negligence by third parties to a contract, and a perception that the direction of policy had turned. The economic arguments once thought to be in favour of the privity rule had weakened.

Donoghue provided the opportunity for reconsideration by the House of Lords of the underlying rationale of the privity rule. In documents submitted to the House of Lords in *Donoghue* by the respondent, Stevenson, accessible online,[150] the respondent asserts that it is firmly established in England and

[148] ibid 479.
[149] ibid.
[150] 'Donoghue v Stevenson', Scottish Council of Law Reporting: www.scottishlawreports.org.uk/resources/donoghue-v-stevenson/appeal-papers/index-of-respondent-s-case/.

Scotland that the supplier or manufacturer of an item 'is under no duty to anyone with whom he is not in a contractual relation'.[151] The decision of *Winterbottom* appears in the margin as authority for this statement. The respondent's submission then immediately goes on to quote from Parke B in *Longmeid* the passage, set out above, beginning that it would 'be going much too far to say that so much care is required in the ordinary intercourse of life between individual and another'.[152] On the other hand, for Mrs Donoghue it was submitted that there were cogent policy reasons for deciding in her favour (though the word 'policy' was not used). This was, of course, necessary, as she was asking the court to depart from established principle. It was said that the respondent had 'regulated his business' in such a way that put his products onto the market 'under conditions which made it impossible for the retailer to interfere in any way with the contents of his bottles, or for the retailer or purchaser to examine their contents'.[153] That the article sold was capable of causing serious injury (indeed, the argument goes so far as to allege potential fatality) if care were not taken in its manufacture was urged upon the court as a ground for a duty of care being imposed on the manufacturer.[154] The question of the policy behind the rules at stake, and the consequences of deciding one way or another, were thus put squarely before the court for consideration.

Lord Atkin was certainly persuaded that the possible consequences of one outcome over the other demanded the recognition of a duty in *Donoghue*:

> It is said that the law of England and Scotland is that the poisoned consumer has no remedy against the negligent manufacturer. If this were the result of the authorities, I should consider the result a grave defect in the law, and so contrary to principle that I should hesitate long before following any decision to that effect which had not the authority of this House. I would point out that, in the assumed state of the authorities, not only would the consumer have no remedy against the manufacturer, he would have none against any one else, for in the circumstances alleged there would be no evidence of negligence against any one other than the manufacturer …
>
> The doctrine supported by the decision below would not only deny a remedy to the consumer who was injured by consuming bottled beer or chocolates poisoned by the negligence of the manufacturer, but also to the user of what should be a harmless proprietary medicine, an ointment, a soap, a cleaning fluid
>
> …
>
> I do not think so ill of our jurisprudence as to suppose that its principles are so remote from the ordinary needs of civilized society and the ordinary claims it makes upon its members as to deny a legal remedy where there is so obviously a social wrong.[155]

[151] ibid 7.
[152] ibid. See above (n 93).
[153] Appellant's Case, 'Donoghue v Stevenson', Scottish Council of Law Reporting: www.scottishlawreports.org.uk/resources/donoghue-v-stevenson/appeal-papers/index-of-appelants-case/ 16.
[154] ibid 17.
[155] *Donoghue* (n 21) 582–83.

He appeared to dismiss most of the authorities relied upon by the respondent as distinguishable or irrelevant. In *The Caledonian*, for instance, he noted that there had been ample opportunity for inspection by the second railway company (the view he had held in *Oliver*).

As with Lord Atkin's, Lord Macmillan's speech shows a clear awareness that times had moved on since the *Winterbottom* decision. As has already been noted in chapter one, he said that 'the conception of legal responsibility may develop in adaptation to altering social conditions and standards. The criterion of judgment must adjust and adapt itself to the changing circumstances of life. The categories of negligence are never closed'.[156]

With respect to *Winterbottom*, Lord Macmillan dismissed this as authoritative because it was, he said, 'a singular fact that the case of *Winterbottom* … is one in which no negligence in the sense of breach of a duty owed by the defendant to the plaintiff was alleged on the part of the plaintiff'.[157] He was also in agreement with Pollock,[158] who had opined by 1887 that the real proposition gleaned from *Winterbottom*, which was correct, was that if A breaks a contract with B, this is insufficient to make A liable to C.

In the minority, Lord Buckmaster, though certainly concerned with existing authority, was also concerned with policy, and appeared to see continued value in the policy considerations at the centre of *Winterbottom*.[159] After briefly setting out the facts of *Winterbottom*, he said:

> This case seems to me to show that the manufacturer of an article is not liable to a third party injured by negligent construction, for there can be nothing in the character of a coach to place it in a special category. It may be noted, also, that in this case Alderson B said … 'The only safe rule is to confine the right to recover to those who enter into the contract; if we go one step beyond that, there is no reason why we should not go fifty'.[160]

Indeed, he picked up this thread later in his speech:

> [T]he duty, if it exists, must extend to every person who, in lawful circumstances, uses the article made. There can be no special duty attaching to the manufacture of food apart from that implied by contract or imposed by statute. If such a duty exists, it seems to me it must cover the construction of every article, and I cannot see any reason why it should not apply to the construction of a house. If one step, why not fifty?[161]

Lord Buckmaster concluded by approving the comments of Lord Anderson in *Mullen* that the potential proliferation of claims against manufacturers where their goods were widely distributed, which would be the consequence of finding

[156] ibid 619.
[157] ibid 608.
[158] See Pollock, *The Law of Torts* (n 22) 449.
[159] On this, see Chamberlain (n 70) 258–59.
[160] *Donoghue* (n 21) 568.
[161] ibid 577.

liability, would be 'little short of outrageous'.[162] Similarly, the quotes selected by Lord Tomlin from *Winterbottom* indicate that he thought some of the warnings given as to the potential consequences of allowing liability equally applicable to the case at hand.[163]

In the close aftermath of *Donoghue*, Pollock criticised Lord Buckmaster for forgetting that he was 'judging in a Court of last resort'.[164] Nevertheless, by a narrow margin, concern for the interests of, and consequences for, injured consumers won out, after 90 years of subservience, over those of the manufacturers of goods.

IV. Conclusions on the Treatment of *Winterbottom*

The outcome in *Winterbottom* must be understood as a product of its socio-legal context. Britain had undergone an industrial revolution and experienced an explosion in industry, trade and commerce, creating novel situations and problems to which courts had to respond. The law of negligence was in its infancy, and courts were forced to act as policy-makers as litigants sought to test the boundaries of the emerging law.

The most plausible explanation for the outcome in *Winterbottom* is that the court, in imposing the privity requirement, was concerned not to expose would-be defendants to the burden of the cost and uncertainty involved in defending, investigating and meeting potentially vast and indeterminate numbers of claims. The doctrine was a convenient mechanism by which to prevent such imposition. This is evident in the wording of reports of *Winterbottom* itself, and is supported by the way *Winterbottom* was understood and applied in subsequent cases and commentary. At least in the middle part of the nineteenth century, contemporaries appear to have understood *Winterbottom* as based on concern for consequences, rather than doctrine or principle. The judges in *Winterbottom*, it seems, were not 'taken in' by any 'logical fallacy', nor forced into a decision on the basis of bad pleading. Instead, the court made a decision based on the consequences that might ensue and decided that public policy required that no liability be imposed.

However, by the later part of the nineteenth century and into the twentieth century, courts approached *Winterbottom* in a more formalist manner. Decisions were, for a time, increasingly based on rigid adherence to the privity rule, rather than consideration of the reasons for the introduction of the rule and consequences of recognising a duty of care to exist.

By the time of *Donoghue*, a tension had developed between the strictness of the privity rule and achieving what was perceived to be a desirable result. By 1932, the

[162] ibid 578, quoting from *Mullen* (n 144) (Lord Anderson) 479.
[163] ibid 600.
[164] F Pollock, 'The Snail in the Bottle, And Thereafter' (1933) 49 *Law Quarterly Review* 22, 22.

concerns that had influenced the *Winterbottom* court's decision were no longer convincing. Times had changed. Reasons for the weakening of policy arguments in favour of the rule will be advanced in chapter three. The rise of a consumer society and the changes it brought to manufacturing meant that production of goods was conducted on a far larger scale. This, together with the wide availability of liability insurance, meant that there was far greater loss-spreading potential than in 1842. Negligence had developed into an established, well-defined tort and, by the beginning of the twentieth century, it was beginning to be distanced from potentially constraining links with morality. A choice was made in *Donoghue*: in 1932, the majority of another consequence-oriented court considered that policy now favoured the plaintiff.

3

A Climate Supportive of Privity's Ousting

The focus of this chapter is the ousting of the privity rule from the law of negligence in 1932 and, in particular, understanding why it was *at this point in time* that this development occurred. It was argued in chapter two that it is possible to see, in case law and commentary leading up to *Donoghue v Stevenson*, a perception that the consequence-based concerns underpinning the introduction of the rule had weakened and were no longer persuasive. This chapter identifies some factors that might explain the cause of this weakening.

Three principal contemporaneous factors can be recognised as creating a state of affairs, external to the law of negligence, supportive of the ousting of privity. The first of these is the difficult issue of married women's legal status and capacity; it will be suggested that the problems created by married women's legal and societal position in *George v Skivington* were no less real in the 1920s and 1930s. The position of children will also be considered. The ongoing difficulties associated with women's and children's contractual capacity is also important for the material revealed in chapter four and the argument advanced in chapter five.

The second external factor is the rise of consumerism; whereas shopping and demand for goods had been the province of the elite before the nineteenth century, by the early twentieth century, consumer demand and consumption of goods had increased dramatically and had reached all levels of British society. This section draws on the work of historians of consumer culture[1] to argue that the rise of consumer culture in the nineteenth century, and its extension to all classes in the early twentieth century, is a development supportive of the recognition of liability for products outside of the contract of sale. The way in which shopping was conducted changed: small specialised shops were increasingly replaced by larger businesses stocking all kinds of goods. With such changes came increased

[1] See, eg, P Gurney, *The Making of Consumer Culture in Modern Britain* (Bloomsbury, 2017) (generally, and see also 87–88); TC Whitlock, *Crime, Gender and Consumer Culture in Nineteenth-Century England* (Taylor & Francis, 2005); ED Rappaport, *Shopping for Pleasure: Women in the Making of London's West End* (Princeton University Press, 2001); ED Rappaport, '"The Halls of Temptation": Gender, Politics, and the Construction of the Department Store in Late Victorian London' (1996) 35 *Journal of British Studies* 58; B Shannon, 'ReFashioning Men: Fashion, Masculinity, and the Cultivation of the Male Consumer in Britain, 1860–1914' (2004) 46 *Victorian Studies* 597; C Wildman, *Urban Redevelopment and Modernity in Liverpool and Manchester, 1918–1939* (Bloomsbury, 2016).

separation between manufacturers and vendors; it became more likely that consumers were buying goods from a party which was not the manufacturer. Of course, the development of non-contractual actions is not a logical *necessity* of these developments. However, it will be suggested that a significant increase in the volume of products in circulation, together with an increased likelihood that ultimate consumers would not have a direct relationship with the manufacturer of a product, is likely to have put pressure on laws restricting the availability of actions by those injured by defective products. Larger-scale manufacturers also had greater loss-spreading ability.

The third external factor is the availability of liability insurance. It has been suggested, in the existing literature on *Donoghue*, that the availability of liability insurance may have been a trigger for the outcome.[2] Adding to this, it will be argued here that the picture created by treatises and advertising of the time is that there was a substantial increase in the availability of liability insurance, beyond employers' liability and motor cars, during the mid-1920s and therefore shortly before *Donoghue*. This development, together with the larger scale on which manufacturing was increasingly conducted, significantly weakened economic arguments in favour of the introduction of the privity rule based on consequences for manufacturers: producers of goods could, from the 1920s, insure against claims by third parties in negligence.

Finally, it will be noted that, at the turn of the century, there was also, *within* the law, an important shift in the way negligence was understood. The distancing of liability in negligence from questions of morality, through the application of external, objective standards, created space for the expansion of the scope of negligence in the 1930s.

The purpose of this chapter is not to conduct a comprehensive analysis of these factors, nor to contribute in a significant way to the scholarship dealing with them. Instead, this chapter borrows from existing scholarship to understand the context in which the removal of the privity rule occurred and to advance our understanding of the timing. It is argued that, in the lead-up to *Donoghue*, these four factors can reasonably be understood as significant contributors to creating the right climate. They are not to be understood as catalysts in the sense of 'but for' causes, of the eventual change. The world is too complex for such an argument to be persuasive. Instead, this chapter identifies some simultaneous and supportive developments, perhaps even accelerators; they contributed to an environment in which the problem arising in *Donoghue* tipped the balance and the law was changed.

[2] See, eg, D Ibbetson, *A Historical Introduction to the Law of Obligations* (Oxford University Press, 1999) 196; DJ Ibbetson, 'The Tort of Negligence in the Common Law in the Nineteenth and Twentieth Centuries' in E Schrage (ed), *Negligence: The Comparative Legal History of the Law of Torts* (Duncker & Humblot, 2001) 258. The argument that the availability of liability insurance might be behind *Donoghue* is a point that was also advanced by Professor Ibbetson in a lecture given at the University of Oxford in 2001.

I. The Effect of Personal Status: Married Women and Children

A. Married Women

One matter potentially influencing legal development in the early twentieth century is the difficult issue of the legal position of the married woman. It is clear that in the late 1800s married women faced difficulties when attempting to sue upon contracts: first, they may not have provided the consideration which, as noted in chapter one, had to move from the promisee; and, second, they may not themselves be a party to the contract but instead an agent for their husbands, creating a privity problem. These obstacles for married women were front and centre in the controversial decision in *George v Skivington*,[3] probably causing the court there to break from established principles to allow the wife a cause of action.[4] Though legal disabilities for married women persisted until 1935, over the course of about 70 years from 1870, the common law position in England of the married woman was amended gradually through legislative intervention. Similar intervention took place in Scotland.[5] Successive legislative developments in England in 1870, 1882 and 1893 undoubtedly gave rise to what Tosh describes as 'a more egalitarian climate'.[6] Nevertheless, it seems that the real change for the majority came only in 1935 with the Law Reform (Married Women and Tortfeasors) Act.[7]

There were three main lines of development that created the complex and confused position of married women in the first decades of the twentieth century: common law qualifications, mitigation by the Chancery courts, and legislative intervention.[8] What follows is a brief discussion of the legal position of women from the late-Victorian period to the early twentieth century, focusing primarily on property-holding and contractual capacity. Developments with respect to married women's insolvency and a husband's liabilities for torts committed by his wife are, of course, related, but beyond the scope of the current focus. The purpose of this survey is to demonstrate that, even by the early 1930s, and therefore shortly before *Donoghue*, it is likely that married women often were not strictly parties to contracts of sale when purchasing goods. While their relative position had improved from what it was in 1842, ongoing complexity for married women with

[3] *George v Skivington* (1869) LR 5 Ex 1. See discussion in ch 1.

[4] See DJ Ibbetson, 'George v Skivington (1869)' in C Mitchell and P Mitchell (eds), *Landmark Cases in the Law of Tort* (Hart Publishing, 2010).

[5] See Married Women's Property (Scotland) Act 1881; Married Women's Property (Scotland) Act 1920; AE Anton, 'Effect of Marriage on Property in Scots Law' (1956) 19 *Modern Law Review* 658.

[6] J Tosh, *A Man's Place: Masculinity and the Middle-Class Home in Victorian England* (Yale University Press, 1999) 161.

[7] See J Lewis, *Women in England, 1870–1950* (Wheatsheaf Books Ltd, 1984) 120–22; L Holcombe, *Wives & Property* (University of Toronto Press, 1983) 219–24.

[8] For a useful overview, see Law Revision Committee, *Fourth Interim Report* (Cmd 4770, December 1934) 4.

respect to privity of contract is likely to have created pressure in favour of the ability to sue, when harmed by defective products, without first having to establish a contractual relationship.

i. At Common Law and before the Courts of Equity

The English common law position was, as described by the Law Revision Committee in 1934, when 'a married woman's position was merged in that of her husband'.[9] A woman's husband, during his life, was entitled to all of his wife's personal chattels (including her money), all of her leaseholds and the rents and profits of her freeholds, and to all of her choses in action.[10]

Wives were also unable to make contracts; this was, as Baker notes, a direct consequence of the inability to hold property.[11] There was, through modern eyes, a disjuncture between married women's position under the law and their expected role in domestic management: despite being unable to enter into contracts, married women were nevertheless expected to procure what was needed for their households.[12] Tradesmen who were willing to give credit to married women acted with some risk: under the common law, there was no way of enforcing this obligation against her through the usual channels of the courts or the prisons.[13] A married woman could only contract as agent for her husband, and in so doing bound *him*. The risk was heightened, Rappaport has pointed out, with new retail practices: women of the nineteenth century were increasingly shopping further from home, which meant that retailers were often selling and extending credit to women (and by extension, to their husbands) whom they did not know personally.[14]

There were some qualifications to this position. The most important for current purposes is the law of 'necessaries'.[15] In effect, at least since the late-medieval period, married women were permitted to contract for the necessaries of life; that is, a husband's consent was implied in his wife's purchasing those goods and

[9] ibid 4. Though, it must be noted, the wife as a separate legal person did not completely disappear: see discussion in GL Williams, 'The Legal Unity of Husband and Wife' (1947) 10 *Modern Law Review* 16, 18.

[10] See, eg, P Mitchell, *A History of Tort Law, 1900–1950* (Cambridge University Press, 2015) 290; Lewis (n 7) 119; ACH Barlow, 'Gifts and other Transfers Inter Vivos and the Matrimonial Home' in RH Graveson and FR Crane, *A Century of Family Law, 1857–1957* (Sweet & Maxwell, 1957) 197; Law Revision Committee, *Fourth Interim Report* (n 8) 4.

[11] J Baker, *Introduction to English Legal History*, 5th edn (Oxford University Press, 2019) 526. See also, eg, Lewis (n 7) 119.

[12] See, eg, M Finn, 'Working-class women and the contest for consumer control in Victorian County Courts' (1998) 161 *Past & Present* 116, 129.

[13] See, eg, M Finn, 'Women, Consumption and Coverture' (1996) 39 *The Historical Journal* 703, 707–08; Rappaport, *Shopping for Pleasure* (n 1) 50–51.

[14] Rappaport, *Shopping for Pleasure* (n 1) 51.

[15] See useful discussion in Finn, 'Women, Consumption and Coverture' (n 13) 709 ff.

services that were suitable to his position in society and his wealth.[16] The idea seemed to be that this was the corollary duty to maintain flowing from his acquiring all of her property. The right to purchase necessaries could be lost through, for instance, a wife's own adultery but may survive if she had good reason, such as his cruelty, to leave her husband.[17] As to what constituted a 'necessary', Wharton, writing in 1853, provided the following list:[18] board, lodgings, suitable apparel, medicines, medical attendance, reasonable expenses during illness, furniture.

Married women had also sought assistance from the Chancellor to soften their position. Avenues were opened in the courts of equity whereby a married woman could exercise some separate control over property settled on her for her benefit.[19] The language of 'separate property' was used. A further device was invented to protect women's separate property, most likely from their husbands, the husband's creditors or indeed, a woman's own acts and 'extravagance':[20] the 'restraint on anticipation'. The restraint on anticipation was a device exclusively used for settlements upon married women; single women and men were not extended the privilege. Essentially, if the appropriate restraining clause were inserted into a settlement or will, the property in question was settled upon the married woman as her 'separate property' and the clause prevented her, during her marriage, from disposing of that property, or placing a charge on the property or income flowing from it.[21] As the Law Revision Committee explained, it most often acted to prevent a married woman from disposing of income in advance, before that income was due to be paid to her. Obviously, the other side of this protective device is that it was a helpful way of avoiding creditors, who could enforce no debt against property the subject of such a restraint (even when it was eventually paid out).[22]

However, as the Committee astutely pointed out, the great majority of married women would have no marriage settlements for which the court of equity could provide protection.[23] Such financial arrangements were limited to the wealthier parts of society.

It is to the final, and most significant, strand of development that discussion now turns: the many legislative changes that slowly chipped away at the legal disabilities of married women from 1870 to 1935.

[16] See, eg, JJS Wharton, *An Exposition of the Laws Relating to the Women of England; Showing their Rights, Remedies, and Responsibilities, in Every Position of Life* (London, 1853) 369; Finn, 'Women, Consumption and Coverture' (n 13) 709–10; Finn, 'Working-class women and the contest for consumer control in Victorian County Courts' (n 12) 130.

[17] See discussion and sources cited in Finn, 'Women, Consumption and Coverture' (n 13) 709.

[18] Wharton (n 16) 369.

[19] See, eg, Law Revision Committee, *Fourth Interim Report* (n 8); Barlow (n 10) 198.

[20] Law Revision Committee, *Fourth Interim Report* (n 8) 10.

[21] See useful overview in Law Revision Committee, *Fourth Interim Report* (n 8) 10. See also, eg, W Cornish, 'Wives: The Quest for Civil Independence' in W Cornish et al (eds), *The Oxford History of the Laws of England, Vol XIII: 1820–1914 Fields of Development* (Oxford University Press, 2010) 757–66, 741–42); W Cornish et al, *Law and Society in England, 1750–1950*, 2nd edn (Hart Publishing, 2019) 349.

[22] Law Revision Committee, *Fourth Interim Report* (n 8) 10.

[23] ibid 6.

ii. The Victorian Legislation: 1870, 1882, 1893

The political fight for married women's property rights is extensively canvassed in the literature elsewhere.[24] For present purposes, the focus is on the effect of the various legislative developments. The first major piece of legislation was the Married Women's Property Act 1870. This Act provided that any money or property acquired by a married woman became her separate property for her separate use. Lewis has suggested that this first Act was passed 'primarily in order to give working class women control over any earnings made'.[25] This accords broadly with comments made by the Law Revision Committee in reviewing the law in 1934.[26] However, the effect of this Act was not truly to confer legal ownership, but rather to give rise to a sort of equitable interest in the property in question.[27] The Act fell significantly short of providing that a married woman's property should be treated as if she were a *feme sole*, a woman without a husband.[28] It was limited to certain kinds of property. While the original Bill would have put married women on par with single women, resistance to a perceived threat to the authority of the husband meant that the final form was watered down.[29]

The next piece of noteworthy legislation was an Act of the same name in 1882. A married woman could, after 1882, acquire, hold and dispose of 'any such real or personal property' as her separate property, as if she were a single woman.[30] The restraint on anticipation device could still be used; the Act did nothing to override the explicit terms of settlements.[31] It also provided that married women could enter into contracts, though only in respect of, and to the extent of, the separate property.[32] In 1882, the relevant property was that which a married woman owned at the date of the contract. Lopes LJ in *Palliser v Gurney*[33] put the matter clearly:

> The disability of a married woman to contract was removed by the Married Women's Property Act, 1882, but only to this extent – that she may now enter into a binding contract, in respect of her separate property. If she has no separate property she still cannot contract
>
> …

[24] See, eg, Holcombe (n 7); ML Shanley, *Feminism, Marriage and the Law* (Princeton University Press, 1989); DM Stetson, *A Woman's Issue: The Politics of Family Law Reform in England* (Greenwood Press, 1982).

[25] Lewis (n 7) 47.

[26] Law Revision Committee, *Fourth Interim Report* (n 8) 6.

[27] Sir Arthur Underhill, *The Law Reform (Married Women and Tortfeasors) Act 1935* (Butterworth & Company, 1936) 15.

[28] See discussion in Shanley (n 24) 68.

[29] See Lewis (n 7) 122.

[30] For a useful overview of the effects of this Act, see, eg, Law Revision Committee, *Fourth Interim Report* (n 8) 7; Underhill (n 27) 16.

[31] See the Married Women's Property 1882 Act, s 19; see also Cornish, 'Wives: The Quest for Civil Independence' (n 21) 763.

[32] See s 1(2) of the 1882 Act.

[33] *Palliser v Gurney* (1887) 19 QBD 519.

> To entitle the plaintiff to succeed he must prove the existence of some separate property at the time of entering into the alleged contract.[34]

By further legislation in 1893, a married woman's 'separate property' was extended to all 'separate property, present or future', even if she had no separate property at the date of the contract.[35] The 1893 amendment removed the problem of determining what, if any, property the wife had at the time of contracting.[36] Prior to this amendment, courts also had to grapple with the *kinds* of property that would be sufficient to be the basis for a contractual relationship. Personal items of small value were insufficient. For example, in *Leak v Driffield*[37] in an action by a firm of drapers to recover a debt said to be owed by a married woman, it was held that clothing was not sufficient. The married woman in *Leak* had property settled upon her for her separate use, but this was subject to a restraint on anticipation. She had, with the income generated from the settlement, purchased some clothing for herself and for her children but had no other property free from the restraint on anticipation. It was said that a married woman's property was not bound by her contracts unless she could be supposed to have contracted with reference to it:

> [T]he question is whether the defendant had separate property with respect to which she could reasonably be deemed to have contracted; and as her only free separate property consisted of the clothes of herself and of her children, which they could not do without, it is clear to me that she could not be deemed to have contracted with reference to that separate property.[38]

As such, the drapers were left without a remedy. The extent to which this particular question was necessary after the 1893 Act is unclear: if future property could be the property with which a married woman contracted, what if she never acquired more than clothing?

Nevertheless, every contract entered into by a married woman was deemed to be with respect to, and to bind, her separate property, unless the contrary were demonstrated.[39] There was, therefore, at least in principle, a presumption operating that a married woman had contracted to bind her separate property and had not contracted as agent for her husband.[40] The presumption of the common law that a wife had authority to pledge a husband's credit for 'necessaries' continued.[41] Even without a husband's express consent, where he had failed to provide for her, a wife could 'pledge his credit' provided the spending was not out of keeping with

[34] ibid 521.

[35] Married Women's Property Act 1893, s 1.

[36] This issue was before the courts in, for example, *Re Shakespear* (1885) 30 Ch D 169 and *Palliser* (n 33).

[37] *Leak v Driffield* (1889) 24 QBD 98. See also Cornish, 'Wives: The Quest for Civil Independence' (n 21) 764.

[38] ibid 101–02 (Mathew J).

[39] Married Women's Property Act 1882, s 1(3).

[40] See, eg, discussion in W Bowstead, *A Digest of the Law of Agency*, 7th edn (Sweet & Maxwell, 1924) 22.

[41] ibid 23.

her husband's social status and lifestyle.[42] She was there deemed to be acting as his agent. However, either the married woman, or her husband, would be a party to the contract; not both.[43] It remained the case that the Acts did not give married women full contractual capacity; they were not bound personally but only to the extent of their separate property.[44]

Reviewing the law in 1934, the Law Revision Committee was critical of these legislative developments. The Committee's report noted that a simple course could have been adopted, whereby 'a woman on marriage would not have changed her status as regards capacity to contract, to hold property and to sue and be sued'.[45] The report continues:

> Instead Parliament took a much more indirect course, with the result that the Married Women's Property Act 1882 was a very complicated measure of 27 sections, and has given rise to much difficult litigation. What was done was to adopt from equity the idea of '*separate property*'. This in itself was harmless enough … [b]ut unfortunately, as some may think, the legislature not only adopted the name by which the Court of Chancery had designated such property, but attached to this statutory separate property many of the other qualities with which the Court of Chancery had endowed it …
>
> The Act … so far from conferring on the married woman the power of contracting as though she were a feme sole, merely gave her a limited power of entering into contracts differing but little from the limited power of entering into engagements that she had acquired in equity, and it was accordingly held that if a woman had no '*separate property*' when she incurred a liability in contract, she could not be made liable at all … This defect was indeed corrected by the Act of 1893, but that Act safeguarded the old rules as to restraint upon anticipation and still left a married woman's liability under her contracts a proprietary and not a personal one (emphasis original).[46]

The idea of 'separate property' thus remained the key to married women's proprietary and contractual rights. If there were a restraint upon anticipation of a settlement, this would not be available as future separate property to be bound by the contract. In effect, the law remained unsatisfactory and outdated, the legislation adding little that could not already be achieved in the courts of equity.

In addition to the legislative provisions themselves, it is apparent from the way in which the Victorian legislative developments were handled by courts

[42] See Lewis (n 7) 120.

[43] According to *Bullen and Leake's Precedents of Pleadings* in 1915, it was 'now practically impossible for both husband and wife to be liable' on a parol contract made by a married woman since the marriage – either the wife was agent, or she was not: see WB Odgers, *Bullen and Leake's Precedents of Pleadings*, 7th edn (Stevens and Sons, 1915) 19.

[44] This was confirmed by Lord Esher MR in *Palliser* (n 33) who said: 'It is said that this [1882] statute makes a married woman personally liable upon contracts entered into by her in her own name; but if that was the intention it is not expressed, though it might easily have been expressed … The section limits the capacity of the married woman to bind herself by the words "in respect of and to the extent of her separate property". It is clear that she is not given an unlimited capacity to enter into and be bound by any contract': 520.

[45] Law Revision Committee, *Fourth Interim Report* (n 8) 7.

[46] ibid 7–8.

that the idea that married women were acting as agents for their husbands was difficult to overcome. Though this may have been to the advantage of women seeking to avoid their debts, it also suggests that, in practical terms, the Acts were not the near-equalising watershed that some contemporaries feared, and that others had sought. The idea that a married woman might be contracting as agent for her husband was considered in the 1906 case *Paquin v Beauclerk*,[47] which resulted in a 2:2 split in the House of Lords. In *Paquin*, a married woman had dealings with Paquin Ltd, dressmakers. She was a regular customer and was extended credit when she purchased items. The bills were sent to her, and for some time she paid regularly by her own cheques. Her husband was later found to be insolvent and absconded. The plaintiffs brought an action against his wife to recover the remaining amount due. The question for the House of Lords was whether she was acting as agent for her husband, in which case the 1893 Act would not apply and he would be liable, or not acting as agent, in which case the 1893 Act might enable her to be sued upon the contract (though she would be bound only to the extent of her separate property).[48] She denied having any separate estate or separate income of any kind. She said that the goods had been bought while she was agent for her husband; she said that they were goods that would be described by the law as 'necessaries' – suitable to her husband's position in society – but also that she had bought them with his direct authority and his knowledge. Lord Loreburn LC and Lord Macnaghten held that, because she had her husband's express or implied authority to purchase the goods, she had contracted on his behalf as his agent. Lord Macnaghten, in particular, appeared unconcerned about any hardship this might bring upon the dressmakers (and others in such a position):

> There is really no hardship on the tradesman who deals with a married woman. He is under no obligation to give credit at all, or to continue or extend the credit, if credit is given. He may make any inquiries he pleases of the customer or of anybody else. If he chooses to trust a lady with unlimited credit, when he is not sure of his ground, he has only himself to blame if anything should go wrong.[49]

Lord Robertson, in dissent, noted that the dressmakers did not know that she had a husband living, nor that she was cohabiting with him. He said:

> Did the appellants deal with the respondent as an agent? As already stated, they certainly did not, for they never heard of the existence of a husband. This being so, I find it legally impossible to hold that the respondent contracted as an agent; for, unless both parties regarded the respondent as an agent, she did not contract as agent.[50]

Lord Atkinson, also in dissent, noted that he did not think that the Married Women's Property Act 1893 had been intended to protect married women from

[47] *Paquin v Beauclerk* [1906] AC 148.
[48] ibid 159.
[49] ibid 164.
[50] ibid 165.

liability, in circumstances where they entered a contract 'apparently as principal'.[51] The outcome of this case, and its effect, was lamented in an article in 1930 published in the *Solicitors' Journal*, the author criticising the apparent ease with which some married women might escape liability at the expense of tradesmen.[52] This indicates that *Paquin* remained good law into the 1930s.

Despite the limitations of the statutes enacted and continued difficulties in practice, the ability to enter into contracts, which bound a woman to the extent of her separate property, was certainly a significant development for married women's independence. However, it was only a limited power to contract.[53] The outcome in *Paquin* suggests that the legal status quo, the woman acting merely as agent for, and with the permission of, her husband, was difficult to escape. Furthermore, any benefits created by the legislative changes would not have been enjoyed by many women of lower socio-economic standing, who may have brought no property to the marriage and had no earnings.

iii. The Law Reform (Married Women and Tortfeasors) Act 1935 and Beyond

The more significant change to women's status came only in 1935, and thus after *Donoghue*, with the passing of the Law Reform (Married Women and Tortfeasors) Act. It was only with the passing of this Act that married women were 'given the same capacity as single women to acquire, hold and dispose of property'.[54] This legislation was the result of an inquiry into the state of the law relating to married women, as part of a larger project of law reform. Viscount Sankey, then Lord High Chancellor, set up a committee, including several prominent judges,[55] which reported in December 1934. As foreshadowed in the Committee's comments outlined above, the report concluded that the concept of 'separate property' ought to be abolished. The report states:

> We cannot see, in modern conditions, any reason for treating the property owned by a married woman in any way differently from that of any other woman or any man, or for keeping alive the idea of '*separate property*'.
>
> …
>
> *Women nowadays, whether married or single, engage in almost all professions, trades and businesses and are eligible to hold and do in general hold every sort of public and official post and exercise every right and franchise*, just as much as men.
>
> …

[51] ibid 166.
[52] 'The Married Woman as Fraudulent Debtor' (1930) 74 *Solicitors' Journal* 427, 429.
[53] See, eg, discussion in M Brown, 'Legislation' (1936) 14 *Canadian Bar Review* 265.
[54] Lewis (n 7) 78.
[55] The Master of the Rolls, Ernest Pollock (Lord Hanworth) was chairman, and was joined by Lord Wright and Lord Justice Romer, amongst others.

> A married woman's liability under a judgment should be personal, not merely proprietary. If she incurs a debt, we cannot see why it should not be enforced against her in the same way as it would be against anyone else. In other words, the conception of the Acts of 1882 and 1893, based on the idea of the wife's '*separate property*' should be abolished by a suitable amendment of the law (emphasis added).[56]

The report is clear in expressing the view that restrictions upon a woman's ability to contract and to hold property, in the same way as single women and men, were out of step with modern society. It was also recommended that the 'restraint on anticipation' practice be abolished through legislation, noting that other protective devices were offered in the law of trusts which were open to men as well.

The resulting legislation of 1935 removed altogether the idea of separate property, and rendered married women able to acquire, hold and dispose of property, and significantly, to bind themselves *personally* in contract, rather than just to the extent of separate property. Therefore, certainly by 1935, a married woman's status, in respect to her ability to incur and enforce obligations, and her ability to hold wealth, was drawing close to that of her husband's, if not equal. However, and importantly for the purpose of this thesis, the same cannot be said of married women before 1935.

The position in Scotland was a little different. Scotland appeared, in fact, to have made more progress towards equality through the Married Women's Property (Scotland) Act 1920. This was the last of a series of statutes that modified the common law position of wives. Two statutes are of particular relevance to the present discussion, the Married Women's Property (Scotland) Act 1881, and the 1920 Act.

As under English law, so under early Scottish law all of a wife's moveables went to her husband upon her marriage, and over other property he was given rights of administration.[57] The 1881 Act provided that a wife's moveables, acquired before and during the marriage, were to remain her separate estate but preserved the husband's rights of administration.[58] No contractual capacity was conferred in 1881. The 1920 Act, however, appears more radical: the husband's right of administration was abolished, and married women were given the same powers of disposal with respect to their property as if they were unmarried. Married women were also, by this Act, able to enter into contracts and incur obligations as if unmarried. After the 1920 Act, in Scotland marriage alone had no legal effect on the property holding of the parties to the marriage.[59]

However, a 1956 piece in the *Modern Law Review* suggested that for wives entering marriage without property, and acquiring little, the equality was purely formal:[60] '[t]he formal rule that the earnings of either spouse remain his or her own property may be translated into the practical rule that the earnings

[56] Law Revision Committee, *Fourth Interim Report* (n 8) 9.
[57] See, eg, Anton (n 5) 653.
[58] ibid.
[59] ibid 656.
[60] ibid 657.

of the husband remain his property'.[61] Unless a wife had a separate income, most of what was purchased by wives, for the family or household, would be considered to be an act of agency for her husband and therefore his property.[62] There was also a legal presumption known as *praepositura* in operation, whereby third parties were entitled to presume that a wife was in charge of her husband's domestic arrangements and therefore had authority to act as his agent in domestic matters.[63] The case of *Smith v Smith*[64] provides a good example of the continuing practical inequality within marriage in Scotland, despite the equality apparent in the statute book. In *Smith*, a marriage had broken down after 40 years and the husband brought an action against his wife to recover £1,000 that was held in a savings account in her name. Certain shares were also claimed, though the £1,000 is of more interest for present purposes. The husband asserted that the funds in question were the product of savings made of the money he had given his wife for the running of the household. The Court of Session found in favour of the husband (subject to some small deductions). The Lord President said: 'Her *praepositura* cannot entitle her to make savings for herself out of that of which she is only stewardess. If, therefore, any accumulations are made, they belong to the husband'.[65]

The position, with respect to household money, was the same in England. A married woman in England would also not have owned the money provided to her by her husband for housekeeping. Even in 1943, any savings a married woman could make by being careful with household expenditure and taking in lodgers remained the property of her husband.[66] The headnote to the report of *Blackwell v Blackwell*[67] in the All England Law Reports series contains an editorial note that the decision was one 'on a point which is really settled by previous authority', but that '[s]ome little doubt ha[d] been felt whether the position ha[d] been affected by social change and the various statutes dealing with the property of married women'.[68] The decision clarified the matter. Mrs Blackwell, who had recently separated from her husband, had saved the sum of £103 by being thrifty with household expenditure. However, the source of that income was found to be the weekly allowance given to her by her husband. It was decided that she could not be said to be carrying on a separate business in taking in lodgers. In the absence of any kind of understanding that the housekeeping money was to be hers as a gift, the money remained his property and he was entitled to reclaim it. The position

[61] ibid.

[62] ibid 657–58.

[63] See P Fraser, *Treatise on Husband and Wife according to the Law of Scotland* (T and T Clark, 1876–78) 605–07; Scottish Law Commission, *Family Law: Report on Outdated Rules in the Law of Husband and Wife* (Scot Law Com No 76, 1983) 16.

[64] *Smith v Smith* 1933 SC 701.

[65] ibid 705. See also, on this point, *Dryden v McGibbon* 1907 SC 1131; *Logan v Logan* 1920 SC 537.

[66] *Blackwell v Blackwell* [1943] 2 All ER 579 (CA); 'Housekeeping Money: Whether Property of Saving Wife' (1943) 196 LT 175. See also discussion in Barlow (n 10) 203.

[67] *Blackwell v Blackwell* (n 66).

[68] ibid 579.

that any savings out of housekeeping remained the husband's property in law continued until 1964.[69]

It was therefore the case in England and in Scotland in the early part of the twentieth century that acquisition of property by women would require something like employment, endowment or gift. It becomes useful, therefore, to consider the nature of marriage and financial arrangements within marriages, and how this may have changed from the mid-Victorian era (the time of *Winterbottom*) through to the 1935 Act (around the time of *Donoghue*).

iv. Women, Money and Marriage: A Continuing Problem

In the absence of domestic servants, a married woman would be the party most often interacting with shop owners and suppliers. However, if a married woman had no wages from employment, and no family settlement (presumably uncommon outside the upper echelons of society), she may not have had any separate property. In England, a woman in such a position was likely not to be a party to a contract of sale that she concluded. Paying out of a household allowance provided by her husband, the money remained her husband's, and she had probably not provided the consideration. She was also likely to be acting as the agent of her husband.

The doctrine of consideration was not present in Scottish law: there was no need for consideration to have passed between parties to form a binding contract.[70] The obligation arose instead from consent; an intention to be bound, clearly expressed.[71] As such, consideration did not constitute the same obstacle for Scottish women as for English. It is also possible that a contractual remedy was available under Scottish law to a third party for whose benefit a contract had been made. There was certainly a historical line allowing claims by third parties, based on the position taken by James Dalrymple, Viscount Stair, who first published his *Institutions of the Law of Scotland* in 1681.[72] However, subsequent case law and commentary was not always wholly consistent with this view.[73] By the nineteenth century, things had become

[69] Married Women's Property Act 1964. See also Cornish et al, *Law and Society in England, 1750–1950* (n 21) 380.

[70] See, eg, WM Gloag, *The Law of Contract* (W Green & Son, 1914) 58.

[71] ibid. Though see also, commenting on aspects of Gloag's work: HL MacQueen, 'Third Party Rights in Contract: Jus Quaesitum Tertio' in K Reid and R Zimmermann (eds), *A History of Private Law in Scotland: Volume Two: Obligations* (Oxford University Press, 2000) 238–39.

[72] See MacQueen (n 71); HL MacQueen and WDH Sellar, 'Scots Law: Ius quaesitum tertio, Promise and Irrevocability' in EJH Schrage (ed), *Ius Quaesitum Tertio* (Duncker & Humblot, 2008); TB Smith, 'Jus Quaesitum Tertio: Remedies of the "Tertius" in Scottish Law' (1956) *Juridical Review* 172. It also seems the basis of the third party rights is that any notions of privity yield to the intention of the parties, and that therefore third party rights may have required an intention to create such enforceable rights, express or implied, as opposed to a third party simply benefiting from the contract: see H MacQueen and J Thomson, *Contract Law in Scotland*, 4th edn (Bloomsbury, 2016) 85–86. See also Smith, 'Jus Quaesitum Tertio', ibid, 10.

[73] See, eg, MacQueen and Sellar, 'Scots Law: Ius quaesitum tertio, Promise and Irrevocability' (n 72); MacQueen (n 71).

uncertain,[74] and by 1932 in *Donoghue*, as we have seen, it was being supposed that Scottish law followed English law in the doctrine of privity of contract, precluding suit by the ultimate consumer against the manufacturer of a product.[75] As such, if a married woman in the early part of the twentieth century were acting as agent for her husband in purchasing goods, it is perhaps possible that she may, in Scottish law, have acquired some enforceable rights if the contract could be said to have been made for her benefit. However, it is more likely that she would not have been able to sue upon the contract concluded, should the goods prove harmful to her.

In England, marriage was, for the entire period covered by this study, the norm and the expected state of women of all classes.[76] For some classes in the nineteenth century, it was essentially an economic necessity, as women's wages were so low.[77] The two world wars had, unsurprisingly, a significant effect upon percentages of women who married: there was a shortage of men, preventing some women from fulfilling the 'natural destiny'.[78] Nevertheless, it remained the expected path. Government agencies and policy-makers operated on the assumption that married women would be financially dependent on their husbands.[79] Indeed, the 'family model' was encouraged, as it was seen as central to economic and community stability, and important for the workforce.[80]

At several points in the Committee's 1934 report, discussed above, it is made clear that married women's position in society had changed, by 1934, from what it was in the 1870s and 1880s.[81] Women, it said, whether married or single, engaged in 'almost all' professions and trades.[82] Histories of women's work in the early twentieth century demonstrate that there were new areas of employment opening up for female workers, such as retail and clerical positions. Opportunities for work in these appear to have been taken up with enthusiasm, during this period, particularly by

[74] See *Robertson v Fleming* (1861) 23 D (HL) 8, 4 MacQ 167; MA Millner, 'Ius quaesitum tertio: comparison and synthesis' (1967) 16 *International and Comparative Law Quarterly* 446, 459. It seems that there may have been a rule in operation that while a third party may enforce their rights to a benefit, they could not sue, on the contract, for defective performance of the contractual terms. However, MacQueen and Sellar suggest that while *Robertson v Fleming* may have introduced into Scottish law some kind of contract/tort fallacy, this was then rejected in *Edgar v Lamont* 1914 SC 277: HL MacQueen and WDH Sellar, 'Negligence' in K Reid and R Zimmermann (eds), *A History of Private Law in Scotland: Volume Two: Obligations* (Oxford University Press, 2000) 537. See also MacQueen and Sellar, 'Scots Law: Ius quaesitum tertio, Promise and Irrevocability' (n 72); MacQueen (n 71).

[75] This has subsequently been criticised. See, eg, Burns, who, writing in 1978, said: '[s]ince the seventeenth century at least, the law of Scotland recognised that the fact that A had a contract with B was no reason why he should not be liable to C in delict if through his carelessness C had been injured. That part of the law had been obscured during the nineteenth century through the grafting on to Scots law of the notion of privity of contract': CB Burns, 'Are we forever to be behind Scotland?' (1978) 12 *Law Teacher* 76, 78.

[76] See, eg, Lewis (n 7) 3.

[77] ibid.

[78] ibid 4.

[79] ibid 45.

[80] ibid 45.

[81] See Law Revision Committee, *Fourth Interim Report* (n 8) 4, 9.

[82] ibid 9.

young women, but they also participated in more traditional forms of employment like domestic service.[83] Nevertheless, in the early twentieth century, the majority of women in England were not in employment, and therefore would not have had wages. Todd reports the percentage of women over the age of 24 in paid work as just 23 per cent in 1921.[84] For married women, percentages are even lower. Marriage bars were also in place, and became more widespread, in many types of employment during the 1920s, such as the civil service, banking and, to an extent, teaching.[85] Many women simply expected to leave their employment upon marriage.[86] Even wartime engagement by women in employment did not mean a significant overhaul of the economic structure of society.[87] After the First World War, there was a perceived need in some quarters to restore the pre-war 'order' and reassert proper gender distinctions and roles.[88] By the 1920s, intense pressure was put on women to leave their work and return to their domestic positions.[89] Lewis puts the percentage of married women in work from 1911 to 1931 at a steady 10 per cent.[90]

The upshot of this survey is that, in the 1920s and 1930s, even if society's perception of women's abilities had developed, as signalled in the Committee's report, it remained the case that the majority of married women did not work in formal employment. Most married women would therefore have been using their husband's money in purchasing goods. This, together with the likelihood of their being treated as an agent for their husbands, suggests that many women were not parties to the contracts they concluded.

In the August 1882 issue of the *Solicitors' Journal*,[91] the difficult situation of married women, raised by *George* (and topical, given the passing of the Married Women's Property Act also in 1882), was identified to argue for a change in the law:

> A married woman goes and buys some hairwash for her own use. Assume that the hairdresser has, through the grossest ignorance or carelessness, put some highly

[83] S Todd, *Young Women, Work and Family in England 1918–1950* (Oxford University Press, 2005) 21–26, 34–43. See also discussion in S Alexander, 'Becoming a woman in London in the 1920s and 1930s' in D Feldman and G Stedman Jones, *Metropolis: London* (Routledge, 1989) 248–56. Todd reports that women under the age of 25 made up almost 50% of the female workforce in the interwar period, and when this figure fell in the 1940s this was because of more married women coming into the workforce, rather than numbers of young women diminishing: Todd, *Young Women, Work and Family in England 1918–1950*, 19–20.

[84] Todd, *Young Women, Work and Family in England 1918–1950* (n 83) 19–20, drawing from 1921 Census information.

[85] K Murphy, 'A Marriage Bar of Convenience? The BBC and Married Women's Work 1923–1939' (2014) 25 *Twentieth Century British History* 533.

[86] See, eg, 'Women in Industry' (1930) 30 *Monthly Labour Review* 71, 72.

[87] See Lewis (n 7) 149 and sources there cited.

[88] See S Kent, *Making Peace: The Reconstruction of Gender in Interwar Britain* (Princeton University Press, 1993) 99–100 and sources there cited.

[89] ibid 101.

[90] Lewis (n 7) 150, also relying on Census figures for the period.

[91] 'Damage to a third person caused by a defective article' (1882) 26 *Solicitors' Journal and Reporter* 665, 667–68.

> deleterious substance in the hairwash by which the wife is injured. The wife cannot contract; in law the husband is the purchaser. Therefore no action lies … Again, a married man goes to a chemist's [shop] to have a prescription made up. The chemist has left a shop-boy entirely unqualified to make up prescriptions. The shop-boy puts some deleterious drug in a draught by mistake. If the husband drinks the draught and is rendered ill, there is a cause of action, but if the prescription was for his wife she has no remedy. The result plainly is that in cases where, if death resulted from the negligence, there might be a case of manslaughter, there is yet no duty to support a cause of action.[92]

While this was written in 1882, the complication in *George* had not been remedied by the early 1930s, despite the passage of more than 50 years. This fact, given the improved status of women in other respects, is likely to have appeared to be out of step with modern society and a contributing factor to the right climate for a change in the law.

B. Children

It is worth briefly considering another category of person whose legal rights and capabilities were limited by the law during the nineteenth and early twentieth centuries: children. This is particularly important for understanding the case law uncovered in chapter four. A person under the age of 21 was an 'infant' under the law until 1970 (when the age of majority was reduced to 18).[93] One is more likely to participate actively in commercial activities – working, buying goods and services – as one nears adulthood, and probably already during teen-age years. That young people were, in the eyes of the law, 'children' until the age of 21 meant that contracts with 'children' must have been concluded with relative frequency.

The common law rule was that infants were not liable upon their contracts, subject to some general exceptions.[94] For example, an infant could be held liable on a contract of marriage and on a contract of apprenticeship.[95] The other major exception was that they could be bound by contracts for the supply of 'necessaries'.[96] At common law, it was said that all other contracts were either void or voidable, with some confusion and complexity as to which sorts of contracts

[92] ibid.

[93] For a useful general discussion of the law concerning Infants during this period, see W Cornish, 'Children' in W Cornish et al (eds), *The Oxford History of the Laws of England, Vol XIII: 1820–1914 Fields of Development* (Oxford University Press, 2010).

[94] See, eg, AH Simpson, *A Treatise on the Law and Practice relating to Infants*, 3rd edn (Stevens and Haynes, 1909) 74–75; WHS Garnett, *Children and the Law* (J Murray, 1911) 209; Cornish, 'Children' (n 93) 806.

[95] ibid.

[96] ibid.

might be the former or the latter.[97] However, Parliament intervened and passed the Infants' Relief Act 1874, which provided, inter alia:

> All contracts … henceforth entered into by infants for the repayment of money lent … or for goods supplied or to be supplied (other than contracts for necessaries), and all accounts stated with infants shall be absolutely void.[98]

As to 'necessaries', it is clear that this term included food and drink, medicine and clothing, but was sufficiently malleable to stretch to jewellery, when deemed appropriate, and was not confined to items that sustained existence.[99] However, food and clothing supplied while the child was living at home were not considered 'necessaries', and a father was not liable for necessaries supplied to the child unless the child had acted as agent in ordering the items.[100] Infants were able to sue upon contracts that were not void; if voidable at common law, it was still binding upon the other party and therefore able to be sued upon by the infant.[101] However, an infant bringing an action on a contract could not appear in person and was required to sue by a next friend.[102]

Children, therefore, had some limited capacity to enter into binding contracts, though only for the procurement of goods and services which could be described as 'necessaries'. They could also sue upon these contracts. However, they were not able to 'enjoy the full fruits of adult status'.[103] The privileges accorded to them, including, for example, a higher standard of care owed in relation to their physical safety under the law of negligence, were, according to one author of the *Solicitors' Journal*, provided to console them for this reduced capacity.[104]

Scotland appears to have had similar rules concerning the capacity of children to contract, though there are some differences. A minor had the capacity to contract, but if the child had curators, their consent was required.[105] A child without curators could enter into contracts and be bound.[106] However, a child with curators but acting without their consent might nevertheless be bound with respect to contracts for 'necessaries'.[107] 'Necessaries' might include, for instance, bread, meat, vegetables and water, but perhaps also, for example, an expensive coat,

[97] Simpson (n 94) 4–7; Garnett (n 94) 209.

[98] Infants' Relief Act 1874, s 1.

[99] Garnett (n 94) 215, citing *Peters v Fleming* (1840) 6 M & W 42, 151 ER 314. The minor in *Peters* was an undergraduate of the University of Cambridge and the 'eldest son of a gentleman of fortune and a member of Parliament'. The jewellery was determined to be fit for his station in life, and thus capable of being 'necessaries'. See also Simpson (n 94) 75–78; AE Randall, *Leake's The Law of* Contracts, 6th edn (Stevens & Sons, 1912) 391–93.

[100] Garnett (n 94) 216, citing *Mortimore v Wright* (1840) 6 M & W 482, 151 ER 502.

[101] Randall (n 99) 393.

[102] ibid 394.

[103] See, eg, 'Privileges of Infancy' (1911) 56 *Solicitors Journal and Weekly Reporter* 81, 82.

[104] ibid.

[105] WF Trotter, *The Law of Contract in Scotland* (William Hodge and Company, 1913) 82.

[106] ibid 81–82, 90.

[107] ibid 83.

if it was needed for the child's trade or calling.[108] A minor was also able to carry on a trade, and therefore to make contracts in the course of that trade without any curator consent.[109] Children could also sue upon contracts.[110]

Still, in England as in Scotland, even if children were able to sue in some circumstances, the fact remains that most children in the early part of the twentieth century would not have had significant money of their own and therefore would most often, if they were purchasing goods, be acting as agent for their parent. Even more often, their parent would be the direct purchaser. If a child were to be injured by a defective item, any ensuing medical fees would also have been paid by their parent. The child would be left to claim against a vendor or manufacturer in negligence alone, which, as was demonstrated in chapter one, may have been difficult.

II. The Rise of Consumer Culture

We have already seen, in cases like *Mullen*, that bringing an action was still difficult by the 1920s for would-be plaintiffs not party to the contract of sale with a vendor, and for those seeking to make manufacturers liable for harm done by a faulty product. Nonetheless, the early twentieth century in England was a period in which an unprecedented array of goods was available for purchase, and shopping was a form of leisure enjoyed by all parts of society – not just the elite. There is a variety of views on the likely cause of the creation of the mass 'consumer culture' that developed from the mid-nineteenth century.[111] It suffices to note here there were several important developments during this period that encouraged and fuelled the creation of a consumer culture. These, it will be argued, are likely to have increased the pressure on the law to recognise a duty owed by manufacturers to consumers, outside of any contractual relationship.

A. Developments in Retail: New Forums and Practices

In the eighteenth century, shopping had been the province of the elite. Most shops operated in traditional ways, offering only a small variety of goods and using credit.[112] New forums for retail came into being during the nineteenth century. Arcades, with covered walkways, developed in the early nineteenth century for the wealthy to purchase luxury items.[113] Perhaps more novel,

[108] ibid 84.
[109] ibid 86.
[110] A curator was, however, necessary for the discharge of certain debts: see discussion in Trotter (n 105) 91.
[111] See discussion in Whitlock (n 1) 18–19.
[112] See, eg, Whitlock (n 1) 18.
[113] ibid 24; Gurney (n 1) 23.

however, were the bazaars springing up around the same time, which catered to the wider public.[114] Co-operative stores also rose to prominence during the nineteenth century, with numbers of co-operative societies peaking in the first few years of the twentieth century, offering everyday goods to primarily working-class customers at affordable prices.[115] The forerunner to the modern department store was the large 'emporium', well established by the 1840s, which began to trade in all kinds of clothing.[116] The adoption of set prices, pioneered by drapers in the early nineteenth century,[117] was particularly important for bringing in lower middle-class customers, as they were then able, at a glance, to determine whether or not their budget could meet the asking price.[118] The rise of emporia marked a change in the scale at which goods were sold and the way in which people consumed.[119] For life's necessities, the expansion of urban centres meant that people were less able to produce their own food,[120] leading to a decline[121] in importance of markets, and the rise of grocery stores selling basic goods to meet working-class needs.[122]

These new forums did not mean that smaller shops died out: more traditional types of shop remained a prominent feature of the Victorian and early twentieth-century shopping landscapes, and proliferated.[123] There was, it seems, simply more of everything: variety of goods, forums and consumers.

Towards the end of the nineteenth century came the department store, which created for consumers a new and luxurious shopping experience. These new establishments provided, as the century wore on, an increasingly wide variety of goods and services – luxury items, clothing, furniture, household goods, groceries, ironmongery, dining facilities, writing rooms.[124] They were also, as Gurney describes it, cathedral-like in their focus upon atmosphere and light, and designed to entice and encourage spending.[125] These new institutions attracted not just the social elite; they catered for a wider clientele and were frequented also by middle-class shoppers.[126] Of course, the largest, and perhaps the most famous, of all department stores was Selfridges, which opened its doors in 1909 under the direction of the American, Harry Gordon Selfridge. Selfridge aimed to sell to the masses but

[114] Gurney (n 1) 23.

[115] ibid 109–15. See also J Blackman, 'The Development of the Retail Grocery Trade in the Nineteenth Century' (1967) 9 *Business History* 110, 111.

[116] Gurney (n 1) 23. See also Whitlock (n 1) 27, 33–34.

[117] Whitlock (n 1) 28–33.

[118] ibid 30.

[119] ibid 33–34.

[120] Gurney (n 1) 25–26, 29–30, 33.

[121] Markets were, however, by no means abandoned: see Gurney (n 1) 25–26.

[122] Gurney (n 1) 25–26.

[123] ibid 25; A Adburgham, *Shops and Shopping 1800–1914* (Unwin Brothers, 1981) 280.

[124] See Gurney (n 1) 87–91; Rappaport, '"The Halls of Temptation"' (n 1) 77; B Lancaster, *The Department Store: A Social History* (Leicester University Press, 1998) 21–23.

[125] Gurney (n 1) 90–91. See also Rappaport, '"The Halls of Temptation"' (n 1) 66; Rappaport describes them as 'palaces'.

[126] Lancaster (n 124) 22–23.

also to promote shopping as leisure; to that end, he used display, advertising and spectacle to great effect.[127]

Another forum rose to prominence in the first part of the twentieth century: chain stores. Chain stores carrying cheap, mass-produced goods such as tinned food, confectionary, toiletries and clothing offered a much wider range of goods to consumers.[128] Many chains still in existence today grew significantly in scale and prominence in this early part of the twentieth century. Woolworths opened its first British store in Liverpool in 1909; by 1929 it had 375 branches and, by 1939, there were 759.[129] Marks & Spencer was also growing in prominence and profit during this time, offering goods affordable to most parts of society.[130] Simon Marks, chairman and managing director of Marks & Spencer, commented in 1936:

> Improvements in the efficiency of production, brought about by inventions, scientific technique and more rational administration, enable us to produce *constantly increasing quantities of goods at lower prices, and to extend the range of commodities manufactured*
>
> …
>
> Goods and services once regarded as luxuries have become conventional comforts and are now almost deemed necessities. A fundamental change in people's habits has been brought about. Millions are enjoying a substantially higher standard of living
>
> …
>
> It is … a mistake to assert that large-scale manufacture has restricted the freedom of choice of the average consumer. It is patent to anyone who compares the average family budget of to-day with that of two decades ago that it provides for a greater quantity and variety of goods and services. The machine age, paradoxical as it may sound to some, has increased and not decreased the demand for the satisfaction of individual tastes and personal services (emphasis added).[131]

B. Consumers of Goods

A clear picture that emerges from studies of shops and consumer culture in the nineteenth century is one of increasing distance between the producer of goods and the ultimate consumer. For example, Gurney notes that farmers who might earlier have travelled to market to sell their own meat came increasingly to operate through middlemen: butchers. This caused the number of butchers in Sheffield, for instance, to rise from 148 in 1825 to 358 in 1861.[132] The new railways enabled

[127] Rappaport, *Shopping for Pleasure* (n 1) 154–57.

[128] Gurney (n 1) 138.

[129] ibid 137, citing A Godley, 'Foreign Multinationals and Innovation in British Retailing 1850–1962' (2003) 45 *Business History* 80, 86.

[130] Gurney (n 1) 138.

[131] *The Times* (26 May 1936), 24, parts of which are also quoted in Gurney (n 1) 138.

[132] Gurney (n 1) 26.

middlemen to buy perishable goods from further afield and to bring them into urban centres to sell.[133]

Another clear picture is that women were perceived to be significant consumers: shopping was considered a female pastime.[134] There was significant concern, during the nineteenth century, that women were being lured into making unwise purchases, behaving undesirably, spending beyond their means and being exploited by the sharp practices of retailers.[135] This seems to have abated by the 1880s, as retailers sought to cleanse the public image of the industry, which, in turn, facilitated more expansion in department stores.[136] The new stores used display and advertising to target female consumers.[137] Though fashion was, of course, not a nineteenth-century phenomenon, as Whitlock describes it, the increased production, competition and forums of sale of the nineteenth century 'democratize[d]' fashion.[138] The new era in retail allowed women *outside* the upper classes to pursue, during the second half of the nineteenth century, fashion and finery in a way that had never before been possible. New technologies and mass production meant that middle-class women, and perhaps also upper working-class women, could enjoy fashionable but affordable clothing.[139] Lace could be made by machine, and steam-driven production in weaving from the late 1700s had led to the wide availability of cheap cotton fabrics.[140] These goods were then sold in emporia to consumers who could not have participated in fashion in the same way even half a century earlier.[141]

Nevertheless, it has been suggested that it was not before the interwar years in the twentieth century that consumer culture really reached all parts of British society.[142] Department store advertising expanded, between the wars, to target lower socio-economic groups as well.[143] That working-class people in the interwar years had greater access to consumer goods is, as Wildman notes, captured nicely by George Orwell in his *Road to Wigan Pier*:

> The two things that have probably made the greatest difference of all are the movies and the mass-production of cheap smart clothes since the war … You may have three halfpence in your pocket and not a prospect in the world, and only the corner of a leaky bedroom to go home to; but in your new clothes you can stand on the street

[133] ibid.

[134] See, eg, Gurney (n 1) 93; Whitlock (n 1) 103–04.

[135] See Whitlock (n 1) 103, 113–14; Rappaport, '"The Halls of Temptation"' (n 1).

[136] Rappaport, '"The Halls of Temptation"' (n 1) 77–83. It seems some concern continued in relation to beauty retail practices: see JP Clark, *The Business of Beauty: Gender and the Body in Modern London* (Bloomsbury Visual Arts, 2020) 1–4.

[137] Rappaport, '"The Halls of Temptation"' (n 1) 77–83.

[138] Whitlock (n 1) 106.

[139] ibid 109–10.

[140] ibid.

[141] ibid 110–11.

[142] See Wildman (n 1) 96–97. See also Alexander (n 83) 245–46, 256–67. See also Gurney (n 1); Lancaster (n 124) 94.

[143] Wildman (n 1) 101.

> corner, indulging in a private daydream of yourself as Clark Gable or Greta Garbo, which compensates you for a great deal
>
> ...
>
> Whole sections of the working class who have been plundered of all they really need are being compensated, in part, by cheap luxuries which mitigate the surface of life.[144]

The increased participation in the consumption of goods, by women and by members of all parts of society, is significant for the aims of the present chapter, as the increased availability and wider reach of potentially harm-causing goods is likely to have put pressure on laws restricting the ability to sue.

C. New Industries

Women were also the principal consumers in the commercial beauty industry, which emerged in the period between the mid-nineteenth century and the early decades of the twentieth. This particular branch of retail was practised discretely in the nineteenth century. Although certainly available then, attitudes towards beautifying goods and those providing beautifying services were not always positive: there were fears that products might be dangerous, but there was also a sense of immorality or lack of respectability around their use.[145] Clark has shown that between the 1850s and 1910s, the scale of the beauty business was transformed.[146] She suggests that the groundwork was laid by Victorian traders, aided by improvements in manufacturing techniques and new forms of transport, for the eventual 'market explosion in the twentieth century'.[147] For example, it has been suggested that hairdressing, as a trade, nearly doubled in size between 1921 and 1931.[148]

Regional newspapers of the 1920s certainly abound with advertisements for beauty products and hairdressing services, and it is evident that consumer demand was high.[149] This was expressed clearly in the *Derby Daily Telegraph* in 1927, where the author of a beauty advice column notes:

> The change in fashion has given rise to what may almost be described as a new industry. Lady's hair-dressing was always an art, but it was not so widely practised as it is to-day,

[144] G Orwell, *The Road to Wigan Pier* (Penguin, 2020) 84–86, quoted in Wildman (n 1) 112.

[145] See Clark (n 136) 1–4.

[146] ibid 4, 165–89.

[147] ibid 4. See also 187.

[148] See S Vincent, *Hair: An Illustrated History* (Bloomsbury, 2018) 220, cited in Clark (n 136) 197.

[149] An advertisement in the *Ripley and Heanor News*, 4 June 1926, asserts that '[o]wing to the Increased Popularity of Ladies' Hairdressing, it has become necessary to open an Additional Private Room Exclusively for Ladies'. One page of the *Journal and North Star*, 29 November 1928, contains no less than seven images of women's hairstyles, around the same number of advertisements for hairdressing services and a lengthy beauty advice column. Of course, being just two examples, this is not conclusive, but these features do suggest an industry faring reasonably well.

> and although the number of businesses has been greatly multiplied, giving employment to thousands of clever men and women, there would appear to be scope for more.[150]

The 'Women's Chat' section of the *Thanet Advertiser* in 1925 noted that the demand for hairdressing services was so great that it became viable for women to set up small private salons for friends and family, in competition with larger salons. The author, described only as 'Olive', notes:

> Bobbing and shingling have brought so much business to the hairdresser that girls are being trained for this profession and are thinking of setting up establishments of their own. Others are training themselves by practising on their sisters, cousins, and aunts, and seeking paying customers outside the family circle. Where there are several girls in a family the constant visits to the hairdresser, *that are now found to be necessary*, amount to no little sum week by week (emphasis added).[151]

It is likely that this column was not designed only for upper-class women; the concern for the amelioration of weekly costs is indicative of a broader readership. This evidence suggests that hairdressing services were no rare luxury, even for those with budgetary constraints. Some advertisements for hairdressing services expressly note that their prices are 'moderate'.[152]

The significant expansion of the beauty industry in the 1910s and 1920s is of particular relevance to this book. It provides an example of an area in which products and services were available on a scale not seen in previous centuries. These were being demanded and consumed by all parts of society, not just the very wealthy. The potential that such products would harm the consumer, as was the case in *George*, may have played a role in holding back expansion of the industry at an earlier date but was an ongoing problem into the twentieth century. Their increased availability, and consumption, is likely to have contributed to the pressure for a change in the law. Indeed, the potential for harm to consumers of beautifying products, and their appetite for legal redress, is central to chapter four, which uncovers and brings together a series of cases brought in the 1920s by women against the creators and purveyors of clothing and cosmetic products.

D. Consumer Products and the Law

Studies of the rise of British consumerism and the changing nature of the retail trade from the nineteenth century into the twentieth century do not suggest particular points of explosive change. Instead, the literature suggests that the period was marked by the steady expansion of a culture of consumerism and innovations in commercial practices that both fuelled and responded to this trend. For present purposes, what is striking is that, despite significant changes in the nature

[150] 'My Lady's Hair' *Derby Daily Telegraph* (10 November 1927).
[151] 'Women's Chat' *Thanet Advertiser* (24 October 1925).
[152] See 'The Bainbridge Hairdressing and Beauty Salons' *Journal and North Star* (29 November 1928).

of manufacturing and the manner and scale of the sale of goods from the 1840s to the 1930s, the law as to liability for products, until *Donoghue*, remained unchanged. In the middle of the nineteenth century, many goods were still being made and sold on a small scale. Fifty years later there was mass-production of goods, and department stores recognisable to modern eyes had taken over the high street. By the interwar period, consumerism had taken hold across all parts of society. Appetite for goods increased, the variety of goods available expanded and the forums in which they might be procured proliferated. There was also increasingly a separation, throughout the period from the mid-nineteenth century to the early twentieth century, between the vendor and producer of products.

With unprecedented access to goods and demand for goods came unprecedented scope for injury through defective goods. The fact that shopping was seen, and marketed, as an activity principally for women would also have exacerbated the ongoing difficulties with married women's contracts. Whenever a contract of sale was concluded between a married woman and a vendor, there may have been a real question as to whether or not the woman was a party to it. If not, and if she were then injured by the product purchased, her opportunities to sue would be limited: no warranty would be owed to her, and her suit in negligence would be barred by the privity rule. Taken together, these factors are likely to have increased the pressure for a change to the legal rules. A law of product liability that recognised only limited circumstances in which someone injured by defective goods might successfully sue appears at odds with a developed consumer society.

III. Liability Insurance

Liability insurance is plainly advantaged by an expansive approach to legal liability. It is not feasible to sell insurance to cover conduct immune from liability.[153] It is also possible, although not universally accepted, that the availability of insurance may render courts more prepared to find that a liability exists.[154] It is unnecessary to delve into this question. It suffices to say that, before liability insurance became available, smaller producers might not have been able to absorb and spread the cost of possibly substantial liability if they were found negligent – or, at least, it was not unconvincing for manufacturers to claim that this was the case.[155] Indeed, as discussed in chapter two, it is this concern that appears to have been

[153] See discussion in KD Syverud, 'On the Demand for Liability Insurance' (1994) 72 *Texas Law Review* 1629, 1633.

[154] See, eg, J Stapleton, 'Tort, Insurance and Ideology' (1995) 58 *Modern Law Review* 820, particularly 824–26. See also F James, 'Accident Liability Reconsidered: The Impact of Liability Insurance' (1948) 57 *Yale Law Journal* 549, 551 and generally for discussion of the potential impact of insurance upon tort law.

[155] J Bell and D Ibbetson, *European Level Development: The Case of Tort* (Cambridge University Press, 2012) 76.

at the forefront of the minds of the *Winterbottom* court and other courts of the mid-nineteenth century. The significant expansion of the availability of liability insurance throughout the 1920s may reasonably be understood as setting up the right climate for the legal change (a widening of liability) created by *Donoghue*.

A. The Development of Liability Insurance

The timing of the development of liability insurance is particularly relevant to the present enquiry. Of the other types of insurance we need say only a little. Eighteenth and nineteenth-century insurance was fragmented; there were, for example, separate markets for marine, life and fire insurance.[156] As Raynes describes it: 'Marine insurance covers losses due to marine perils; fire insurance covers loss due to fire; life assurance provides payments on the happening of … contingencies involving human life; accident insurance … cover[s] loss sustained by any other events'.[157]

Accident insurance, as a category, came to include insurance against personal accident, employers' liability, public liability, burglary and motor vehicle accidents, to name just some.[158] Emerging in the 1840s,[159] its earliest form was insurance against personal accident, where a policy might be purchased such that, in the event of sickness, blindness or other unfortunate event, a sum would be paid to the insured person regularly during recovery or for longer.[160] Lobban attributes this development to the 'railway age';[161] Dinsdale suggests that it arose in response generally to the 'changed conditions of life and human activity … [springing] from the Industrial Revolution'.[162] Accident insurance grew in importance from its inception and was, by the early part of the twentieth century, a significant and well-publicised category of insurance on offer.[163] What is perhaps particularly striking to modern eyes is that in the aftermath of the First World War, coupon accident insurance was advertised daily in newspapers.[164] These had been conceived in the 1880s, and could operate in different ways: either a premium was paid by the proprietors of the newspaper, and the 'Insured' reader simply had to

[156] See M Lobban, 'The Law of Insurance' in WR Cornish et al (eds), *The Oxford History of the Laws of England, Vol XII: 1820–1914 Private Law* (Oxford University Press, 2010) 674–77 and sources there cited. See also, generally, HE Raynes, *A History of British Insurance*, 2nd edn (Pitman & Sons Ltd, 1964).
[157] Raynes (n 156) 275. Though the author goes on to note that the division is artificial and there is much overlapping: 275.
[158] WA Dinsdale, *History of Accident Insurance in Great Britain* (Stone & Cox, 1954) iii.
[159] See, eg, Lobban, 'The Law of Insurance' (n 156) 677; Cornish et al, *Law and Society in England, 1750–1950* (n 21) 485; Dinsdale (n 158) 1, 37.
[160] Dinsdale (n 158) 53.
[161] Lobban, 'The Law of Insurance' (n 156) 677.
[162] Dinsdale (n 158) 37.
[163] See, eg, various advertisements in *The Times*: 'Insurance Companies' *The Times* (13 September 1898); and 'Special Articles' *The Times* (2 May 1912).
[164] Dinsdale (n 158) 68–69.

complete the coupon, or the 'Insured' reader would pay a registration fee and send in the completed coupon to the insurance company.[165] One example of coupon insurance from 1919 even offers 'Free' broad-brush insurance, covering damage by things such as fire, burglary, death by accident to the insured and also covers claims by third parties for accidents occurring on the insured's premises.[166] All that was required was that the reader fill out and post the coupon. These newspaper coupon schemes were only discontinued in 1939 upon the outbreak of war and the consequent increased risk of loss.[167] The schemes were, it seems, mainly intended as advertisement, but they did offer some limited protection if the strict conditions were satisfied.[168]

Liability insurance emerged later than other forms of insurance; its origins lie in the late nineteenth century.[169] Product liability insurance, of particular relevance to this book, developed within the broader category of public liability insurance.[170] It is therefore worth considering the development of the broader category. Available from 1875, the first public liability insurance policies outside marine insurance were drivers' (of carts) insurance policies.[171] However, it was really with the introduction of the Employers' Liability Act in 1880 that liability insurance become more widespread. The common law had, it will be recalled from chapter two and the discussion of *Priestley v Fowler*,[172] adopted a chilly attitude towards the liability of employers to their employees.[173] The 1880 Act limited the availability of the defence of 'common employment', imposed new obligations upon employers and, from there, liability insurance 'blossom[ed]'.[174] Earlier in the century, the sale of such insurance had been seen as morally objectionable and was not permitted on public policy grounds.[175] By the end of the 1800s, attitudes seem to have shifted.[176] Motor vehicle insurance provides an interesting example for considering the magnitude of the change in attitude: this type of insurance, including third-party indemnity, had been introduced and began to be offered by

[165] ibid.

[166] See, eg, 'Free Insurance' *Edinburgh Evening News* (28 February 1919).

[167] Dinsdale (n 158) 69.

[168] ibid.

[169] See, eg, Dinsdale (n 158) 177; KS Abraham, 'The Rise and Fall of Commercial Liability Insurance' (2001) 87 *Virginia Law Review* 85, 86–87.

[170] EA Heppell, *Products Liability Insurance* (Pitman & Sons Ltd, 1967) 1, 4.

[171] See Dinsdale (n 158) 179–80; M Davies, 'The end of the affair: duty of care and liability insurance' (1989) 9 *Legal Studies* 67, 75.

[172] *Priestley v Fowler* (1837) 3 M & W 1, 150 ER 1030.

[173] See, eg, *Priestley*, ibid. See also, for example, K Oliphant, 'Tort Law, Risk, and Technological Innovation in England' (2014) 59 *McGill Law Journal* 819; P Bartrip, 'The impact of institutions and professions on compensation for occupational injury in England' in P Mitchell (ed), *The Impact of Institutions and Professions on Legal Development* (Cambridge University Press, 2012).

[174] Cornish et al, *Law and Society in England, 1750–1950* (n 21) 486. See also Dinsdale (n 158) 41; M Lobban, 'Workplace Injuries' in WR Cornish et al (eds), *The Oxford History of the Laws of England, Vol XII: 1820–1914 Private Law* (Oxford University Press, 2010) 1018.

[175] See AW Baker Welford, *The Law Relating to Accident Insurance*, 2nd edn (Butterworth & Company, 1923) 432. See also Cornish et al, *Law and Society in England, 1750–1950* (n 21) 486; Davies (n 171) 75.

[176] See, eg, Baker Welford (n 175) 432.

several companies around the turn of the century and, by 1931, *compulsory* third-party motor vehicle insurance was introduced.[177]

Dinsdale has proposed several reasons for the growth of public liability insurance. One is the increased appreciation by the public of their legal rights.[178] An article published in *The Policy-Holder*, a specialist insurance journal, in January 1933 supports Dinsdale's suggestion that there was an increasing awareness of legal rights and the potential for compensation following misfortune. The article, describing the content of a lecture given by a representative of the Royal Insurance Company, Liverpool, states that

> accidents of employment and road accidents have educated the public to make claims and have developed the compensation complex … The old time state of unsophistication has gone, and if anyone is injured now thoughts turn very rapidly towards legal remedies.[179]

It is useful for the present enquiry to consider two principal questions: first, *when* did liability insurance grow into a substantial, frequently-used category of insurance; and second, against which sorts of liabilities was insurance offered and sought in the first part of the twentieth century? These questions are considered below.

i. Prevalence

Material sourced from *The Times* and regional newspapers indicates that the availability of liability insurance increased significantly from the early to mid-1920s. In November 1924, the *Northern Whig and Belfast Post* published an article, which must surely have been sponsored by the many insurance companies for which details are provided, entitled 'Insurance that Shields!' and urging upon the readership the benefits of insurance. Relevantly for our purposes, the opening comments included the following:

> While for marine, fire, and life purposes the great developments of the system occurred during the nineteenth century, *it is within the twenty years of the twentieth century* that some of what are now very important forms of insurance have originated … such as have arisen from new conditions as in motor car and accident liability insurance.
>
> To-day it is possible to insure against any kind of risk … which may affect an individual, a company or a community financially (emphasis added).[180]

[177] See discussion in Dinsdale (n 158) 177; Raynes (n 156) 304–05; PWJ Bartrip, 'Pedestrians, Motorists, and No-Fault Compensation for Road Accidents in 1930s Britain' (2010) 21 *Journal of Legal History* 45, 52. Compulsory third-party insurance was introduced by the Road Traffic Act 1930. It was from 1969 that employers, too, were required to take out compulsory insurance against their liability: Employers' Liability (Compulsory Insurance) Act 1969. See also Oliphant (n 173) 839.

[178] Dinsdale (n 158) 178.

[179] 'Third Party Liability: Interesting Examples' *The Policy-Holder: An Insurance Journal* (25 January 1933) 125.

[180] 'Insurance that Shields!' *Northern Whig and Belfast Post* (29 November 1924).

Similarly, a 1937 report in *The Policy-Holder* provides:

> Third party insurance is quite young compared with some of the other branches of insurance, although policies providing a limited indemnity in respect of certain legal liabilities for accidents to third parties were issued towards the end of the last century. This century, however, *particularly since the war* – has seen a considerable expansion in the demand for insurance protection of this nature, and a rapid development of this class of business has taken place (emphasis added).[181]

These sources indicate that it was during the first decades of the twentieth century that liability insurance became widely available, with demand (and corresponding availability) increasing after 1918.

A report in *The Times* in 1925 of the progress of the Ocean Accident and Guarantee Corporation includes the following:

> The income of the public liability department also showed an advance over that of any previous year. The corporation issues policies covering a very great variety of contingencies and *there is no doubt that the necessity for this class of cover is becoming more widely appreciated* (emphasis added).[182]

This report marks 1925 as the most lucrative to date in the area of liability insurance. Another article in *The Times* in 1926 by RC Gask emphasised the importance of liability insurance in light of the current state of the law of negligence. He wrote:

> The importance of public liability insurance, both as a means of public protection and as a commercial necessity, is indicated by the immensity of the field of risk covered. By the Common Law of the country every individual is under obligation so to conduct his affairs as to avoid involving others in injury to their persons or damage to their property, the same principle applying also to every firm, company, or other body. Any breach of this obligation represents negligence which … constitutes liability.
>
> …
>
> The possibility of such negligence is to be regarded as a kind of contingent liability which may or may not arise, but without provision for which complete financial security must very often be absent
>
> …
>
> Where the risk in any one connexion, such as motoring, is especially important, insurance may be specialized under a separate branch, the policies issued being distinct from the general public liability policy as it is known in the insurance world.[183]

The author goes on to outline 'Examples of Liability', one of which is 'Ptomaine Poisoning', where it is commented that all owners or occupiers of premises, such as manufacturers, shopkeepers, and hotel proprietors, have risks to consider which

[181] 'Third Party Insurance: Development of Third Party Insurance' *The Policy-Holder: An Insurance Journal* (25 August 1937) 1388.
[182] 'Company Meetings: Ocean Accident and Guarantee Corporation' *The Times* (29 April 1925).
[183] RC Gask, 'Public Liability' *The Times* (28 April 1926).

may be the subject of insurance cover.[184] 'Ptomaine poisoning' was a term given to forms of food poisoning from the late nineteenth century to the first half of the twentieth century.[185]

One possibility for this significant growth was the confirmation in the courts around this time that indemnities for the consequences of accidents would be enforced by the courts, even in the case of gross negligence, and were not against 'public policy' and thus liable to being struck down. In 1921, a novel question was raised before the King's Bench following a fatal motor vehicle accident: where negligence is gross, a man is killed and the crime of manslaughter is committed, can a defendant claim an indemnity under an insurance policy covering such liability, or is it against public policy to indemnify a person against the civil consequences of his criminal act?[186] The case was *Tinline v White Cross Insurance Association*.[187] The insurance policy held by the plaintiff and issued in 1920 covered 'sums which the assured shall become legally liable to pay to any other person … as compensation for accidental personal injury … sustained or caused through the driving of the automobile'. Bailhache J found that the policy was an insurance against negligence, whether slight or great, and covered the case at hand. However, he also explained that the outcome would have been different if there had been some *intentional* wrongdoing:

> It must of course be clearly understood that if this occurrence had been due to an intentional act on the part of the plaintiff, the policy would not protect him. If a man driving a motor-car at an excessive speed intentionally runs into and kills a man, the result is not manslaughter but murder. Manslaughter is the result of an accident and murder is not, and it is against accident and accident only that this policy insures.[188]

As to the argument raised about public policy, he seemed to dismiss this as something that existed in principle but was not pursued. He acknowledged that it was generally 'true to say that it is against public policy to indemnify a man against the consequences of a crime which he knowingly commits',[189] with 'crime' including breach of statutory duties for which a fine might be imposed. Driving at excessive speed was such a breach. Indeed, the objection, he explained, could apply to most driving accident cases. It was, however, 'notorious that the defence is never raised … by common consent, these third party indemnity insurances have been treated as valid and effective'.[190]

A similar case arose in 1927, *James v British General Insurance Company*.[191] Roche J held that, where an act carrying criminal responsibility was done by negligence, rather than intentionally, the degree of criminality that would make

[184] ibid.
[185] See, eg, B Bynum, 'Discarded diagnoses' (2001) 357 *The Lancet* 1050.
[186] *Tinline v White Cross Insurance Association* [1921] 3 KB 327.
[187] ibid.
[188] ibid 332.
[189] ibid 331.
[190] ibid.
[191] *James v British General Insurance Company* [1927] 2 KB 311.

indemnification contrary to public policy is not present. In *Tinline*, it had been excessive speed that caused the accident and, in this case, drunkenness. In neither case did the insured intend the injury. The availability of insurance was therefore unaffected. *Tinline* was approved and followed.

Liability insurance was certainly widely available by 1923. In that year, Baker Welford wrote in his treatise on accident insurance:

> Insurance against liability seems to have been first introduced in marine insurance, for the purpose of protecting the assured, in the case of a collision, against his liability to pay damages … The business of insuring against liability has, however, been extended until, at the present day, it is possible to effect an insurance against nearly every conceivable liability.[192]

The author went on to suggest that there was a question as to whether or not liability insurance, which was essentially 'insurance against the consequences of wrongful acts', offended the rule that no action could lie upon a contract of indemnity against 'liability arising from the doing of an act which is manifestly unlawful or which the doer … knows to be unlawful, as constituting either a civil wrong or a criminal offence'.[193] He suggested that there may be a question as to whether or not such contracts, providing for liability insurance, were capable of being enforced.[194] The author was writing after *Tinline*, though before *James*. He notes that *Tinline* was the first time the question of their legality was 'definitely' raised before the courts.[195] Nevertheless, he appeared not to see *Tinline* as providing a full answer. Baker Welford went on to distinguish insurances 'against liability arising out of contract', which were valid (and had always been so) because, he explained, they were insurances on property and are not, strictly speaking, insurances against liability.[196] Employers' liability insurance was acceptable, he said, as it had been recognised by statute.[197] He appeared to conclude that while *wilful* conduct by the insured may preclude valid indemnity for the consequences, *negligence* was not treated in the same manner.[198] *Tinline* is cited many times, and particularly for the notion that the doctrine of public policy has no application in respect of negligent acts.[199] However, the argument is also advanced that a distinction ought to be drawn between degrees of negligence.[200]

Despite Baker Welford's concerns about the enforceability of some potential forms of liability insurance, it is clear that at the time of writing, liability insurance

[192] Baker Welford (n 175) 428.
[193] ibid 429.
[194] ibid 431.
[195] ibid.
[196] ibid. Most of the cases cited concern insurance policies taken out by carriers of goods, the rest concern fire insurance.
[197] Baker Welford (n 175) 432.
[198] ibid 433–35.
[199] ibid 435–36.
[200] ibid 436.

was an important and substantial category. Baker Welford devotes over 200 pages in his 1923 treatise to the combined topics of liability insurance generally, public liability insurance, driving accident insurance and employers' liability insurance. We can contrast this with Morrell's *Insurance: A Manual of Practical Law*, published in 1892, which contains no parts devoted to liability insurance, even in the employment context.[201] McGillivray's 1912 treatise gives just three pages of around 1,200 to employers' liability policies, and two paragraphs to 'Third Party Risk Policies'.[202] Interestingly, Porter's sixth edition of *The Laws of Insurance*, published in 1921, contains only a very short discussion of employers' liability and its insurance, under the heading of 'Accident Insurance'.[203] There is no discussion of other forms of liability insurance.

The 1937 report in *The Policy-Holder*, considered above, suggests reasons for the expansion of the liability insurance business, including an increase in the use of machinery and 'mechanically propelled vehicles' and the consequently increased risk of accident, and the introduction of 'a considerable amount of legislation dealing with factories and … accidents to employees … [which] had the effect of bringing to the notice of the ordinary public that they owe a duty of care to their fellowmen'.[204] There also appears to be some concern about a developing compensation culture:

> [R]ecent years have evidenced a marked tendency to resort to litigation to obtain redress in the event of accident, and the consequent reports of the legal proceedings in the daily press have proved a decided incentive to traders and employers to obtain insurance protection in respect of third party risks.[205]

The connection between the growth of the liability insurance industry and the size of damages awards, and also the publicity given to such awards in the press, was also made in later reports in the *Post Magazine and Insurance Monitor*.[206]

Whatever the reason, from the general absence of the subject in treatises of the very early 1920s and the content of the newspaper material considered, it is likely that we can place the significant expansion of the liability insurance business in the mid-1920s. That liability insurance became widely available in the few years before *Donoghue* is significant. While it is not possible to suggest any direct causation, the development of a means by which manufacturers of products might, with relative ease, protect themselves from the consequences of a successful claim against them in negligence, is likely to have increased the pressure on the law to change.

[201] CF Morrell, *Insurance: A Manual of Practical Law* (Adam and Charles Black, 1892).

[202] EJ MacGillivray, *Insurance Law relating to All Risks other than Marine: including Life, Fire, Accident, Guarantee, Burglary, Third Party Risks, and Employers' Liability* (Sweet & Maxwell, 1912) 966–70.

[203] JB Porter, *The Laws of Insurance: Fire, Life, Accident and Guarantee*, 6th edn (Gilbert Stone, 1921).

[204] 'Third Party Insurance: Development of Third Party Insurance' (n 181) 1388.

[205] ibid.

[206] See, eg, 'Reflections on Public Liability Insurance' *Post Magazine and Insurance Monitor* (19 August 1939); 'Third Party Insurance' *Post Magazine and Insurance Monitor* (3 February 1940).

ii. Liability Insurance for Products

It is also likely that specific policies were increasingly available for suppliers and producers of all kinds of goods in the 1920s. It is possible to get a sense of the types of liability insurance available at different time periods from a perusal of some insurance policy proposals held by the Aviva Group Archive. However, it has not been possible to ascertain whether or not these are the earliest or first of their kind made available. As such, they are helpful in providing a general impression only.

Liability insurance for 'Licensed Victuallers', offered by the General Accident Fire and Life Assurance Corporation, is the subject of a 1909 proposal, which contains the following statement:

> The liability of Shopkeepers, Traders, etc, to compensate customers and others not in their service who may be injured on their premises through the negligence of the Proprietor or his servants applies specially to Licensed Victuallers. The daily visitors to licensed premises are numerous and often hurried, and the lurking danger of a worn mat, a defective step, an unsecured trap-door … may at any moment cause an accident for which the Proprietor may have to make a heavy payment by way of compensation.
>
> Injuries, entailing heavy damages, sustained through the carelessness of waiters, *bursting bottles, aerated water bottle corks*, and accidents of this nature are of frequent occurrence.
>
> The General Accident Fire and Life Assurance Corporation, Limited, will insure against this liability for a premium so moderate that no innkeeper need be without this protection (emphasis added).[207]

This proposal shows that, even as early as 1909, it might be possible for vendors to protect themselves from the consequences of a successful claim against them, in the event that they supplied products causing harm. Similarly, a 1914 proposal issued by the same corporation offers protection for grocers, in respect of 'Liability to Public for Accidents, Either in or about the Shop or by the Sale of Goods'.[208]

Insurance for liability for ptomaine poisoning may have been available as early as 1910.[209] It is clear from a brief report in the *Aberdeen Daily Journal* that, by 1922, ptomaine poisoning insurance was so widely available that insurance providers were competing for business. The report notes a recent meeting of the Aberdeen District Grocers' and Provision Merchants' Association, and its consideration of several schemes for insuring against ptomaine poisoning in order to find the most favourable terms.[210]

A 1931 proposal also issued by the General Accident Fire and Life Assurance Corporation, entitled 'Cinema Proprietors Public Liability Insurance', states that it covers accidental bodily injury to members of the public, accidental property

[207] General Accident Fire & Life Assurance Corporation Ltd, *Specimen and completed proposal documents*, Aviva Group Archive (Norwich), GA863. Permission to reproduce this content has been granted by the Aviva Group Archive.

[208] ibid.

[209] Dinsdale (n 158) 183.

[210] See, eg, 'Aberdeen Grocers: Ptomaine Poisoning Insurance' *Aberdeen Daily Journal* (5 April 1922).

damage and, relevantly: '[b]odily injury or [i]llness caused by poisonous, foreign or deleterious matter in food or drink served in the Auditorium'.[211]

Food and beverage products were not the only products capable of causing harm. It has already been noted, in section II of this chapter, that, in the early twentieth century, goods became available on an unprecedented scale and all parts of society could engage in their consumption. In the 1920s, indemnities were sought against claims for damages with respect to dermatitis caused by the purchase (and wearing) of inexpensive furs.[212] The *Yorkshire Post* reported in 1925 that:

> [Fur dermatitis] had … become so common that there was a special insurance policy available for the members of that section of the trade which dealt in such things, indemnifying them against damages. The disease … was a comparatively new one, and was traceable to the cheaper imitation furs.[213]

There was widespread concern about an 'epidemic' of dermatitis connected to the wearing of fur, which reached such a level that an inquiry was instituted and a report made by the Ministry of Health.[214] Liability for dermatitis-inducing fur garments is considered in chapter four.

B. Liability Insurance and Legal Change

The picture created by examining the various policy proposal examples and newspaper reports, and by comparing the content of treatises from before and after this period, is that there was an upward trend during the 1920s of insuring for all kinds of legal liabilities. Significantly for present purposes, this increase in availability occurred in the 10 or so years leading up to the decision in *Donoghue*. It is no great leap to suggest that this may have had an impact on the courts' attitudes towards compensation. Certainly, the arguments advanced in *Winterbottom* as to the dire consequences for defendants if they were to be saddled with liabilities beyond their agreed contractual relationships appear far weaker in a world where loss-spreading through insurance is not only possible, but increasingly commonplace. The majority speeches in *Donoghue*, and three of the judgments in *Mullen*, appear to contemplate a different world from that which existed when the privity rule was introduced.

Insurance bodies were certainly keeping an eye on cases like *Donoghue*. In January 1933, *The Policy-Holder* published an article entitled 'Third Party Liability,' in which significant attention was given to *Donoghue*. In a discussion of the types

[211] General Accident Fire & Life Assurance Corporation Ltd, *Specimen and completed proposal documents*, Aviva Group Archive (Norwich), GA863.

[212] Dinsdale (n 158) 182.

[213] 'Skin Disease from Fur Collar' *Yorkshire Post and Leeds Intelligencer* (27 June 1925).

[214] See Ministry of Health Report on Public Health and Medical Subjects (No 27, 1924). See also Heppell (n 170) 6; 'Fur Dermatitis' *Western Daily Press* (4 September 1924).

of third-party liability cover available, the article notes that '[a] recent case has widened considerably the liability of manufacturers'.[215] It goes on:

> Until a short time ago it was generally believed that whilst manufacturers were liable in certain cases to reimburse traders in respect of claims arising out of goods … they could escape direct claims on the part of persons injured, because they (the manufacturers) did not owe them any duty. This was dealt with in an interesting case where a lady who in consuming some ginger beer also consumed a dead snail.[216]

IV. The Morality of Negligence

At the end of the nineteenth century and moving into the twentieth century, there was also a change *within* the law that contributed to creating a climate in which an expansion in liability was more likely. This change concerned the perception of negligence and its connection to notions of morality.

In the mid-nineteenth century, there was a lack of consensus amongst jurists and treatise writers as to the theoretical basis for liability in negligence: did it concern a failure to meet an external standard, or was it based upon the defendant's mental state?[217] Another matter that was unclear was whether or not it mattered that the conduct did or did not conform to a moral standard.[218] John Austin[219] and Jeremy Bentham,[220] for example, preferred to treat negligence in terms of *mens rea*, a particular state of mind being necessary for liability.[221] It appears not to have been about morality for Austin and Bentham, though, but rather about pragmatism: liability required knowledge for the sanction to be effective.[222] Oliver Wendell Holmes, however, understood Austin's theory to have a moral dimension.[223] Well into the twentieth century, it was this form of the theory that was taken up by Salmond:

> Negligence … is conduct different from that of a prudent and reasonable man; therefore it is imprudent and unreasonable conduct – viz., conduct unaccompanied by that anxious consideration of consequences which is called care
>
> …

[215] 'Third Party Liability: Interesting Examples' (n 179) 128.
[216] ibid.
[217] D Ibbetson, 'The tort of negligence in England' in N Jansen (ed), *The Development and Making of Legal Doctrine* (Cambridge University Press, 2010) 49.
[218] ibid.
[219] J Austin, *Lectures on Jurisprudence* (J Murray, Vol 2, 1863) 144; see also discussion in Ibbetson, 'The tort of negligence in England' (n 217) 50.
[220] J Bentham, *Introduction to the Principles of Morals and Legislation* (Clarendon Press, 1879) 90–96; see also discussion in Ibbetson, 'The tort of negligence in England' (n 217) 50.
[221] See OW Holmes, 'Trespass and Negligence' (1880) 14 *American Law Review* 1, 1: Holmes notes that this was Austin's theory of negligence.
[222] See discussion in Ibbetson, 'The tort of negligence in England' (n 217) 50.
[223] See OW Holmes, *The Common Law* (Little, Brown and Company, 1881) 82; Ibbetson, 'The tort of negligence in England' (n 217) 50.

> Attempts are sometimes made to define negligence as a purely objective fact involving no characteristic or essential mental attitude at all … This, however, is a defective analysis of the conception. To cause harm by a failure to take precautions is not necessarily want of care or negligence, for it may be intentional wrongdoing or a mere accident. Which of these three things it is cannot be ascertained save by looking into the mind of the defendant
>
> …
>
> No man can be judged in this respect, save by reference to what he knew, or foresaw, or would have known or foreseen had he been in his own heart sufficiently careful and anxious to do no harm to others.[224]

However, another way of thinking about negligence seems to have risen to prominence in the late nineteenth century, and to dominance by the twentieth:[225] that negligence was about the application of external standards to a situation. This was an idea put forward by Oliver Wendell Holmes, who had rejected the idea that liability required subjective fault.[226] There was no need to consider what had passed through the defendant's mind at the time of acting, and fault did not mean some personal moral short-coming;[227] instead, it was necessary to consider what, given the circumstances of the case, would be blameworthy according to the average, prudent man.[228] Taking the Holmesian approach would mean negligence became *unmoralised*; the external standards to be applied reflected the morals of a society that required, for general welfare, certain conduct to be avoided, but liability did not require personal immorality.[229] He explained:

> Notwithstanding the fact that the grounds of legal liability are moral to the extent above explained, it must be borne in mind that law only works within the sphere of the senses. If the external phenomena, the manifest acts and omissions, are such as it requires, it is wholly indifferent to the internal phenomena of conscience. *A man may have as bad a heart as he chooses, if his conduct is within the rules*. In other words, the standards of the law are external standards, and *however much it may take moral considerations into account, it does so only for the purpose of drawing a line between such bodily motions and rests as it permits*, and such as it does not (emphasis added).[230]

This understanding of negligence gained supporters in England. In February 1880, Pollock wrote to Holmes, responding to his reading of the article in which the above quote appears:

> I quite agree with your thesis that legal negligence is not a state of mind (as somebody says in Year Book quoted in Blackburn on *Contract of Sale*, the thought of man is not

[224] JW Salmond, *The Law of Torts*, 2nd edn (Stevens and Haynes, 1910) 22–23. See also discussion in Ibbetson, 'The tort of negligence in England' (n 217) 50.

[225] Ibbetson, 'The tort of negligence in England' (n 217) 51.

[226] See Holmes, *The Common Law* (n 223) 96; see also M Lobban, 'Negligence' in WR Cornish et al (eds), *The Oxford History of the Laws of England, Vol XII: 1820–1914 Private Law* (Oxford University Press, 2010) 941.

[227] Holmes, 'Trespass and Negligence' (n 221) 21.

[228] See Holmes, *The Common Law* (n 223) 96; see also Lobban, 'Negligence' (n 226) 941.

[229] Holmes, 'Trespass and Negligence' (n 221) 21–23.

[230] ibid 23.

> triable, for the devil himself knows not the thought of man) but falling short of an objective standard.[231]

Thirteen years after this letter was written it seems that Holmes's view of negligence had gained traction, causing Pollock to write:

> But Nemesis is upon us. The reasonable man and the 'external standard' have filtered down to the common examination candidate, who is beginning to write horrible nonsense about them.[232]

By the 1920s, as Ibbetson has observed, Beven's *Negligence in Law* and Salmond's *Law of Torts* had been amended, under new editorship, and commentary in favour of the objective approach was added.[233]

On the subjective view of negligence, where the defendant's state of mind is central, a finding of liability was a moral condemnation of a defendant: liability meant that they were personally at fault and had a blameworthy state of mind when acting. However, on Holmes's external standard view, the defendant could be liable without being quite so reprehensible – the defendant had not necessarily had a blameworthy state of mind but had simply acted in a way the reasonable person would not. Holmes welcomed the consequence that an external standard would make private law less about moral wrongdoing. This separation of legal principle from morality would continue into the twentieth century; it was by no means complete by the 1930s and indeed Lord Atkin's judgment in *Donoghue* has, as the underlying principle, the moral assertion that one ought to love one's neighbour, and therefore take care not to injure them.[234]

The increasing availability of liability insurance also suggests a view of liability in negligence that is more practical than moral – legal liability was not something that only happened to 'bad' people; it was, instead, a feature of the modern world and something that prudent businesses and individuals sought protection against.

The gradual move towards the *de*-moralising of the negligence enquiry, beginning with Holmes's ideas in the late nineteenth century, would thus have created a climate in which it was more likely courts would expand liability. There was less at stake for the reputation of the defendant.

[231] F Pollock, 'February 10, 1880' in M De Wolfe Howe (ed), *Holmes–Pollock Letters: The Correspondence of Mr Justice Holmes and Sir Frederick Pollock 1874–1932, Vol I* (Harvard University Press, 1942) 13.

[232] F Pollock, 'August 31, 1893' in M De Wolfe Howe (ed), *Holmes–Pollock Letters: The Correspondence of Mr Justice Holmes and Sir Frederick Pollock 1874–1932, Vol I* (Harvard University Press, 1942) 46.

[233] See T Beven, *Negligence in Law*, 4th edn (Sweet & Maxwell, 1928) 183; JW Salmond, *The Law of Torts*, 7th edn (Sweet & Maxwell, 1928); Ibbetson, 'The tort of negligence in England' (n 217) 51.

[234] See discussion in Ibbetson, 'The tort of negligence in England' (n 217) 64. There were, of course, then objective standards applied to limit the potential scope of this principle – reasonable care and foreseeability.

V. A Climate for Change

The purpose of discussion in this chapter is not to argue for any definite causal connection between these factors and the eventual outcome in *Donoghue*. The world is a complex place. Rather, it is suggested that these factors were contemporaneous developments or states of affairs that together, created a climate that was *supportive* of the removal of the privity doctrine in 1932.

Each of the factors identified – the difficult position of married women (and perhaps also children), the sale of goods on an unprecedented scale, often by retailers who were not also their manufacturers, the increasing availability of loss-spreading and liability insurance, and the move away from moral condemnation in a finding of negligence – would have contributed to pressure or stress, or, at any rate, would not have *reduced* the stress, upon the law. They contributed to a climate in which Mrs Donoghue's case might tip the balance and cause a change.

Several strands of development identified in this chapter are also central to the evidence revealed in chapter four. The case law uncovered, principally from regional newspaper reports of the 1920s, suggests that, with the new retail practices and increased demand for cheap goods, there was also an appetite for suing the vendors and makers of harm-causing products. It has already been noted above that claims against purveyors of cheap furs were sufficiently numerous to encourage the creation of special insurance policies against such liability. The plaintiffs in the claims revealed in chapter four were most often women, and sometimes children. The claims were also sometimes against manufacturers. What is striking, given the privity rule and the ongoing difficulties with respect to married women's contractual capacity, is that they often met with success. This is compelling evidence of a climate ripe for a change in the law.

4

Product Liability in the Early Twentieth Century

With the exception of the law concerning 'dangerous goods', which will form the basis of discussion in the final chapter of this book, there appears to have been little development of the law concerning liability for defective products in between the late nineteenth century and *Donoghue v Stevenson*. Cases like *Cavalier v Pope*[1] in 1906 and *Blacker v Lake and Elliot*[2] in 1912, which have been considered already, confirmed the strict application of the privity rule. Prominent treatise writers, too, appear not to have perceived any change in the law.[3]

We might look at *Preist v Last* in 1903.[4] The plaintiff, Mr Preist, purchased from the defendant, a retail chemist, a rubber hot-water bottle. He had asked the chemist if it could stand boiling water, and the defendant told him that it was intended to carry hot water but would not stand boiling water. However, when his wife used it some days later, it burst and she was burned. An action was brought against the defendant chemist by Mr and Mrs Preist. At trial, judgment was given in favour of Mr Preist on the basis that section 14 of the Sale of Goods Act 1893 applied and that the plaintiff had relied on the seller's skill and judgement. There was an implied condition that the article should be fit for the purpose of holding hot water. The jury found that it was not so, and therefore the implied warranty was breached. However, particularly important for present purposes were the decision and the comments made by Walton J as to Mr Preist's injured wife. The jury had assessed damages at £140: £40 for the expenses incurred by Mr Preist, and £100 for Mrs Preist's pain and suffering.[5] The question for Walton J was then what judgment ought to be entered. He noted that there was no evidence of any contract

[1] *Cavalier v Pope* [1906] AC 428.

[2] *Blacker v Lake and Elliot* (1912) 106 LT 533.

[3] See, eg, F Pollock, *The Law of Torts* (Stevens and Sons, 1887) 443–49, and compare F Pollock, *The Law of Torts*, 8th edn (Stevens and Sons, 1908) 541–47; T Beven, *Negligence in* Law, 2nd edn (Stevens and Haynes, 1895) 58–65, and compare T Beven, *Negligence in Law*, 3rd edn (Stevens and Haynes, 1908) 50–57.

[4] *Preist v Last* [1903] 2 KB 148. See also *Preist v Last* (1903) 89 LT 33, (1903) 47 *Solicitors' Journal and Weekly Reporter* 566.

[5] (1903) 89 LT 33, 34.

between Mrs Preist and the defendant, and that *Longmeid* appeared to be directly on point. He went on:

> It is true that in ordinary language the husband may be said to have bought the bottle for his wife; that is to say, he bought the bottle because his wife wanted it; but he was not acting as his wife's agent. He bought the bottle on his own account, and the contract was between him and the defendant. Therefore, as to the £100 damages, I think the plaintiffs' case fails, because there was no contract between Mrs Preist and the defendant.[6]

There was therefore judgment for Mr Preist only, in the amount of £40. The appeal by the defendant chemist was unsuccessful. The outcome of this case is wholly unsurprising. It is not surprising that a husband cannot claim in contract for his wife's suffering. It is also unsurprising that no claim was pursued in tort. What is of interest for present purposes is that there appears to have been no significant change from the late nineteenth century to the early twentieth century in the formal rules concerning liability for products in tort. The interest of this feature is explored below.

This chapter reveals that, alongside ostensible continuity of the law in the books, there was an apparent proliferation of successful claims for injuries caused by defective products in the 1910s and 1920s in circumstances where it is very unlikely that there was any privity of contract between plaintiff and defendant. These are reported, principally in regional newspapers, as cases in county courts and before single judges of higher courts. The impression these reports provide is that courts were increasingly results-oriented, rather than being doctrine-focused; a way was being found to provide a remedy to certain injured parties.

How was this occurring? The brevity of reporting is unsurprising; the average reader of a regional newspaper would care little for legal technicalities. Yet this brevity means that it is necessary, with most of the reported claims revealed in this part, to speculate about the legal arguments involved. The cases collated are examples of such cases reported in the mass of local newspapers in circulation at this time. There may well be further examples that remain hidden.

The structure adopted in this chapter is based on categories of harm-causing goods appearing in the reported cases, with each example presented in, broadly, chronological order. Instead of imposing any thesis on this evidence from the start, this chapter seeks principally to present and collate the evidence. It is in chapter five that an explanation will be advanced.

I. Fur Dermatitis in the Courts

While the wearing of animal fur coats and accessories might, in the modern age, leave you vulnerable to condemnation, a rather different concern emerged

[6] ibid.

in mid-1920s Britain. Dermatitis, caused by contact with cheap, treated fur, left consumers with a painful, debilitating rash. Cheap fur garments were an extremely popular commodity, particularly among working-class women, around the time of the First World War and during the interwar years.[7] The incidence of fur dermatitis also became a problem for manufacturers and vendors, as these claims began to sound in damages, often many times the value of the item originally sold. As has already been noted in chapter three,[8] it was considered a problem significant enough that insurance providers offered specific liability insurance for vendors of fur.

Relevantly for the focus of this chapter, reports in regional newspapers of courts' activities in the 1920s reveal significant numbers of married women suing, ostensibly in tort and contract, after contracting dermatitis from wearing inexpensive fur garments. It is often difficult to tell, owing to the nature of the reporting, the exact nature of the claim: it could be in tort or in contract, depending on the circumstances. Most seem to have alleged both negligence and breach of warranty. Some sue as co-plaintiffs with their husbands, some alone. Most are successful in obtaining compensation for personal injuries.

A 1923 report in *The Scotsman* noted:

> Mrs Edith Grace Norrington, of Camberwell, was awarded £12 damages at Lambeth County Court yesterday against a costumier. She bought a coat with a fur collar from the defendant for £2, 12s, and after wearing it three days contracted dermatitis. Dr T.C. Bull, of King's College Hospital, said between 30 and 40 cases of skin trouble, all due to wearing cheap furs, had been treated at the hospital.[9]

This was the tip of the iceberg. Claims became increasingly expensive for defendants and continued for several years to come. The phenomenon, and not merely the cases, was reported in the press. Earlier in 1923, the *Sunderland Daily Echo* had reported on the issue, with the dramatic heading 'Cheap Furs Danger: Skin Eruption Caused by Chemicals'.[10] The piece warns that chemicals used in the preservation and cleaning of cheaper furs were causing an 'outbreak' of dermatitis. In March 1923, the *Nottingham Evening Post* reported that 'Manchester, in common with London and other [cities], is suffering from an epidemic of skin-poisoning cases among women, caused by wearing furs'.[11] The matter became such a widespread concern that an inquiry was commenced, and, as noted in the previous chapter, a Ministry of Health report

[7] See, eg, S Alexander, 'Becoming a woman in London in the 1920s and 1930s' in D Feldman and G Stedman Jones (eds), *Metropolis: London* (Routledge, 1989) 256, 265. See also, eg, 'Women's Chat' *Thanet Advertiser* (24 October 1925), in which the fashion for fur coats and fur-trimmed garments is noted, along with the comment that '[o]vercoats fashioned of cheaper pelts abound' and a warning that 'tweed may be the wiser choice'.

[8] See ch 3, nn 212–13.

[9] 'Skin Trouble from Fur' *The Scotsman* (18 July 1923). See also 'Collar Gives Disease: Many Cases of Skin Complaint Set Up by Cheap Furs' *Leeds Mercury* (18 July 1923).

[10] 'Cheap Furs Danger: Skin Eruption Caused by Chemicals' *Sunderland Daily Echo* (9 February 1923).

[11] 'Fur Poison: Doctor Thinks It Due to Arsenic' *Nottingham Evening Post* (16 March 1923).

written on the subject.[12] *The Scotsman*, summarising the report, noted that 'virtually all' of the furs concerned were produced and dyed in foreign countries (Belgium, France, Germany and the United States).[13]

The cases concerning single women are straightforward. Miss Bertha Hart, reported as being a watercolour artist, was awarded £75 and costs in her action against the vendors of a fur-collared coat.[14] The case was not argued on the basis of negligence but, rather, of implied warranty. As a 'Miss', Bertha Hart was a *feme sole* and could thus freely contract and sue under that contract.

More curious are the cases where negligence and breach of warranty are alleged by married plaintiffs. Several newspapers reported that 'Mrs. Sarah Fox, wife of a Liverpool Corporation employee', brought an action against the defendant outfitter and furrier.[15] The nature of the action is not specified. Of course, the lack of detail means that it is only possible to speculate about the possible defences and doctrinal difficulties.[16] The reports go on to say that the defendant's own medical witness, Dr Alec Waugh, said that, after hearing the plaintiff's evidence, he did not doubt that it was a dye in the fur causing the trouble. Counsel for the defendant thereafter withdrew the defence and instead asked the jury to award only nominal damages. The generous award demonstrates that the jury refused to do so. The withdrawal of the defence suggests that any argument based on lack of privity was felt to be unlikely to succeed. This may be because Mrs Sarah Fox was clearly a party to the contract, bound to the extent of her separate property. However, separate property would not be typical.

As we have already discussed in the previous chapter, many married women in 1920s Britain did not work, and had little, if any, money available to them outside that allocated by their husbands to defray housekeeping expenses and to clothe and educate the family. Even money put aside from the housekeeping allowance belonged to the husband.[17] Any money truly belonging to a married woman would come from work, a gift or an endowment. The furs causing dermatitis were not expensive furs, which one might expect wealthy women to purchase with a pool of separate funds, but cheaper furs that needed chemical treatments to be saleable. It is particularly likely that these kinds of fur coats, relatively

[12] *Ministry of Health Report on Public Health and Medical Subjects* (No 27, 1924).

[13] 'Skin Disease and Furs: Cheapness and Danger' *The Scotsman*, 4 September 1924.

[14] 'Skin Disease From Fur Collar: Woman Artist Awarded Damages' *Nottingham Evening Post* (24 March 1926).

[15] See, eg, 'Dermatitis From Fur: £100 Damages Against a Shopkeeper' *Northern Daily Mail* (22 July 1926); 'Dangerous Fur Dyes: Jury Awards £100 Damages' *The Scotsman* (22 July 1926).

[16] One report records that the judge, Sir WFK Taylor, KC, 'pointed out that there was no evidence of negligence on the part of the defendant': 'Skin Rash from Fur' *Liverpool Post and Mercury* (22 July 1926). This might suggest that the tort action failed, and success was based on a contractual claim (for which negligence is not necessary). However, it is difficult to draw firm conclusions; another report notes that, following the judge's comment as to evidence, the defendant's expert witness gave evidence that the dye was a 'fairly dangerous' substance: 'Disease caused by a fur collar' *Liverpool Echo* (21 July 1926).

[17] See ch 3, and, for example, *Smith v Smith* 1933 SC 701, and *Blackwell v Blackwell* [1943] 2 All ER 579 (CA).

inexpensive yet still a luxury, would have been purchased by a husband for his wife, or, if physically purchased by the wife, purchased, *in law*, as agent for her husband. A report in the *Hull Daily Mail* on the weekly budgets of working-class households in a 'populous district' of London provides an idea of the distribution and control of money in a working family.[18] One 'house-wife of the district' interviewed by the newspaper is reported to have said the following:

> My husband earns three pounds a week, we pay 17s for rent, and he allows me £1 12s, which has to cover not only food, but gas, fuel and sundries such as bus fares, washing and cleaning materials, household goods and stamps. Luxuries come out of the remainder, after allowing for clothes and insurance.

Some reports of cases suggest that it was indeed the husband who made the purchase, or funded the purchase, and therefore the one who sued on the contract. Perhaps most telling is a 1929 report in the *Norwood News* of a case before the Wandsworth County Court.[19] The article notes that a Mr William Laceby and his wife, Mrs Adelaide Laceby, claimed damages from Messrs Risman Ltd, presumably the vendors, with regard to a fur coat which allegedly caused Mrs Laceby to suffer from dermatitis. The report continues:

> Plaintiffs claimed £45 and damages for breach of warranty, and 15s. 2d. for medical attendance, and Mrs. Laceby claimed £39 for personal injury sustained by the alleged breach.
>
> Defendants denied that Mrs Laceby contracted the disease, and paid into court £75 in satisfaction of the claims.

The case was settled out of court. It seems that Mr Laceby might have been suing on the contract for breach of warranty, while Mrs Laceby claimed in negligence.

In a Bristol case in the same year, Mrs Colley, 'wife of Alfred Colley, chemist' sued Mr Vanderplank, a furrier.[20] Mr Colley was joined as 'co-plaintiff' after the trial had commenced. This appears to be a pleading practice of the time. Bullen and Leake's *Precedents of Pleadings* advises that, although the husband need not be joined with the wife in an action for a tort to her person or property, he may be joined as a co-plaintiff where he has claims of his own against the defendant.[21] The pleading example provided includes, as the husband's claim, a claim for expenses involved in medical attendance and loss of a wife's society. Mrs Colley's claim, however, failed on the evidence: there were no traces of dye on the fur tested.[22]

[18] 'Life on £3 a week' *Hull Daily Mail* (24 April 1930).

[19] 'Story of a Fur Coat: Dermatitis Alleged in County Court Case' *Norwood News* (21 June 1929).

[20] 'Fur Coat Bought at a Sale: Allegations of Skin Disease Infection' *Western Daily Press* (13 February 1929).

[21] WB Odgers, *Bullen and Leake's Precedents of Pleadings*, 7th edn (Stevens and Sons, 1915) 334. As was noted in the previous chapter, earlier in the same work it was said that it was 'now practically impossible for both husband and wife to be liable' on a parol contract made by a married woman since the marriage: either the wife was agent, or she was not: see Odgers, *Bullen and Leake's Precedents of Pleadings*, ibid, 18–19.

[22] 'The Bristol Fur Case' *Western Daily Press* (14 February 1929).

In all of these reports, the women's status as married women is made clear. They are not described as having any profession or employment. While it cannot be concluded that this means they had none, one might contrast this with the way other cases of fur dermatitis are reported: in 1924, a Mrs Marion Outred, 'a Croydon tailoress', was reported to have sued a West Croydon firm after she purchased a fur collar and contracted dermatitis.[23] Mrs Outred, being employed, would clearly have a pool of 'separate property' with which to contract. She might be the appropriate party to sue on a contract, and in negligence. The case is less clear for a married woman without employment.[24] If they were suing on the contract for breach of warranty, we might query their ability to do so given the limited capacity of married women to enter into contracts. If, on the other hand, they were suing in negligence, we might also query their ability to do so, owing to the privity rule.

Some cases seem clearly to have proceeded on the basis of a contract between vendor and purchaser. In 1929, Mrs Adelaide Glenfield is reported to have brought an action in Margate County Court against Mr and Mrs FT Bates, ladies' outfitters, when she contracted a skin disease after wearing a fur-trimmed coat purchased from the defendants. It is noted that, in summing up, 'His Honour said the action cast no reflection upon Mr. and Mrs. Bates, who were in the hands of the manufacturers from whom they obtained the coat'.[25] Nevertheless, damages of £25 were awarded to the plaintiff. Here the claim is clearly contractual: absence of fault is irrelevant to the legal liability.

There are some few reports in which the manufacturers, rather than the vendors, are sued. However, the plaintiff in such cases is sometimes a party with whom the manufacturer contracted – for example, the vendor. In one such example, from the county court, the reader is told that the plaintiffs had sold to Mrs Ellen Bushell a fur collar and cuffs, and that she had subsequently contracted dermatitis.[26] She claimed against the plaintiffs, and they paid her £25 in settlement. The plaintiffs then claimed against the wholesale furrier that had supplied the fur in question, alleging negligence in the cleaning and dyeing of the fur, namely the use of unsuitable chemicals. The wholesale manufacturer denied liability, stating that all cases in the past had been Belgian rabbit, rather than American opossum, as in this case. Ultimately, the claim failed on evidential grounds: no noxious chemicals or chemical substances were found in the fur that would give rise to dermatitis. In giving judgment, the judge said that the plaintiffs had been 'too hasty' in paying Mrs Bushell.[27]

[23] 'Injurious Dye in a Fur Collar' *The Scotsman* (8 July 1924).

[24] Census records for these married plaintiffs records their employment status as doing 'unpaid domestic duties', or similar wording: see *The 1921 England Census*, and *The 1939 England and Wales Register*, available at: www.ancestry.co.uk.

[25] 'Disease from Furs: Risks Run by Women' *Thanet Advertiser* (8 November 1929).

[26] '"Too Hasty": Northampton Woman, Firm that Compensated Fail in County Court' *Northampton Mercury* (3 July 1925).

[27] ibid.

In the Westminster County Court, Mrs Effie Bussey was awarded £50 in her action against the vendor of her fur-collared coat; £45 pounds for loss, pain and suffering, and £5 for breach of warranty.[28] It was alleged that Mr Sugarman, the vendor, had represented that the collar was real mink when in fact it was not. Mr Sugarman did not appear before the court and had been debarred by the Registrar from defending the claim, after failing to put in particulars of defence.[29] It is very likely that Mrs Bussey was not a widow in 1931; the census records Mr James and Mrs Effie Bussey as living together in Sheffield in 1939.[30] Apart from this likelihood, we know little else about this case. Nevertheless, claims like this by married women raise interesting questions about who the party to that contract of sale might have been, and how strictly the courts were enforcing the privity rule with respect to contract and negligence claims.

Even if light on detail, the reports suggest that plaintiffs generally fared well in the courts. As an unmarried woman, it is unsurprising that Isabella White, of West Lothian, Scotland, encountered no difficulty suing the general draper who had supplied her with the fur in question.[31] Lord Blackburn in the Court of Session was prepared to find that the fur had contained some poisonous matter, even if the analyst had not managed to discover it. She recovered £100 in damages. It was later reported that the draper had successfully sued the supplier of the furs, which had, in turn, sued another firm involved in the process.[32]

Many of these reports are so brief that it is not always possible to tell with certainty whether the claim is in tort or in contract. Even if the case is reported as concerning a claim for 'breach of warranty', we cannot know for certain if this was or was not argued alongside a negligence claim, and which was successful. However, the result is generally the same: the woman receives damages for personal injuries.

II. More Dermatitis: Cosmetic Products

Cheap fur was not the only product behind the many dermatitis claims of the 1920s. The manufacturer of the hair dye 'Inecto Rapid', Inecto Limited, 'attained some notoriety'[33] after being successfully sued, in 1922, by a Miss Rivette for the

[28] 'Fur Collar: Sheffield Purchaser Awarded £50 Damages' *Yorkshire Post* (16 July 1931); 'Skin disease from fur collar' *Sheffield Daily Independent* (16 July 1931).

[29] Skin disease from fur collar' (n 29).

[30] Entry in *The 1939 England and Wales Register*, available at: www.ancestry.co.uk. The plaintiff, Mrs Bussey, was a Sheffield resident: 'Fur Collar: Sheffield Purchaser Awarded £50 Damages' (n 28) 16 July 1931.

[31] 'Danger of Cheap Dyed Fur' *Evening Telegraph* (14 May 1925). See also, eg, 'Outer House: A Dyed Fur Danger' *The Scotsman* (15 May 1925); 'Risk of Cheap Furs' *The Herald* (22 May 1925); 'Action against Broxburn Draper: Risk of Cheap Furs' *Linlithgowshire Gazette* (22 May 1925).

[32] 'Fur Dermatitis: Important Development in Broxburn Case' *Linlithgowshire Gazette* (24 June 1927).

[33] 'Compulsory Winding-Up of Hair Dye Company' *The Times* (5 July 1922).

rash-like injuries she sustained after using the dye.[34] Miss Rivette, a music hall artist, brought an action in the King's Bench against Inecto, and also the hairdresser who had applied the preparation. Miss Rivette was awarded £200 in damages against Inecto. Her claim against the hairdresser was dismissed on the basis that he had not been negligent.[35]

Another claim against Inecto was brought in 1922 in the King's Bench by Mrs Lillie Pendry, said to be the wife of a wholesale provision merchant.[36] The hairdresser, from whom she had purchased the product, was also a defendant in the action. Her claim is reported to be for breach of warranty or negligence.[37] Application of the dye caused sores, which lasted several weeks. Curiously, it is reported that, after this first application, her hair was turned green rather than the desired black, and she was persuaded to apply the product again. The sores appeared again. A pamphlet was said to have accompanied the product, asserting that the preparation was safe to use on healthy skin. While the evidence of the doctor who treated Mrs Pendry was that he had never seen a case of 'hair dye poisoning' before, another witness, Dr John Bunch, a skin specialist, said that 'from the effects of Inecto which he had seen on patients he considered it a poison'.[38] It seems that, after the medical evidence was given, proceedings were halted and an 'arrangement' between the parties reached (though no detail is provided).[39] Important additional information is provided in a report of the case in the *Chemist and Druggist*, a specialist periodical for chemists. It is reported that:

> Mr Higgins, for Inecto, Ltd, said the company took up the position that they were not liable in contract, and they were not defending the action so far as they might be liable *in tort*. He admitted however, that there had been complaints from other people, who alleged they had suffered through using Inecto. Mr Harold Morris, for [the hairdresser], while denying that that was an admission against his client, said he had had an opportunity of consulting [his client] and counsel for the plaintiff, and they had come to terms which embraced both defendants, and which would be endorsed on counsel's briefs (emphasis original).[40]

[34] 'Injury Caused By a Hair Dye: Rivette v. Inecto, Ltd' *The Times* (28 February 1922).

[35] By 1955, it had been held that a contract between hairdresser and customer, involving the application of hair dye, was a contract of work and materials, and that there was an implied term in the contract, analogous to the corresponding term in the sale of goods (pursuant to s 14 of the Sale of Goods Act 1893), of fitness for purpose: *Ingham v Emes* [1955] 2 QB 366. However, that a contract of work and materials was subject to an analogous implied term seems not to have been settled before the 1930s: see *GH Myers v Brent Cross Service Company* [1934] KB 46 (KB). In *GH Myers* it was argued (in the end, unsuccessfully) for the defendant that such a contract required only the exercise of reasonable care and skill.

[36] See, eg, 'Effects of a Hair Dye: Lady's Painful Experience' *Yorkshire Post* (12 January 1922); 'Woman's Hair of Many Hues' *Daily Mirror* (12 January 1922); 'Hair Turned Green: Effect of a Poisonous Dye' *Hull Daily Mail* (12 January 1922).

[37] ibid.

[38] 'Effects of a Hair Dye: Lady's Painful Experience' (n 36).

[39] ibid; 'Woman's Hair of Many Hues' (n 36); 'Hair Turned Green: Effect of a Poisonous Dye' (n 36).

[40] 'Hair-dye claim' *Chemist and Druggist* (14 January 1922).

The manufacturer's decision not to defend the claim in tort is striking. The position with respect to the contractual claim is understandable: it is difficult to see how the claim of breach of warranty would be available as against the manufacturer, given that the plaintiff did not purchase the dye from the manufacturer. We can speculate, plausibly, that the legal argument against any contractual liability must have been based on privity. Even if, looking at the case with modern eyes, we might see that some kind of warranty, akin to that recognised years later in *Shanklin Pier v Detel Products*,[41] might, at a push, have been arguable between Mrs Pendry and the manufacturer, this does not appear to have been pursued in the 1920s. The settlement reached appears to have been based on the strength of the claim in tort.

In the same year, a similar accident from use of the same product had resulted in an award of £532 damages to Mrs Gladys Havelock Bostock.[42] Mrs Havelock Bostock's daughter, Evelyn, was a famous Hollywood actress in the 1930s.[43] The defendants to Mrs Havelock Bostock's claim were, in this case, the hairdressers. Mrs Havelock Bostock's claim appears to have been in negligence alone; it was described as such, including in reports in *The Times*, and it seems that Mrs Havelock Bostock paid nothing for the service.[44] An appeal to the Court of Appeal in 1924 was dismissed by the Master of the Rolls, Warrington LJ and, notably, Atkin LJ.[45] The arguments advanced for the appellants were that the trial judge had misdirected the jury as to the issue of negligence, and that, in any case, the damages awarded were excessive. The Master of the Rolls, with whom Warrington LJ and Atkin LJ concurred, is reported to have said that he saw no reason to complain of the summing-up.[46] He explained that the negligence complained of might arise from one or both of two sources. First was the failure to apply a test: the directions for the use of Inecto hair dye said that a preliminary test ought to be made in every case before using it, even if the dye had been previously used with success upon the same person. Second, carelessness in application. The learned judge had put both possibilities before the jury, and there was no reason for suggesting that he had misplaced the onus of proof.[47]

Before McCardie J and a jury in the King's Bench in 1923, Mrs Minnie Akerman and her husband, James Akerman, a painter and decorator (and said

[41] *Shanklin Pier v Detel Products* [1951] 2 KB 854. The court in *Shanklin* treated the question before it as novel.

[42] See, eg, 'The "Inecto" Hair Dye Case Result' *The Times* (29 May 1924).

[43] See 'Hollywood Probe into English Star's Death' *Daily Mirror* (Sydney, Australia, 30 November 1944), available at the Trove database: trove.nla.gov.au, and entry for Mrs Gladys Havelock Bostock in *The 1921 England Census*, available at: www.ancestry.co.uk.

[44] See, eg, 'Another "Inecto" Hair Dye Case' *The Times* (28 May 1924); 'The "Inecto" Hair Dye Case Result' (n 42). Of course, the lack of payment does not preclude the existence of a contract, but one might expect some discussion of whether or not a contract existed if the action were founded on contract.

[45] 'Court of Appeal: "Inecto' Hair Dye' *The Times* (27 November 1924); 'Appeal Dismissed: Aftermath of Dyed Hair' *The Scotsman* (27 November 1924).

[46] 'Court of Appeal: "Inecto" Hair Dye' (n 45).

[47] ibid.

to be co-plaintiff), sued a hairdresser in Enfield.[48] Mrs Akerman had purchased the dye from the hairdresser, and had applied it at home with disastrous effects: her injuries were so extensive that she had to receive medical treatment, and the doctor 'almost despaired of her life'.[49] The action is reported as being for negligence or for breach of warranty, and the jury found in favour of Mrs Akerman, awarding £50 in compensation.[50] Her success was apparently interesting enough to the general public that a large picture of Mr and Mrs Akerman arriving, with their daughter, at the Law Courts was published in the *Daily Mirror*.[51]

Another manufacturer, Permanol Limited, was sued successfully in the King's Bench in 1924 by Mrs Louise Barber.[52] The hairdresser, Madame Ennis, was also a defendant in the action. The claim was said to be for negligence or breach of warranty.[53] It is reported that Permanol 'denied negligence or warranty, or that Permanol was a noxious and dangerous preparation', and Madame Ennis disclaimed the allegations made against her.[54] The jury found for Mrs Barber, who was awarded £300 in damages against Permanol and one farthing against Madame Ennis.[55] It is reported in some newspapers that it was 'intimated that Permanol … were not represented and were not defending the action'.[56] Mrs Barber's appeal against the award of one farthing was dismissed by the Court of Appeal; Bankes LJ (Scrutton LJ and Sargant LJ concurring) found that there were reasonable grounds for the verdict.[57]

In 1926, Mrs Esme Gozney, 'wife of the stationmaster of Princes Risborough',[58] successfully sued the manufacturer of the Inecto hair dye, now Rapidol Ltd,[59] in the King's Bench.[60] A claim for breach of warranty and negligence was reported.[61] She had purchased the hair dye from a chemist[62] and alleged that, a few hours after applying the hair dye, she developed acute dermatitis, swelling and temporary

48 'Judge on Women's Hair: Charm of a Little Grey' *Northern Daily Mail* (18 October 1923); 'Judge and Woman's Glory' *Nottingham Evening Post* (18 October 1923); 'The Charm of the Grey Hair', *Westminster Gazette*, 18 October 1923; 'Judge on Grey Hair' *Leeds Mercury* (18 October 1923).

49 'Hair-dye Damages' *Chemist and Druggist*, 20 October 1923.

50 ibid.

51 'Hair Dye Illness' *Daily Mirror* (18 October 1923).

52 'Women's Use of Hair Dye' *Westminster Gazette* (29 March 1924).

53 ibid.

54 ibid.

55 ibid. See also 'Another Hair-Dye Case' *The Times* (28 March 1924); 'Danger of Hair Dyeing: £300 Damages' *The Times* (29 March 1924).

56 See, eg, 'Hair Dye Action: Woman's Claim for Damages' *The Scotsman* (28 March 1924).

57 'Court of Appeal: A Hair Dye Case' *The Times* (26 July 1924).

58 See, eg, 'Hair Dye Poison' *Leeds Mercury* (19 May 1926); Untitled, *Cornishman and Cornish Telegraph*, 26 May 1926.

59 It appears that Rapidol Limited had purchased the assets, and carried on the business, of Inecto Limited after the latter was wound up in 1922: see 'Compulsory Winding-Up of Hair Dye Company' (n 33).

60 See, eg, 'Hair Dye Case: Woman Awarded £544 Damages in Action' *Aberdeen Press and Journal* (20 May 1926); 'Poisoned by Hair Dye' *Evening Telegraph* (18 May 1926).

61 See, eg, 'The "Inecto" action: £500 damages' *The Times* (19 May 1926).

62 See, eg, 'Lady's Injuries from Hair Dye' *Bucks Herald* (22 May 1926); 'Woman's Hair Dye Ordeal' *Daily Mirror* (18 May 1926); 'Poisoned by Hair Dye' (n 60).

blindness lasting several days. She had her hair cut off and 'her heart was … affected'.[63] The manufacturer unsuccessfully argued that Mrs Gozney was to blame for failing to heed the instructions and warnings provided when she had applied the dye.[64] Mrs Gozney did not purchase the dye from Inecto but from a chemist, so it is difficult to see how a claim for breach of warranty would be available. This must, therefore, have been a claim in tort. Yet why was the legal point about privity not taken by the defendant, or by the court? The jury found in her favour and awarded the impressive sum of £544 in damages.[65]

As with fur dermatitis, actions of this sort were also being brought in Scotland. Mrs Christina Macrossan, of Glasgow, claimed the enormous sum of £750 in her action against a Glasgow hair specialist when she contracted a skin disease following the application of hair dye by the defender's employee.[66] The defender denied fault and said there was no negligence but the jury found for the pursuer, albeit awarding only £450 – still not a trifling sum.

Given the widespread incidence and extensive newspaper reporting of the fur dermatitis 'epidemic' and of hair dye dermatitis, it is plausible that 1920s dermatitis put pressure on courts in their handling of the cases and, in turn, on the law itself. What is striking about the dermatitis claims reported in the 1920s is that the probable lack of privity on the part of the married woman seems to have posed no complication. There are several examples of manufacturers being sued directly. Nor does the probable contract between the vendor and the husband, which, pre-*Donoghue*, ought to preclude a claim in tort by the wife, seem to have been problematic. The general impression afforded by these cases is that these claims by married women were generally successful – even where warnings, or instructions to test before use, had been given by the unfortunate vendors and manufacturers.

It is possible that the married women in these reports had all themselves provided the consideration, made up of money constituting their separate property. However, as we have already seen, in this chapter and in the previous, it is more likely that the husband was the true party to the contract. It is improbable that there was a contract with manufacturers. These women were, then, successfully suing, notwithstanding the existence of a contract to which they were not a party.

III. Bottled Surprises

Ginger beer seemed to pose a particular difficulty to manufacturers and consumers in the early part of the twentieth century. In January 1908, *The Times*

[63] 'Lady's Injuries from Hair Dye' *Bucks Herald* (22 May 1926).

[64] 'Hair-Dye Case' *Chemist and Druggist* (22 May 1926).

[65] See, eg, 'Hair Dye that Hurt' *Dundee Advertiser and Courier* (19 May 1926); Untitled, *The Cornishman and Cornish Telegraph* (n 58) 26 May 1926.

[66] 'Hairdresser to Pay £450 Damages' *Dundee Courier and Advertiser* (23 June 1928).

reported a matter before Grantham J, of the King's Bench, in which a young girl sued the manufacturer of ginger beer.[67] Miss Martha Oldfield had been working as a barmaid and had been seriously injured when a bottle had exploded in her hand. The bottle had been supplied by the manufacturer to her employer. Counsel for the defendant manufacturer submitted, it is reported, that there was no negligence and, more significantly, that there 'was no duty imposed upon the defendants to confine the ginger-beer in such a way as not to cause injury to the public at large',[68] citing *Winterbottom* and *Longmeid*. It was argued that there was no case to go before the jury. However, Grantham J 'declined to withdraw the case from the jury'.[69] Why he did so is not explained in the report. The case nevertheless failed as no negligence in the manufacturing process had been made out.

A similar case occurred in 1913. *The Times* reported that Mr Bates 'sued both on his own behalf and on behalf of his son, a boy of 12 years old, for damages for personal injuries to the latter and expenses of his own'.[70] The defendants were, again, the manufacturers of the ginger beer. The bottle had burst while the boy was trying to open it, and he was injured to the extent that he lost the use of his right eye. However, judgment was given for the defendants, as they had not known of the defect in the bottle.[71]

While exploding ginger beer incidents may not have been leading to successful claims, there is another type of case worth considering that is familiar to every lawyer and law student: foreign objects in bottled beverages. What the regional newspapers of the 1920s suggest is that the situation and, perhaps more surprisingly, the outcome in *Donoghue* were not novel. In 1920, a boy of seven, through his father, Giuseppe Camelo, brought an action in the King's Bench against White and Sons Ltd.[72] The defendants denied liability. Several newspaper reports describe the case as one of breach of warranty, and, more reliably, so does the *Law Times*.[73] Mr Camelo had purchased bottled drinks from the defendants. His seven-year-old son had, one day, wanted a drink, and had taken a bottle of lemon squash from a crate. The drink did not taste as it should: the father looked into the bottle and discovered that it contained, as well as squash, a dead mouse. The boy allegedly became ill with gastroenteritis following the incident, and was under the care of a doctor for some time.[74] Salter J found for the plaintiffs, awarding £11 7s 6d to the father for expenses incurred, and, curiously, £15 to the boy as compensation, for

[67] 'Law Report, Jan 17' *The Times* (18 January 1908).

[68] ibid.

[69] ibid.

[70] 'Injury Through the Bursting of a Bottle' *The Times* (26 June 1913).

[71] *Bates v Batey* [1913] 3 KB 351, 355–56. See further discussion of this case in ch 5.

[72] See, eg, 'Mouse in Bottle of Lemon Squash' *Dundee Evening Telegraph* (24 June 1920); 'Dead Mouse in Lemon Squash: Bottled Shock for Thirsty Boy' *The Globe* (24 June 1920); '£26 For a Dead Mouse Found in Lemon Squash' *Daily Herald* (25 June 1920).

[73] See (1920) 149 LT 397.

[74] See, eg, 'Dead Mouse in Lemon Squash: Bottled Shock for Thirsty Boy' *The Globe* (24 June 1920).

'pain, suffering, and sickness due to the defendants' negligence'.[75] It is reported that the judge held that the bottle was delivered by the defendants with the mouse in it, and that the defendants had committed a breach of warranty 'because the mouse could not have remained in the bottle except by their negligence'.[76]

We have two plaintiffs here. On a strict interpretation of the law as it stood in the books, and, indeed, as the minority in *Donoghue* understood the law, the son should have no claim. The father was a party to the contract; the son was not. Mr Camelo was in the position of Mrs Donoghue's 'friend', who purchased her drink. Nevertheless, the son apparently brought an action as well, and received the lion's share of the damages. Though the action is said to be breach of warranty, the son is unlikely to have been a party to the contract of sale and damages were expressly awarded on the basis of a finding of negligence. There is no mention of this case in *Donoghue*, despite the factual similarity. Perhaps we can attribute this to a tradition in the courts of focusing only on 'higher', or Court of Appeal, decisions, at least when a trial in the King's Bench is not properly reported.

We can contrast the *Camelo* case with the outcome in the 1929 case of *Mullen*, considered in previous chapters. This was properly reported. In *Mullen*, it will be recalled, some children became ill after consuming ginger beer containing a dead mouse but the action against the manufacturer, brought through their parent, was unsuccessful. The Lord Justice-Clerk expressed his regret that no remedy could be granted but noted this was irrelevant to his decision.[77] Lord Ormidale asserted that he would have found that a duty of care existed on the part of the manufacturer if not constrained by authority against such recognition.[78] This case demonstrates nicely the growing tension between the legal doctrine to be applied and the increasing acknowledgement by courts that plaintiffs had suffered losses that would, without the support of the law, be left without remedy. It seems that, in certain cases, like that of the Camelo boy, an alternative route to a remedy was simply found by a court wishing to do justice for the injured party. The alternative pathway is, however, unclear. Was it a case of a court's ignoring the law – whether *Winterbottom*, privity, or legal disabilities? Is another explanation available?

IV. Contaminated Food and Non-Purchasers

The consumption of food and beverages could be a risky business in the early part of the twentieth century. The food or drink product itself might be harmful for a vast array of reasons, from lack of refrigeration to tampering by unscrupulous retailers. In 1875, Parliament had enacted the Sale of Food and Drugs Act, which

[75] 'Mouse in Bottle of Lemon Squash' *Dundee Evening Telegraph* (24 June 1920); 'Mouse in Bottle of Lemon Squash' *Leeds Mercury* (25 June 1920).
[76] 'Dead Mouse in Lemon Squash' *Edinburgh Evening News* (24 June 1920).
[77] *Mullen v Barr* 1929 SC 461, 470.
[78] ibid 471.

was intended to protect consumers against the sale of dangerous food. Section 6 of that Act provided:

> No person shall sell to the prejudice of the purchaser any article of food or any drug which is not of the nature, substance, and quality of the article demanded by such purchaser, under a penalty not exceeding twenty pounds.

The Act offered protection to consumers by providing a clear definition of 'adulteration', which, as is evident in the above extract, included both non-harmful but fraudulent sales (where additional but harmless material had been added, for example water to milk) and dangerous mixtures.[79] Further legislation concerned with food safety was also passed in 1907.[80] Certainly, retailers found to be selling foods unfit for consumption and likely to cause illness were fined by authorities if discovered.[81] Illness contracted from food was common, and sometimes fatal, even where there was no lack of care and no wrongdoing by any party involved.[82] Nevertheless, even a cursory examination of regional newspapers in the early part of the century discloses many examples of illness caused by contaminated food and leading to claims for breach of warranty and negligence. This is not surprising, given the food preparation and storage practices of the day and the absence of the technology available now. Indeed, as noted in the previous chapter, liability insurance for 'ptomaine poisoning', what we now call food poisoning, seems to have been available by the end of the first decade of the twentieth century. What is interesting for present purposes is the evidence of some courts' apparent willingness to award damages to people external to the contract between purchaser and vendor or manufacturer.

A 'curious and interesting'[83] case in the Watford County Court, against the caterers of a wedding party, was unsuccessful 1908.[84] The defendant was a Mr Gilham, baker and confectioner, who had provided Mr and Mrs Rainbow a wedding breakfast for their son's wedding. The offering consisted of a variety of foods, including chicken patties, sweets and blancmanges, and was served to guests in the local schoolroom.[85] The unsuccessful plaintiffs were

[79] See discussion in J Phillips and M French, 'Adulteration and Food Law, 1899–1939' (1998) 9 *Twentieth Century British History* 350, 350–55; J Bell and D Ibbetson, *European Level Development: The Case of Tort* (Cambridge University Press, 2012) 75–76.

[80] Public Health (Regulations as to Food) Act 1907, enacted to enable the making of regulations 'for the prevention of danger arising to public health from the importation, preparation, storage, and distribution of articles of food or drink': s 1.

[81] See, eg, 'Pork Pie Perils' *Evening Standard* (4 June 1908).

[82] There are vast numbers of reports of such occurrences in the regional newspapers. See, eg, 'The Ptomaine Poisoning Case' *West Sussex Journal* (30 September 1902) 'The Poisoning Cases' *Daily Derby Telegraph* (16 September 1902) (concerning pork pies); 'Ptomaine Victims' *Nottingham Evening News* (17 August 1910) (pork pies, kippers).

[83] 'Wedding guests ill: allegations of ptomaine poisoning' *Shipley Times and Express* (2 October 1908).

[84] 'Litigation after a wedding breakfast' *West Herts and Watford Observer* (17 October 1908); 'Wedding Party Sequel: Action against caterer for alleged poisoning' *Cheltenham Chronicle and Gloucester Graphic* (17 October 1908).

[85] 'Wealdstone Wedding Sequel' *Harrow Gazette* (2 October 1908).

Mr and Mrs Smith; Mrs Smith and her daughter, Miss Smith, had become unwell after the wedding. The basis of the claim seems to be personal injury and pecuniary loss.[86] It is also said in some reports that Mr Smith was bringing the action on behalf of his daughter.[87] They sought £100 in damages. However, this lack of success was not, as one might expect, because the parties were guests at the wedding and in no contractual relationship with the caterer. Instead, it failed on the facts: the judge said that there was no evidence of 'apparent putrefaction … and the doctors had stated that it was extremely difficult to detect ptomaine'.[88] Counsel for the plaintiff had argued that a prima facie case was made out, and was said to have 'quoted the bun case, in which it was held by the Judge that when a stone in a bun was responsible for breaking a person's tooth, negligence had been proved'.[89] No mention was made of the privity problem – perhaps because, failing on the evidence, it was not necessary, but also perhaps because it was not perceived to bar the claim. It was said that there was 'no dispute at all as to the principles upon which [the judge] had to give his decision' and that the 'only point at the present moment before him was whether the plaintiff's case was complete in so far that it had raised a *prima facie* case of negligence'.[90] The reporting of this case suggests (though, again, this must be speculative) that a defence based on lack of privity might not have been relied upon.

In 1911, the *Whitby Gazette* reported the 'interesting verdict' in an action between a purchaser and the vendor-manufacturer of some pork pies.[91] The plaintiff had purchased three pies, given one to his wife and shared the final pie among his three children. The entire family became ill. The plaintiff's wife had not recovered, nine months later, and one of the children had died. The jury found for the plaintiff, awarding just over £13 for expenses caused by the illness and £5 for the loss of his wife's services. Importantly, however, a sum of £15 was also awarded to the wife herself. The report quotes the *Medical Press* in stating:

> This case suggests that, in future, it may be a more hopeful matter to fix upon the vendor of bad food responsibility for the damage caused thereby. In the case under notice, the

[86] ibid.

[87] See, eg, 'Poison at a wedding' *Weekly Times & Echo* (4 October 1908).

[88] 'Wedding Party Sequel: Action against caterer for alleged poisoning' (n 84).

[89] 'A wedding breakfast: alleged poisoning' *Harrow Observer* (16 October 1908). The case referred to was the 1905 case brought by solicitor Mr George Chaproniere/Chapronier against the confectioner, Mr Mason, after he had broken a tooth while eating a bun made by Mr Mason due to a concealed stone inside the bun: *Mason v Champronier* (1905) 21 TLR 633, discussed in JF Clerk and WHB Lindsell, *The Law of Torts* (Sweet & Maxwell, 6th edn (1912) 507. See also, for example, 'Stone in a Bun' *Derby Daily Telegraph* (28 June 1905). The plaintiff's claim was in negligence. At trial, the verdict had been for the defendants, the jury somehow finding that the bun was fit for purpose and of merchantable quality. However, on appeal before Collins MR, Romer LJ and Mathew LJ, the plaintiff was successful in having a new trial ordered. It was said that presence of the stone was said to be clear prima facie evidence of negligence, and the trial judge had been wrong to guide the jury in the way he did: see, eg, 'A Stone in a Bath-Bun' *Newcastle Daily Chronicle* (29 June 1915).

[90] 'Litigation after a wedding breakfast' (n 84).

[91] 'Damages for Meat Poisoning' *Whitby Gazette* (3 November 1911).

> task of bringing home the proof was rendered easier by the fact that the defendant was both maker and vendor of the [contaminated?[92]] pies.[93]

The difficulty of suing manufacturers is thus acknowledged. However, the lack of privity between the wife and the manufacturer is not.

On the other hand, in 1913 a claim in the Doncaster County Court concerning the death of a miner's wife after she consumed food and drink at the annual tea party given by the local co-operative society was unsuccessful.[94] The claim had been brought by the husband of the deceased, Mrs Smith, against the co-operative society. This was reported as being a test case. A charge of sixpence was levied for attendance at the tea but 'at the close something was returned to them of about the same value'.[95] After attending the tea, Mrs Smith had been diagnosed with ptomaine poisoning. Twenty other attendees were also taken ill. Unlike the case of the 1911 pork pie, there seems to have been extensive discussion before the Court about the existence or not of a contractual relationship between Mrs Smith and the co-operative society. It was argued for the plaintiff that, because Mr Smith was a member of the co-operative society, he or his wife was entitled to attend the tea and the contract extended to his wife.[96] If any harm came to his wife, it was argued, there was a breach of contract. Alternatively, it was suggested that negligence would enable the husband to recover under the Fatal Accidents Act 1846.[97] For the defendant society it was submitted that there was no case to answer; there was no evidence of negligence, and further, there was no contract of sale – Mrs Smith had not been a purchaser.[98] Judgment was given for the defendant.[99]

Marmalade was the offending item in a 1916 action in the Scottish Court of Session.[100] The pursuer, George Ryall, had purchased a tin of marmalade made by the defenders from a grocer's shop and, after eating some, reportedly became so unwell that he had to give up his employment as the manager of a commercial firm in Glasgow. He claimed £300 in damages. According to the analyst's report submitted in evidence by Mr Ryall, the marmalade also contained the unappealing additional ingredients of 'brown paper, newspaper paper, mouse excrement, mouse hair, straw, woody fibre, and flock'.[101] The defenders, John Moir and Son Ltd, 'preserved provision manufacturers', denied the suggestion that their marmalade was not in 'sound condition', pointing out that the analysis was dated more than a month after the tin was said to have been opened by the pursuer. They also alleged that the pursuer was

[92] The word is unclear on the image available from the British Newspaper Archive database.
[93] 'Damages for Meat Poisoning' (n 91).
[94] 'The Co-op Tea: Interesting Denaby Case at the County Court' *South Yorkshire Times* (8 November 1913).
[95] ibid.
[96] ibid.
[97] ibid.
[98] ibid.
[99] ibid.
[100] 'Had Mice Been Tasting the Marmalade?' *Aberdeen Weekly Journal* (1 December 1916).
[101] ibid. See also Untitled, *Forward* (9 December 1916).

not in regular or responsible employment.[102] Lord Anderson in the Court of Session was asked to give judgment on the relevancy of the action; that is, on whether or not the facts (as yet unproven), if true, gave rise to a viable action, or if it should be dismissed. Lord Anderson allowed the case to go to proof, saying that a 'chain of causation had been set forth by the pursuer, in which his lordship was unable to discover a flaw'.[103] The case was not, then, dismissed immediately because there was no privity of contract between Mr Ryall and the manufacturers. However, the action ultimately failed because there was no evidence of negligence on the part of the manufacturers.[104] According to reports in some regional newspapers, Ryall's action was raised by Mr Morton KC for Mrs Donoghue before the House of Lords.[105] However, it did not find a place in their Lordships' reasons.

High-end meals served in restaurants were also the subject of litigation in the 1920s. Mr and Mrs Cecil Bishop sued the owners of the famous Frascati's Restaurant, London, in the King's Bench after they had dined at the restaurant and became ill with 'ptomaine poisoning' – Mrs Bishop seriously so.[106] The couple were said to have been out together for the first time since Mrs Bishop had given birth to their fifth child. The maligned meal was one of fried kidneys, bacon, potatoes and a rum omelette. The defendants told the Court that 3,000 meals had been served on the day in question, with no other person complaining of illness.[107] After some joking in the courtroom about the plaintiffs' choice of meal,[108] judgment was given by Darling J in their favour. Mr Bishop was awarded £50, as he 'had the doctor's bill to pay',[109] and Mrs Bishop was awarded £80, as her 'suffering had certainly been greater'.[110] Some newspaper reporting asserts that the cause of action was 'breach of warranty',[111] while others suggest that it was negligence.[112] It may be the case that Mr Bishop, who likely purchased the meal, was suing on the contract for breach of warranty, while his wife's claim was in negligence. Curiously, though, Darling J commented that he had not the slightest doubt that the defendants did their best to supply wholesome food, and that there had been no suggestion to the contrary.[113]

A widely reported incident occurred in a London restaurant in 1924 involving fragments of glass in a mince pie.[114] This was not the first time such an event had made it to the courts and the papers; a similar matter was brought before the

[102] 'Had Mice Been Tasting the Marmalade?' (n 100).
[103] ibid.
[104] 'The Marmalade Not Guilty' *Daily Record and Mail* (19 May 1917).
[105] See, eg, 'Snail said to be in Ginger-Beer' *Sheffield Independent* (11 December 1931).
[106] See, eg, 'Illness that Followed a Restaurant Meal' *Yorkshire Evening Post* (28 October 1921).
[107] 'A Bad Dinner' *Nottingham Journal* (29 October 1921).
[108] See, eg, 'A Dinner at Frascati's' *Leeds Mercury* (29 October 1921).
[109] 'Law Report, Oct 28' *The Times* (29 October 1921).
[110] ibid. See also 'Rum Omelette and Kidneys' *Daily Herald* (29 October 1921).
[111] See, eg, 'Kidneys and Bacon to Blame' *Gloucester Citizen* (29 October 1921).
[112] See, eg, 'Illness that Followed a Restaurant Meal' (n 106).
[113] 'Law Report, Oct. 28' *The Times* (29 October 1921).
[114] See, eg, 'Glass in a Mince Pie' *The Times* (5 December 1924); 'Mince Pie and Glass' *Liverpool Echo* (4 December 1924); 'Glass in Mince Pie' *Daily Herald* (5 December 1924); 'Mince Pie Law Suit: Was There Glass in It?' *Lancashire Daily Post* (4 December 1924).

Shoreditch County Court in 1911.[115] However, the 1924 case is more interesting for our purposes because of the party injured. McCardie J and a jury in the King's Bench heard how Mrs Esther Davis became aware of something sharp and gritty in her mouth after eating the pie. She claimed to experience severe internal pain and her condition became life-threatening. Mrs Davis and her husband were awarded £130. Negligence and breach of warranty were the reported causes of action. It was noted that:

> Mr. Justice McCardie, in summing up, said that in his view everyone supplying food to the public was bound to take full measures to see that it was suitable for human consumption. He was of opinion, and counsel for defendants had not contradicted it, that there was negligence in this case and breach of warranty in the sale of the mince-pie.[116]

It is very likely that Mr Davis was the contracting party; Mr and Mrs Davis had gone out for lunch together when the incident occurred. Nevertheless, Mrs Davis was able to recover for her injuries.

V. A Chemist's Remedy

A curious case in the King's Bench concerning the supply of cough mixture was widely reported in 1922.[117] Mr and Mrs Holt brought an action against Mr Northen, a chemist, alleging negligence or, alternatively, breach of contract. Mrs Holt had taken empty bottles to Mr Northen's shop in order to purchase and collect some cough mixture. Mr and Mrs Holt had both taken some of the mixture. They became seriously ill after doing so. It was later discovered that the mixture contained strychnine. The dispute before the Court appeared to be whether or not the strychnine taken by the plaintiffs was the result of the mixture supplied by the chemist. Judgment was given for the plaintiffs, and £150 damages awarded. The report in *The Times* provides some detail as to the Court's reasoning. Darling J is reported to have said that it was unclear if the strychnine had reached the cough mixture through the chemist's negligence or not, but that, either way, the defendant would still be liable.[118] If there was no negligence, the ground for liability was breach of warranty. The report continues:

> If his decision in the case rested on the ground of an implied warranty only the male plaintiff would be entitled to recover, but *if the decision was based on negligence, then*

[115] See 'Glass in Mincemeat' *Daily News* (11 July 1911). The plaintiff in this case was a Mr Bernard Ellis, who had consumed the pie containing glass. The defendants were the vendors of the pie. Judgment was given for the plaintiff, and £10 in damages awarded.

[116] 'Glass in Mince-Pie' *Western Mail* (5 December 1924).

[117] See, eg, 'Strychnine in Cough Cure' *Pall Mall Gazette* (18 May 1922); 'Old-Fashioned Cold Cure' *Halifax Daily Courier* (18 May 1922); 'Chemist's Sale of Strychnine by Mistake' *The Times* (19 May 1922); 'Chemist Sued' *Chemist and Druggist* (27 May 1922).

[118] 'Chemist's Sale of Strychnine by Mistake' (n 117).

> *both plaintiffs would be entitled to do so*. If the male plaintiff alone recovered under the implied warranty, the only head of damage to be deducted would be for the pain and suffering endured by Mrs Holt. [Darling J] did not propose to consider separately what damages he should award under that particular head apart from anything else, and he gave judgment for the plaintiffs for £150 damages and costs (emphasis added).[119]

This is curious. Mrs Holt went to the shop to purchase the cough mixture. She contracted as agent for her husband. It is clear, from Darling J's comments as to breach of warranty, that Mrs Holt was not a party to the contract. However, there is no indication that he perceived her lack of privity to be a problem for a claim in negligence.

VI. No Privity, No Problem?

This book aims to better understand the path of the privity rule in the law of negligence, and its eventual rejection in *Donoghue v Stevenson*. It has already been suggested that several strands of development, both within and outside the law, may be identified that, taken together, created a climate where Mrs Donoghue's problem could become the tipping point for legal change. The privity rule was introduced for policy reasons into the law of negligence at the height of the Industrial Revolution, yet, even as late as 1929, superior courts were applying the rule (albeit reluctantly, in the case of several judges in *Mullen*) to restrict the scope of negligence liability. The rule meant that manufacturers causing injury would rarely be successfully sued. Manufacturers were increasingly distant from the final consumer. Even if the vendor were the desirable party to sue, for success in the highest courts the plaintiff had to be a party to the contract of sale. A married woman or child was likely not to have been a party to the contract of sale, and therefore strictly precluded from suing. If, instead, a husband was the contracting party, application of the privity rule would demand that any action to recover damages (beyond expenditure incurred by the husband himself) for a wife's injuries should fail. The picture we have from cases like *Donoghue* is that the privity rule in tort was strictly enforced, requiring a bold step from a majority in the House of Lords to deliver justice to otherwise remediless plaintiffs.

We would expect, therefore, that product litigation in the 1910s and 1920s would convey a fairly uniform story of failure. Yet newspaper reports of courts' decisions from this time suggest that many plaintiffs were not remediless, after all. There is little evidence of any complication arising from the privity rule in product litigation. In the examples discussed, married couples' or parents' and children's actions are frequently joined; actions in contract are heard together with actions in negligence. The lack of discussion of privity does not seem the result of pleading rules. Contrary to what might be expected, evident in these reports of

[119] ibid.

the dermatitis and product-based litigation in the 1910s and 1920s is a significant appetite for compensation for injury following the purchase of defective goods and that, contrary to the law 'in the books', the claims of women and children frequently met with success.

The impression one gets is that there is a marked awareness of victims' interests during this period. There was clearly significant awareness about the potential harms products might cause: the problem of fur dermatitis received attention at the highest levels; newspapers eagerly reported on the risks and victims of hair dye; and illness-inducing food was a constant challenge. In some of the cases discussed, evidence of negligence was scant, yet liability was found and the plaintiff's suffering emphasised. If these claims were brought in *contract* and the goods were not fit for purpose, it would be irrelevant that the seller was not at fault. However, at least some of the claims were clearly brought in tort. Result-orientation and apparent sympathy for victims is not limited to women and children, though these seem to make up a significant proportion of successful plaintiffs.

It must be acknowledged that these cases might not be a representative sample; we are not necessarily seeing the cases where the claim has failed. Unsuccessful claims are less newsworthy. Nevertheless, what this survey demonstrates is that results similar to the outcome in *Donoghue* were being reached without any formal legal change to the rules. The majority of these cases are English cases. There are only two cases from Scotland of the same nature – though the English cases are widely reported in Scottish newspapers.

Questions arise upon the observation of this trend. How was this happening? Was there simply a practice of ignoring the privity rule? If so, why was the practice not debated and discussed in solicitors' journals, or in the courts themselves? It seems incredible that so many defendants' legal advisers would choose not to pursue the privity point that would, we would anticipate, win a client's case. The final chapter of this book addresses these questions.

5

'Dangerous Things': An Alternative Path to Success

This book has, so far, suggested that in the lead up to the 1932 decision in *Donoghue v Stevenson*, several combining factors can reasonably be understood to have created a climate apt for the removal of privity from negligence. Numerous reports in regional newspapers of cases before county courts and higher courts in the 1910s and 1920s suggest that plaintiffs succeeded in negligence when they were not party to the contract so ought, on a strict application of the privity doctrine, to have failed. The claims and outcomes outlined in chapter four appear at odds with the law 'in the books'. This chapter proposes an explanation as to how and why.

It is possible that, given the scant reporting in the early twentieth century of county court decisions, and even of matters heard by a single judge of the King's Bench, some courts developed their own practice with respect to the supply of harm-causing products. Without significant reporting of outcomes, or, in particular, detailed decisions, it is just possible that this development could be occurring out of the sight of the higher courts and the treatise authors. This possible explanation is considered in the first part of this chapter.

However, it will be suggested that another explanation is available. In 1912, the decision in *Blacker v Lake and Elliot* signalled that, to have any prospect of success, a claim similar to that in *George v Skivington* must be formulated as one involving the sale of a dangerous item. The recharacterisation of *George*, the suppression of any alternative understanding of that case, and the development of a low threshold for what might be considered 'dangerous' together opened a pathway to success for plaintiffs within the orthodox law. This explanation is the principal focus of this chapter and is considered in the second part of this chapter.

I. Deliberate Divergence?

Is it possible that there was, among the judges and lawyers of county courts, and some judges of the King's Bench, in the early twentieth century, a practice of turning a blind eye to the problem of privity in negligence actions? Restrictive privity rules may have seemed out of step with contemporary society. We might speculate that the difficulties surrounding married women's legal position, outlined in chapter three, contributed to a judicial willingness to allow actions that, if the strict letter of the law were upheld, ought not to be allowed in the form in which they were brought.

In order to properly evaluate this argument, it is useful to consider the nature of county courts, as these were the courts in which numerous claims surveyed in chapter four were brought. In 1846, a new type of court was created to deal with small claims.[1] Unlike many local courts before the reform, the new county courts had legally trained, experienced and salaried lawyers sitting in judgment. However, despite increasing similarities with the Westminster courts, as Polden notes:

> The county court bench never carried anything like the same prestige as the superior courts – it was not so much a lower division as a lesser league. The poor quality of many nineteenth-century appointments ensured that its status remained low for a long time, that 'friends' would express surprise when a barrister of eminence joined its ranks.[2]

Over time, it seems, the 'quality' improved,[3] and county court judges were occasionally called upon to afforce King's Bench judges on circuit.[4] Nevertheless, there was still an idea that these appointments were for successful but burned-out barristers seeking to enjoy a quiet life, those who had missed out on High Court positions, or perhaps those lacking some qualities necessary to reach greater heights.[5]

Relevantly for current purposes, Polden describes the nature of work for a county court judge in the following terms:

> In busy courts it involved the endless, rapid processing of debt cases, a form of judicial drudgery even less elevating than the work of a London police magistrate. Judges had to seek stimulation in the rich variety of human stories they encountered rather than the intellectual challenge of knotty points of law, and their satisfaction in protecting the poor from oppression rather than elucidating the law.[6]

Finding a solution to people's problems, engagement with the human side of a dispute, seemed to be at the core of the job, rather than a strong focus on legal doctrine. Finn has suggested that county courts were more flexible in relation to testimony of married women in their husband's disputes than were the superior courts.[7] While the superior courts, 'in deference to the principle of coverture', would not permit wives to appear on behalf of their husbands, the county courts 'deferred instead to the logic of the law of necessaries' and allowed

[1] P Polden, *A History of the County Court, 1846–1971* (Cambridge University Press, 1999) ch 1. See also County Courts Act 1846.

[2] Polden (n 1) 243.

[3] ibid. Applications were numerous and selection reasonably rigorous, involving referees and interviews: see, eg, Polden (n 1) 242–46.

[4] Polden (n 1) 258.

[5] ibid 243–44.

[6] ibid 273.

[7] M Finn, 'Working-class women and the contest for consumer control in Victorian County Courts' (1998) 161 *Past & Present* 116, 130.

wives to appear together with, or in place of, their husbands in claims for small debts.[8]

Could the nature of the county courts at the beginning of the twentieth century, then, have resulted in county court judges accepting and encouraging a practice with respect to product liability that simply ignored rules perceived to be out of step with modern values? Even if county court judges might be expected to be more engaged than their common law counterparts with the 'human stories' involved in litigation, it seems unlikely – particularly by the 1910s and 1920s, when these judges sometimes sat in other, higher, courts as well. While the speed with which some county court judges may have been required to work might have led to loose or sloppy practices, it seems unlikely that this would have led to deliberate divergence from rules set down by courts further up the hierarchy. It is also clear that it was not just county courts that allowed actions where we would expect the rules of privity, applied strictly, to preclude success. There are several instances, outlined already, in the King's Bench.

An explanation based on lower courts' ignoring the law altogether is not plausible. Nevertheless, it is possible that at least some of the cases discussed in the previous chapter might be explained by *some* level of judicial insubordination, in county courts and by single judges of the King's Bench. One case considered shows a glimmer of rebellion: Grantham J of the King's Bench in 1908 refused to withdraw the case from the jury when it was argued for the defendant that there was no duty of care and so no viable case.[9] This could have been an instance of judicial caution, reserving the point for a higher court. Yet it is also possible that Grantham J and others may have felt a powerful sympathy for plaintiffs and a distaste for the doctrinal obstacles to consumer claims. These attitudes may have led to rather crude distinctions being drawn to avoid the effects of *Winterbottom v Wright*. Nevertheless, this can also only account for some of the cases outlined above. The fact that many solicitors were drafting claims for clients injured by defective products suggests that there must have been a coherent argument available. It is to this explanation that discussion now turns.

II. *George v Skivington* and the 'Supply of Dangerous Things'

A more plausible explanation – certainly more than overt and widespread judicial insubordination – is available. This alternative explanation is based on the law concerning the supply of dangerous articles.

It is useful, at this point, to return to some case law discussed in the first chapters of this book. In the nineteenth century, the law of negligence was

[8] ibid.
[9] 'Law Report, Jan 17' *The Times* (18 January 1908).

still developing, and there were pockets where liability had been recognised following the supply of harm-causing chattels. The plaintiff in *Langridge v Levy*[10] was ultimately successful because of the fraudulent nature of the defendant's representation. No duty was owed by the defendant in *Longmeid v Holliday*[11] as there was no privity of contract between Mrs Holliday and the defendant, and no fraud. The judgments in both cases expressed a concern about the potential and 'unsafe' consequences of extending the law to allow actions by third parties. Where, as in *Farrant v Barnes*,[12] there was an undertaking to *carry* dangerous goods, lack of privity did not preclude a duty of care from being recognised. In *Parry v Smith*,[13] Lopes J found that there was no need to rely on privity of contract, or fraud, where 'the plaintiff's right of action is founded on a duty which … attaches in every case where a person is using or is dealing with a highly dangerous thing'.[14] It was not, he said, an action based on contract, but misfeasance independent of contract. However, Lopes J went on to acknowledge that there was no direct authority on this point.[15] Perhaps the most significant of all the early cases is *George v Skivington*.[16] Mrs George was able to recover for her injuries, despite being a stranger to the sale of the hair-wash. However, *George*, insofar as it laid down a general duty owed by the makers of products to consumers, was doubted.[17]

Importantly, and as will be explained here, in the first few years of the twentieth century, an alternative legal argument was confirmed to be available, outside and unimpeded by the law of contract, for parties injured after purchasing harmful products. This argument was based on the principles concerning the 'supply of dangerous things'. The 1912 decision in *Blacker v Lake and Elliot*[18] shut down, in strong terms, the possibility that *George* might be authority for a duty owed to the final consumer with respect to the negligent supply or manufacture of a good. However, another route was signalled to be open: in order to succeed, a claim similar to that in *George* must be formulated as one involving the sale of a dangerous item. The understanding of *George* as a case of the 'supply of a dangerous thing', the rejection of any alternative understanding and an expansive approach to what might be considered 'dangerous' together opened a pathway to success within the orthodox law.

The development and discussion of this alternative pathway in cases, treatises and commentary in the *Solicitors' Journal* will be surveyed in the first part of this

[10] *Langridge v Levy* (1837) 2 M & W 519, 150 ER 863.
[11] *Longmeid v Holliday* (1851) 6 Ex 761, 155 ER 752.
[12] *Farrant v Barnes* (1862) 11 CBNS 553, 142 ER 912.
[13] *Parry v Smith* (1879) 4 CPD 325.
[14] ibid 327.
[15] ibid.
[16] *George v Skivington* (1869) LR 5 Ex 1. See also DJ Ibbetson, 'George v Skivington (1869)' C Mitchell and P Mitchell (eds), *Landmark Cases in the Law of Tort* (Hart Publishing, 2010).
[17] See, eg, *Heaven v Pender* (1883) 11 QBD 503 (Cotton LJ) in the Court of Appeal.
[18] *Blacker v Lake and Elliot* (1912) 106 LT 533.

section. On the basis of this material, it will be suggested that the availability of the 'supply of dangerous things' argument would have been widely appreciated in the legal community and is thus likely to have been taken up by lawyers in framing their clients' claims.

Despite some ongoing lack of clarity as to the precise nature of the principles, the 'supply of dangerous things' argument provided, and was being utilised as, an alternative route to success for those seeking a remedy for damage done by a defective product. This plausibly explains the cases revealed the previous chapter.

A. The 'Supply of Dangerous Things' Route Developed

i. George v Skivington *in the New Century*

There is a subtle but important change in the treatment of *George v Skivington* between the second edition of Beven's *Negligence in Law*, published in 1895, and the third edition, published in 1908. The 1895 edition suggested that *George* did not contradict *Winterbottom*, but was, rather, 'only the natural outcome of the same principle'.[19] Emphasis was placed on the fact that this was a case where the plaintiff or his wife had no duty to examine the goods. The outcome was explained as follows:

> The profession of a special skill by the defendant, and the description of the hairwash as a chemical composition, which implied that ordinary persons would be unable to test it, even if desirous to do so, were circumstances that exonerated the plaintiff from the duty of any independent examination in the matter.[20]

It was also noted that it was a decision on demurrer and could not be said to establish more than that there was a state of facts that raised no implication of a duty on the part of the plaintiff to examine. The section dealing with *George* followed immediately after consideration of an American case, *Heizer v Kingsland and Douglas Manufacturing Company*.[21] That case concerned the principle that the maker of machinery is not liable to parties other than the purchaser for injuries caused by a breakdown in the machine, 'unless such machinery is of an inherently dangerous character, and the maker has failed to make known its true nature'[22] or has sold it without disclosing a known defect. In the 1895 edition, there was no suggestion that *George* concerned a similar principle and a substance which would be dangerous without an accompanying warning.

[19] T Beven, *Negligence in* Law, 2nd edn (Stevens and Haynes, 1895) 65.
[20] ibid.
[21] *Heizer v Kingsland and Douglas Manufacturing Company* (1892) 110 Mo 605, 33 Am St R 482.
[22] Beven, *Negligence in* Law, 2nd edn (1895) (n 19) 65.

However, in the 1908 edition, *George* is treated as involving the supply of a dangerous thing:

> *George v Skivington* was treated in the Divisional Court in *Heaven v Pender* as irreconcilable with *Winterbottom v Wright*. It is not so, but quite consistent. Moreover, the consequences of using the thing were dangerous in the sense just defined.[23]

The remainder of the discussion is similar to that of the previous edition. Nevertheless, the 1908 edition signals that *George* is perhaps to be properly understood as a case of the supply of a dangerous thing, justifying maintenance of the wife's action, notwithstanding the absence of privity.

What was the reason for this subtle difference in treatment? The answer may lie in an additional paragraph inserted into the 1908 edition, between discussion of *Heizer* and discussion of *George*. Since the 1895 edition, two further relevant cases had come before the Court of Appeal of the King's Bench; both are referred to in this additional paragraph. The first is *Clarke v Army and Navy Co-operative Society*,[24] in which both *George* and *Winterbottom* had been raised in argument. The principle in *Winterbottom* was also central to the decision in the second case, *Earl v Lubbock*.[25]

Clarke, it may be recalled, concerned the sale of a tin of disinfectant powder. Mrs Clarke, whose husband was a member of the co-operative, purchased from the defendant owners a tin of chlorinated lime.[26] When she opened the tin with a spoon, some powder flew up into her face and caused injury to her eye. The Clarkes' cause of action was either breach of warranty, or breach of a duty 'arising under the circumstances to warn a purchaser of the explosive or otherwise dangerous character of the article sold'.[27] The remaining tins in stock were sent back to the manufacturer after this incident. With respect to tins already sold, it was alleged that similar accidents had occurred to other purchasers.[28] A Mrs Stebbing's experience had been communicated to the defendants' manager at the store in question before Mrs Clarke's accident.[29] The defendants' manager had instructed his assistants to warn customers, urging care in opening the tins. A warning was, however, not given to Mrs Clarke. The jury found that there was no explosion but that the tins were dangerous, and that the defendants were negligent in not taking further steps. There was a verdict for the plaintiffs.[30]

On appeal, the defendants argued that because the jury found that there was no explosion, they were entitled to a verdict in their favour: the statement of claim only alleged that there had been an explosion. The defendants also argued

[23] T Beven, *Negligence in Law*, 3rd edn (Stevens and Haynes, 1908) 57.
[24] *Clarke v Army and Navy Co-operative Society* [1903] 1 KB 155.
[25] *Earl v Lubbock* [1905] 1 KB 253.
[26] *Clarke* (n 24) 161.
[27] ibid 155.
[28] ibid 156, 165.
[29] ibid 156.
[30] ibid 160.

that, between parties to a contract of sale, all obligations were to be found in the contract itself. However, if there was any duty to warn the purchaser of the dangerous character of goods sold, that duty only arose in a case of goods *necessarily* dangerous, where the danger is obvious to the defendants; they said this was not the case here.[31] They cited *George* as an example of a duty's being owed to a person not party to the contract of sale by 'a vendor of a dangerous article'.[32] *Langridge* was also discussed. It was suggested that these cases involved some 'active negligence or misfeasance' – the preparation of the hair-wash by the defendant in *George*, and the fraudulent misrepresentation of the gun as safe in *Langridge*.[33] They argued that these cases did not show that the vendor would be liable for mere passive negligence in respect of the character of the goods supplied. Conversely, it was the plaintiffs' argument that the authorities demonstrated that a duty was imposed upon anyone who supplies or delivers an article which they know, or ought to know, to be dangerous. The existence of a contract was said not to prevent the existence of that duty.[34] Both Brett MR's comments in *Heaven* and the decision in *George* were cited in support.[35]

The Court of Appeal preferred the arguments of the plaintiffs as to liability in this case. Collins MR thought that the statement of claim covered a cause of action based upon the tin's being dangerous because of some explosive quality and because of a defect in the tin, having regard to the nature of what was inside.[36] The central question, he said, was whether or not the tin with its contents was, to the knowledge of the defendants, dangerous.[37] The defendants here knew the tins to be potentially dangerous to open and therefore owed a duty to take care to prevent injury to purchasers.[38] Romer LJ and Mathew LJ delivered brief separate judgments along similar lines. The application was therefore dismissed. Romer LJ put the duty owed here in the following terms:

> I think that, apart from any question of warranty, there is a duty cast upon a vendor, who knows of the dangerous character of goods which he is supplying, and also knows that the purchaser is not, or may not be, aware of it, not to supply the goods without giving some warning to the purchaser of that danger.[39]

Mathew LJ appeared to see it as sufficient that the defendants 'through their officers *knew, or had the means of knowing*, that the tin supplied to the female plaintiff was likely to be dangerous' (emphasis added).[40]

[31] ibid 158.
[32] ibid.
[33] ibid.
[34] ibid 159.
[35] ibid 160.
[36] ibid 162.
[37] ibid.
[38] ibid.
[39] ibid 166.
[40] ibid 168. See also discussion in WTS Stallybrass, 'Dangerous Things and Non-Natural User of Land' (1929) 3 *Cambridge Law Journal* 376, 388.

The decision in *Clarke* is one of the first where this duty between vendor and consumer is explicitly recognised and applied. There had, of course, been other cases alluding to the possibility of such a duty – indeed, the parties and the court considered that the authorities supported such an argument – but no prior case seems so explicit in its confirmation. In 1837, *Langridge* turned on a false representation made as to the safety of a gun. Caution was expressed against laying down a precedent that would be an 'authority for an action against the vendors, even of such instruments and articles as are dangerous in themselves, at the suit of any person whomsoever into whose hands they might happen to pass, and who should be injured thereby'.[41] *Longmeid* also turned on misrepresentation. Parke B in *Longmeid* noted that there were types of cases, besides those involving fraud, where a person not a party to the contract might nevertheless be owed a duty.[42] He went on:

> And it may be the same when any one delivers to another without notice an instrument in its nature dangerous, or under particular circumstances, as a loaded gun which he himself loaded, and that other person to whom it is delivered is injured thereby, or if he places it in a situation easily accessible to a third person, who sustains damage from it. A very strong case to that effect is *Dixon* v. *Bell* (5 M. & Selw. 198). But it would be going much too far to say, that so much care is required in the ordinary intercourse of life between one individual and another, that, if a machine not in its nature dangerous, – a carriage for instance, – but which might become so by a latent defect entirely unknown, although discoverable by the exercise of ordinary care, should be lent or given by one person, even by the person who manufactured it, to another, the former should be answerable to the latter for a subsequent damage accruing by the use of it.[43]

A limited exception was therefore recognised but not (by 1851, in *Longmeid*) extending to latent defects which could be discovered through the exercise of ordinary care by the vendor. *Dixon v Bell*,[44] to which Parke B refers above, concerned the accidental discharge of a gun. An action on the case was brought by the plaintiff, whose son and servant were injured when the defendant's young servant girl accidentally discharged the gun. The defendant had sent her to fetch the gun, with verbal instructions that the person handing it to her was first to take out a component part and render the gun safe. A Mr Lemon, in handing over the gun, apparently followed the instruction and examined the gun but, finding that relevant part already gone, did nothing further. This proved an ineffective safety precaution. Lord Ellenborough CJ and Bayley J found that more care was required of the defendant. In 1900, Labatt had noted, referring to *Dixon*, that stringent obligations were incurred by those who used or left about 'in such a way as to cause danger an instrument which is dangerous in itself'.[45]

[41] *Langridge* (n 10) 531; 868.
[42] *Longmeid* (n 11) 767; 755.
[43] ibid.
[44] *Dixon v Bell* (1816) 5 M&S 198, 105 ER 1023. See also (1816) 1 Stark 286, 171 ER 475.
[45] CB Labatt, 'Negligence in Relation to Privity of Contract' (1900) 16 *Law Quarterly Review* 168, 176.

He said that the precise reasons for the outcome in *Dixon* had become immaterial, given subsequent treatment, and that the duty to deal with dangerous things carefully was 'owed to all the world'.[46] It was not, though, expressly linked to the *sale or supply* of dangerous goods. Labatt also commented that, at the time of writing, the rule as to 'dangerous things' in England had been narrowly confined – perhaps restricted to explosives – though he thought perhaps it might be extended to poisonous drugs, if the courts were given the opportunity (referring to the American case *Thomas v Winchester*).[47] Certainly, the principle set out in *Clarke* appears not to have been clear in 1900; Labatt is left to advance an argument as to how a principle involving 'dangerous things' might usefully be employed to inject consistency into the law of negligence.[48] *Clarke* marked an important development.

The 1869 case of *George* was cited by the plaintiffs and defendants in *Clarke* for the existence of a duty in circumstances involving the sale of dangerous items, but, as will be explored shortly, was not apparently universally understood as such in contemporary texts and commentaries.[49] The decision in *Clarke* was therefore also significant in putting into general circulation this understanding of the decision in *George*; it could be understood as authority for the proposition that the supply of an item that carried a danger of injury, without an appropriate accompanying warning, could give rise to a duty independent of contract.

Earl was handed down just two years later. The defendant wheelwright had contracted with a firm to keep its vans in good repair, and the plaintiff was a driver employed by that firm. The plaintiff was injured when a wheel came off the cart after it had supposedly been serviced by the defendant's employees. As discussed in chapter one, Collins MR held that the principle in *Winterbottom* was conclusive of the matter.[50] After quoting Parke B in *Longmeid*, he said:

> Here there is the case of a carriage which, so far as the evidence goes, was not visibly out of repair. Apparently the wheel required oiling, and for that purpose the cap was removed, and, as it was defective, a piece of zinc was nailed on to the wheel. That had nothing to do with the accident, but was done to supply a better means of oiling the wheel; and, in my opinion, the van cannot fall within the category of dangerous articles to which Parke B. alludes.[51]

Stirling LJ was of the same opinion. He noted that, to succeed, the plaintiff would have to show either that the thing was dangerous in itself, or that, to the knowledge of the defendant, the van was in such a condition as to cause danger, not necessarily

[46] ibid 177.
[47] *Thomas v Winchester* (1852) 6 NY 397.
[48] See Labatt (n 45) 178, 183–84.
[49] Writing in 1928, Stallybrass lists a number of cases from the nineteenth century in which *George* had been understood as a case involving the supply of a dangerous chattel, including *Cann v Willson* (1888) 39 Ch D 39: see Stallybrass (n 40) 379.
[50] *Earl* (n 25) 256.
[51] ibid 257.

incident to its use.[52] This the plaintiff could not do. Mathew LJ agreed that the appeal must be dismissed.[53]

It follows that, shortly before the publication of the third edition of Beven's treatise, the Court of Appeal of the King's Bench had twice confirmed the existence of this 'supply of dangerous things' exception to the privity rule in relation to negligence. Looking beyond Beven's text, the 'supply of dangerous things' principle, linked with *George*, began, after *Clarke*, to appear in other legal treatises as well. Already in the 1889 edition of *The Law of Torts*, Clerk and Lindsell cited *George* for the proposition that:

> if A. in breach of contract supplies to B. a chattel dangerous by reason of a latent defect, and B. using it in the way contemplated by the parties, entrusts it to C. who thereby suffers damage, C. has an action of tort against A.[54]

Nevertheless, Clerk and Lindsell appear to be among the minority, rather than the majority, of treatise writers linking with *George* such a principle before the early 1900s.

The 1901 edition of Pollock's *The Law of Torts* contains a discussion of the 'supply of dangerous things' principle, but the treatment suggests that it was not yet clearly taken up by courts and adopted into law. There is some discussion of duties associated with dangerous animals and dangerous items such as firearms,[55] and *George* is discussed briefly, but it is noted that the Court of Exchequer seems to have treated the case 'as in the nature of deceit'.[56] *Thomas*, Pollock says, does not seem to have been known either to counsel or to the court. He goes on:

> In the line actually taken one sees the tendency to assume that the ground of liability, if any, must be either warranty or fraud. But this is erroneous, as the judgment in *Thomas v Winchester* carefully and clearly shows. Whether that case was well decided appears to be a perfectly open question for our courts. In the present writer's opinion it is good law, and ought to be followed. Certainly it comes within the language of Parke B. in *Longmeid* … which does not deny legal responsibility 'when any one delivers to another without notice an instrument in its nature dangerous under particular circumstances, as a loaded gun which he himself has loaded, and that other person to whom it is delivered is injured thereby; or if he places it in a situation easily accessible to a third person who sustains damage from it'. In that case the defendant had sold a dangerous thing, namely an ill-made lamp, which exploded in use.[57]

Pollock noted that, on these facts, as lamps are not in their nature explosive, it was quite rightly held that the defendant could only be held liable on the contract and not to third parties.

[52] ibid 258.
[53] ibid 259.
[54] JF Clerk and WHB Lindsell, *The Law of Torts* (Sweet & Maxwell, 1889) 3. See also 364–65, 368.
[55] F Pollock, *The Law of Torts*, 6th edn (Stevens and Sons, 1901) 480–86.
[56] ibid 488.
[57] ibid 489.

However, a new section was added to the seventh edition published in 1904, discussing *Clarke*. In this new section, Pollock noted that a 'much more decided step' (presumably towards recognising a duty in cases involving the supply of dangerous things) was recently taken by the Court of Appeal in *Clarke*, as compared to the 'rather hesitating step' taken earlier by the Court of Exchequer in *George*.[58] He noted the facts of the case, before quoting the section of the judgment of Romer LJ that asserts that there is a duty upon a vendor who 'knows of the dangerous character of the goods which he is supplying, and also knows that the purchaser is not, or may not, be aware of it'.[59] This duty, he said, though arising out of a contract of sale, was independent of contract, and could extend to situations where there is no contract at all. The 1908 edition appears to be materially the same.[60]

Addison's *A Treatise on the Law of Torts* is another publication in which a change in the treatment of *George* is discernible after 1905. The seventh edition was published in 1893.[61] *George* is dealt with in the chapter entitled 'The wrong of fraud'. It is cited, along with *Langridge*, among other authorities, for the proposition that:

> Where a gun had been delivered by the defendant to the plaintiff for the purpose of being used by him, with an accompanying representation that he might safely use it, and that representation was false to the defendant's knowledge, and the plaintiff, acting upon the faith of its being true, used the gun, and received damage thereby, it was held that he was entitled to recover compensation for the injury from the defendant.[62]

It is also cited, after *Longmeid*, as authority for the proposition that, if a vendor of a lamp represents the lamp to be 'fit and proper to be used, knowing that it is not', any person injured in using the lamp would be entitled to 'an action for the deceit, upon the principle that, if anyone knowingly tells a falsehood with intent to induce another to do an act which results in his loss, he is liable to that person in an action for deceit'.[63] The 1893 edition of Addison therefore understands *George* as a case of misrepresentation leading to liability.

However, a change is evident in the eighth edition of Addison's *Treatise*, published in 1906.[64] In this edition, *George* has been removed from the footnotes to the discussion of *Langridge* and *Longmeid* in the chapter on fraud.[65] Instead, *George* appears in the new chapter devoted to the law of negligence.[66] *George* is

[58] F Pollock, *The Law of Torts*, 7th edn (Stevens and Sons, 1904) 496–97.
[59] ibid 497–98.
[60] F Pollock, *The Law of Torts*, 8th edn (Stevens and Sons, 1908) 507.
[61] CG Addison, *A Treatise on the Law of Torts*, 7th edn (Stevens and Sons, 1893).
[62] ibid 740.
[63] ibid 741–42.
[64] CG Addison, *A Treatise on the Law of Torts*, 8th edn (Stevens and Sons, 1906).
[65] ibid 824.
[66] ibid, Preface.

cited for the proposition that a duty 'rests upon him who for his own benefit invites others to use or handle goods which he knows or ought to know, and which they have no reasonable means of knowing, to be dangerous'.[67] It is noted, citing *Clarke*, that the seller of goods that are not ordinarily dangerous will owe no duty, except towards a purchaser, to inform himself as to whether any particular article is actually dangerous or not. Knowledge of the danger is necessary for liability to a third party injured by it.[68]

Salmond's *The Law of Torts* was first published in 1907, after *Clarke* and *Earl* were decided. This first edition sets out the principle that, where A sells or gives a defective chattel to B, who sells it or gives it to C, who is injured by it, A will be liable only in two cases. The first is where the defendant fraudulently represents the chattels to be safe, and 'misleads the recipient into causing damage to the plaintiff'.[69] *Langridge* is cited for this principle. The second case is where the defendant has actual knowledge of the dangerous nature of the chattel. The case of *Farrant*, and liability arising from the delivery of the carboy of nitric acid in that case, is provided by way of example.[70] It is stressed that, save these two cases – fraud and non-disclosure of known dangers – there will be no liability to third persons, even where a duty exists by contract with the recipient to make the chattel safe. For this, *Winterbottom* and *Earl* are cited.[71] The author says that it is 'perhaps to be regretted that so narrow a view has been taken as to the liabilities of those who negligently put dangerous chattels in circulation to the hurt of other persons'.[72] *George* appears in a footnote, where the author notes that, since *Earl* confirmed the authority of *Winterbottom*, 'it seems impossible any longer to maintain the authority of such cases as *George* … and *Elliott v Hall*'.[73]

[67] ibid 721.

[68] Curiously, *Winterbottom*, discussed extensively in earlier chapters, is cited for this knowledge requirement, alongside *Longmeid* (n 11).

[69] JW Salmond, *The Law of Torts* (Stevens and Haynes, 1907) 362.

[70] ibid 362–63.

[71] ibid 363.

[72] ibid.

[73] ibid. In *Elliott v Hall* (1885) 15 QBD 315, the plaintiff had been unloading coal in the course of his employment with the Leicester Coal Consumers' Company (LCCC). He climbed into the truck to unload but then fell out of the truck when the door gave way, and thereby sustained injuries. The defendant was the proprietor of a colliery, supplying coal under contract to the LCCC, and had rented the truck from another company, the Midland Waggon Company. It was the task of the waggon company to repair the waggons. Nevertheless, it was found by a jury that the defendant had been negligent in allowing the truck to leave the colliery in a defective state. The judge at trial declined to give judgment, leaving the parties to move for judgment. The plaintiff did so, and the defendant applied, by cross-motion, for a new trial, arguing that there was no duty of care owed. The plaintiff was ultimately successful. Grove J opined that this was 'a stronger case in favour of the plaintiff than the case of *Heaven v Pender*': 319. However, he also said that the plaintiff was entitled to recover 'quite independently' of *Heaven*: it had been contemplated by the defendant that the truck would need to be unloaded by the purchaser's servants, and therefore a duty arose on the part of the defendant towards the plaintiff. Smith J likened the case to *Foulkes*, describing the basis of the duty in that case, despite the absence of a contract between railway and passenger, as being based on the defendants having 'allowed [the plaintiff] to come into their carriage': 322.

The second edition of Salmond was published just three years later, in 1910, but there is a difference in the way that these principles, and *George*, are treated. The author is much less certain in identifying the relevant principles: he notes, after setting out the 'A sells or gives to B' scenario, that to this question 'it is impossible, as the authorities at present stand, to give any complete or confident answer'.[74] The mere fact of breach of contract is said not to be sufficient to give rise to liability to a third party, for which proposition *Earl* is cited.[75] The author then goes on to outline three circumstances (rather than the two in the 1907 edition) in which a cause of action will be available to a person who is not a party to an existing contract.[76] Fraud and the delivery of a chattel with actual knowledge of its dangers are the first two categories of case, the third category (and new addition) identified is where the defendant 'has been guilty of an act of negligent misfeasance in actually creating the source of danger, and not merely of the non-feasance of omitting to make the chattel safe or to ascertain whether it was safe or not'.[77] The author goes as far as to say that the defendant is *probably* liable in such a case.[78] The author notes that, if there is liability in such a case, 'the rule in *Earl* ... must be construed as limited to cases in which the breach of contract complained of consists merely in the passive failure to discover and put an end to existing dangers, and not in the positive act of negligently creating dangers which did not already exist'.[79] The examples provided are of *creators* of dangerous goods. Rather than including a footnote saying that *George* can no longer be supported as in the 1907 edition, *George* is, in this edition, provided as an example of a case in this third category: 'the defendant was a chemist who negligently manufactured a deleterious hair-wash, which he sold the plaintiff's husband, knowing that it was to be used by the plaintiff'.[80] *Thomas* is also discussed as an example of liability in this kind of case. The formulation of this third category, and the rehabilitation of *George* in this manner, flagged a pathway for would-be litigants seeking compensation for an injury-causing chattel.

ii. Blacker v Lake and Elliot *(1912)*

The next major case was *Blacker*. As set out in chapter one, the plaintiff in *Blacker*, a bicycle maker, sustained serious burns through contact with ignited paraffin oil when a brazing lamp burst. The defendants were the makers of the lamp. There was no contract between these two parties, as the plaintiff had purchased it from a third-party vendor. The vendors, Hobday Bros,[81] were apparently not sued and

[74] JW Salmond, *The Law of* Torts, 2nd edn (Stevens and Haynes, 1910) 373.
[75] ibid.
[76] ibid 375.
[77] ibid 376.
[78] ibid.
[79] ibid 377.
[80] ibid 378.
[81] See 'Mr Blacker's Accident: Appeal Case' *Harrow Observer* (9 February 1912).

receive little attention in the report. A regional newspaper notes only that 'no claim [was] … made for breach of warranty against the seller'.[82] It is unclear why this choice was made.[83] The plaintiff's case against the manufacturers was that the lamp was a 'dangerous thing', 'either by reason of its general character or by reason of the specific condition in which it is sent out', imposing on the maker a duty to 'see that it shall be safe'[84] as far as is possible, or to take care in its manufacture and 'to provide themselves with the best knowledge in existence at the time'.[85]

The judge at first instance, when directing the jury, had instructed that the jury might find for the plaintiff if the lamp was 'dangerous in itself', or if the defendant ought to have known it was dangerous.[86] The lamp was found to be a 'dangerous thing for the purpose for which it was intended to be used' and the plaintiff was entitled to recover.[87] It was decided that the defendants, as reasonable men, ought to have known that the lamp was dangerous.

The appeal was heard by Hamilton and Lush JJ, in the King's Bench Divisional Court. Both concluded that the judge had misdirected the jury. Hamilton J (later, Lord Sumner) referred to the various 'circumstances and conditions'[88] in which a plaintiff might recover in tort for injuries sustained by defective chattels, and said that it was a question of law, rather than fact, whether or not a certain case came within one category or another. Therefore, it was for the judge to decide if the lamp was 'a thing dangerous in itself' (and therefore belonging to that established category creating a duty).[89] The trial judge erred in leaving it to the jury to decide. Hamilton J also took the view that the lamp was not a 'dangerous' item: it had worked safely for almost a year.[90] He found that although the evidence suggested that 'more care in its manufacture might have produced a more durable article', he did not think that it brought the lamp within 'the category, so far as it has been defined, of a dangerous object, the dealing with which *per se* imposes any special legal liability'.[91] He noted that, even if it could be made stronger, this would likely be more expensive and there was no law against selling a cheap lamp. It was, Hamilton J concluded, not an item dangerous *per se* but only *sub modo* – that is, under some conditions. The defendants did not know, he said, that the lamp was unsafe and had no reason to believe it so. However, 'had they been wiser men

[82] ibid.

[83] Advertising in regional newspapers suggests that Hobday Bros were still trading later in the 1910s: see, eg, 'Situations Vacant' *Essex Newsman* (8 July 1916). We can only speculate as to the reason; the lack of suit may perhaps be linked to some express provision in the sale or the passage of around one year between purchase and accident: see, eg, discussion in JP Benjamin et al, *A Treatise on the Law of Sale of Personal Property*, 5th edn (Sweet & Maxwell, 1906) 664.

[84] *Blacker* (n 18) 536.

[85] ibid.

[86] ibid 534.

[87] ibid 534–35.

[88] ibid 535.

[89] ibid.

[90] ibid.

[91] ibid.

or more experienced engineers they would then have known what the plaintiff's experts say that they ought to have known'.[92] That they were not so did not make them liable.

Attention turned to *George*. Hamilton J said that this was a decision 'that a person who makes a hair wash owes a duty to persons for whose use he sells it to take care that the wash shall not injure those who use it'.[93] One possible view was that the judges deciding the case believed it to be a case of misrepresentation or fraud. Hamilton J went on to say that, if that were so, *George* had nothing to do with the present case. Nevertheless, a second interpretation of *George* was open: namely, that it was decided upon the ground of negligence, upon a duty owed to the ultimate user and, as such, 'an authority to which every attention must be paid'.[94] Hamilton J suggested that certain passages within the reports made it clear that the ground was *negligence*, not fraud or misrepresentation, and that the focus was upon a lack of care in preparation rather than any dishonesty.[95] He concluded that *George* was not a case that he was able to follow, it having been 'dealt with in later cases in a way which comes as near express disaffirmance as is possible without its being actually overruled'[96] and being in conflict with *Winterbottom*.[97]

The other member of the King's Bench in *Blacker* was Lush J. He opened by acknowledging that he also felt that the judge had misdirected the jury, and that this was sufficient, but wished to express his wider views given that this was one of a 'class of cases which are so constantly coming before the courts' and so many 'questions of general importance ha[d] been raised'.[98] He asserted that cases like *Earl v Lubbock*[99] had established that negligence in the manufacture of ordinary chattels, not 'in themselves dangerous', could not found an action where there was no contractual duty.[100] In *Earl*, Collins MR had held the principle in *Winterbottom* to be conclusive in rejecting a duty of care by a wheelwright to the driver of a cart.[101] The privity rule and the enduring authority of *Winterbottom* were thus confirmed, in *Blacker*, also by Lush J. Commenting on *George*, he said that it was often relied upon as establishing that a party who undertakes to do work under a contract could be sued for the breach of that duty by a non-party if the defendant knew that the person was going to use the thing made.[102] However, this, he said, was inconsistent with *Winterbottom* and subsequent authority. He

[92] ibid 537.
[93] ibid.
[94] ibid.
[95] ibid 537–38.
[96] ibid 538. See, eg, *Heaven v Pender* (n 17) 516–17.
[97] *Blacker* (n 18) 539.
[98] ibid 540.
[99] [1905] 1 KB 253.
[100] *Blacker* (n 18) 540.
[101] *Earl* (n 25) 256. Collins MR said that the decision in *Winterbottom*, 'since the year 1842 in which it was given, ha[d] stood the test of repeated discussion'.
[102] *Blacker* (n 18) 540.

said it was now impossible to follow *George* as it could not be regarded as good law, in so far as it laid down that general proposition.

Lush J provided an overview of the situations in which a stranger to a contract could be permitted an action. He outlined three ways in which a duty might exist: first, if there was fraud on the part of the vendor as to safety; second, where the chattel was known to be dangerous and no warning was given; and, third, where the thing supplied was a public nuisance.[103] There was discussion of the rules concerning chattels of the 'dangerous' class. He commented:

> If a person … manufactures two different articles, one being a deadly poison and the other safe, and through a careless blunder labels as safe an article which *he ought to have known was of the other category and sells it under that description*, I should be slow to say that in such a case he would not be responsible to persons who he knew would use the article (emphasis added).[104]

Lush J concluded that Blacker's case was not a case in which a dangerous article had, through negligence, been 'passed … off' as safe.[105] He then returned to *George*, suggesting that its facts had perhaps warranted its proceeding as such a case of selling 'a thing dangerous in itself knowing that others will use it without disclosing its real character'.[106] If *George* had proceeded in this way, he did not 'think it would have been in conflict with any of the authorities … cited'.[107] It would, he said, have been consistent with the New York Supreme Court case of *Thomas v Winchester*,[108] which had been recently cited by Lord Dunedin in the Privy Council.[109]

The outcome in *Blacker*, and the reasoning of the court in the pre-*Donoghue* legal landscape, seems unsurprising. Nevertheless, the significance of *Blacker* is twofold. First, the decision of the Divisional Court renders *George* unavailable to litigants as an authority establishing or confirming a general duty owed to consumers with respect to injuries caused by defective chattels. The Court is strong in its rejection of such a principle, finding it to be inconsistent with other authorities. To the extent that the decision in *George* could be understood as based on such a principle, and, being not overruled, potentially still available to litigants, this line of argument was effectively closed down. The Court appeared to be seizing the opportunity to make a definitive statement to this effect.

However, another line was affirmed, and this is the second way in which this case is significant. Certainly in the judgment of Lush J we see the suggestion that

[103] ibid 540–41.
[104] ibid 541.
[105] ibid.
[106] ibid.
[107] ibid.
[108] *Thomas* (n 47). In *Thomas*, a chemist sold a medicine which contained belladonna, but which had been labelled 'extract of dandelion' by the supplier. A third party became seriously ill, and the supplier was held liable.
[109] See *Dominion Natural Gas Company v Collins* [1909] AC 640, 646.

the outcome in *George*, even if not described explicitly as such at the time, may be understood ex post facto as justified by the 'supply of dangerous things' exception to the privity rule in relation to negligence. This was important for would-be plaintiffs. After *Blacker*, if a party injured by a defective product could demonstrate that the item carried a non-obvious risk of injury and there was no reasonable chance of inspection, then *Blacker* and *George* (recharacterised) suggested that a duty might be owed. This duty was owed wholly outside of contract and restricted neither by the privity rule nor, it seems, from the reasoning of Lush J, by a requirement that the defendant subjectively *knew* of the danger (if they ought to have known). A negligently prepared hair-wash is not as clearly *dangerous* as, say, the deadly poison provided in Lush J's example. Nevertheless, it was identified in *Blacker* as falling within this exception.

*iii. Post-*Blacker*: Some Confusion, Wide Recognition*

This view of *George* and the confirmation of a 'supply of dangerous things' argument appears, post-*Blacker*, in judgments, treatises and journals. The discussion to be found there, examples of which are set out below, reveals that there was indeed a pathway to a successful claim available to those injured by defective goods but not party to the contract of sale, but it lay not in the ordinary principles of negligence. Rather, to succeed, such a party needed their claim to fall into a particular category: the supply of dangerous items. It was also confirmed that this duty did not arise from a contract; it was a tortious duty.

There was, however, ongoing lack of clarity as to the precise nature of the exceptional category. When would something be 'inherently dangerous', rather than dangerous because of a defect?[110] Of particular trouble, too, was the knowledge requirement. Would a defendant have to have actual knowledge of the danger posed by the item supplied, or was it sufficient that they ought, if they had taken sufficient care, to have known? This appears to have been an ongoing point of confusion and had not been resolved even by the time of *Donoghue*, as Lord Macmillan's discussion suggests.[111] Writing in 1929, Stallybrass opined that there was 'considerable authority for saying that in these cases constructive knowledge is equivalent to knowledge'.[112] He cited for this proposition, amongst other things, Mathew LJ's reasoning in *Clarke* and the decision of Lush J in *White v Steadman*.[113] He noted that Horridge J in *Bates v Batey*[114] had taken the opposite view, and did not think that liability could be found if a defendant might, by the exercise of reasonable care, have discovered the defect.[115]

[110] See discussion in Stallybrass (n 40) 387–89.
[111] *Donoghue v Stevenson* [1932] AC 562, 616.
[112] Stallybrass (n 40) 388.
[113] *White v Steadman* [1913] 3 KB 340.
[114] *Bates v Batey* [1913] 3 KB 351, which was considered in ch 4.
[115] Stallybrass (n 40) 389.

The alternative mechanism involving the 'supply of dangerous things' is clearly employed in the 1913 case of *Bates*.[116] In *Bates*, discussed in chapter four, the principal plaintiff was a boy of 12 who purchased a bottle of ginger beer from a local shop. The shopkeepers had, in turn, purchased the ginger beer from the defendant beverage manufacturers. The boy was injured when, as he tried to open the bottle, it burst. The injuries were so severe that he lost his right eye. The boy claimed against the defendants for these personal injuries, and his father also claimed in respect of certain expenses incurred in relation to the accident.[117] The jury found that the defective bottle had caused the accident, that it was not a latent defect that would not have been discoverable with due care, and that the defect was brought out by the negligence of the defendants.[118] Any further inferences necessary to resolve the case were left to Horridge J.[119]

The plaintiffs sought to argue before Horridge J that the bottle of ginger beer was in itself a dangerous thing, or that this particular bottle (with its defects) was a dangerous thing.[120] He concluded it was not a dangerous thing of the first type – an inherently dangerous thing:

> In my judgment a bottle of ginger beer is not in itself a dangerous thing, and further, if it be so, it was a thing which Wallis, who purchased from the defendants, must equally have known to be a dangerous thing, as he would be fully acquainted with the explosive quality of ginger beer, and therefore there was no duty to warn him.[121]

He noted that several decisions, including *Cavalier* and *Blacker*, confirmed that there could be no action where the person injured was aware of, or had notice of, the danger.

However, Horridge J concluded that it was a dangerous thing of the second type: this bottle was a dangerous thing owing to the defect. There was then the question of the defendants' knowledge of the nature of the bottle. It was not suggested, and Horridge J said he would not find, that the defendants actually knew that the bottle was defective.[122]

It was argued that, if the defendants had the *means* of knowledge, they were as much responsible as if they had actual knowledge.[123] Noting the outcome in *Earl*, Horridge J observed that the negligence alleged in that case had been a failure properly to inspect the wheel and to report that it was defective. He went on:

> If, however, the failure to obtain knowledge which could by reasonable care have been obtained is equivalent to knowledge, it seems to me the Court of Appeal would have sent that case down to the county court judge to be heard by him on the question of whether or not the defendant must be taken to have knowledge because he failed to

[116] *Bates* (n 114).
[117] ibid 351.
[118] ibid 352.
[119] ibid.
[120] ibid 353.
[121] ibid.
[122] ibid.
[123] ibid 353–54.

> make proper use of the means of discovery at his disposal; and I think this case is a direct decision of the Court of Appeal, following *Longmeid v. Holliday* … that even where the defect is discoverable by the exercise of ordinary care the defendant is not liable, apart from contract, unless he in fact had actual knowledge.[124]

Thus, Horridge J found that it would not be sufficient for liability that the defendants could, by the exercise of reasonable care, have discovered the defect rendering the item dangerous. It was necessary that they had actual knowledge of the defect. This is consistent with the preservation of a clear distinction between fraud and negligence.

He noted that Lush J in *White*[125] held that, in the case of a skittish horse which had caused injury to a non-contracting party,

> a person who has the means of knowledge and only does not know that the animal or chattel which he supplies is dangerous because he does not take ordinary care to avail himself of his opportunity of knowledge is in precisely the same position as the person who knows.[126]

However, Horridge J brushed this aside, saying that he did not think that Lush J could have intended to decide that

> where a thing not dangerous in itself becomes dangerous through a defect occasioned by breach of contract in its manufacture or delivery, the person handing it over must be held liable to a third party because, although he did not know, he might by the exercise of reasonable care have known its condition.[127]

The reason, he said, was that Lush J had been party to the decision in *Blacker* (above), in which Hamilton J had said that it was insufficient for a finding of liability that, if the defendants had been 'wiser men or more experienced engineers', they would have known that the lamp in question was not perfectly safe.[128]

Horridge J's position might seem surprising: Lush J in *White* specifically asked counsel for the defendant for argument on this point. He noted that he had said in *Blacker* that

> if a person hands over an article of a dangerous nature which he knows to be dangerous to somebody else who is ignorant of its true nature, it is his duty to warn him of its

[124] ibid 355.

[125] *White* (n 113). One of the plaintiffs in this case, Mr White, had hired from the defendant a landau (a type of cart) with a horse and coachman for the purpose of taking an afternoon drive in the country. Mrs White, the other plaintiff, was also to come along for the drive. While on the drive, the horse showed signs of being startled by motorised vehicles. Mr White at one point asked the coachman to get someone to lead the horse past a traction engine, but the coachman thought that he could pass safely without such a precaution. When they passed the traction engine, the horse shied and got out of control, and both plaintiffs were injured. The plaintiffs brought an action for damages for negligence and breach of duty. One of the arguments advanced was that the horse was known by the defendant and his servants to be an unsafe horse, due to its propensity to shy when meeting motor vehicles: 345–46. Judgment was given for both plaintiffs, Lush J finding that a duty was also owed to Mrs White: 350.

[126] *Bates* (n 114) 355.

[127] ibid.

[128] ibid 355–56.

> character, and if he does not do so he commits a breach of duty not only to the person who contracts with him, but also to all persons who to his knowledge may use it.[129]

He then asked counsel directly if that duty extended to a case where the defendant did not know a horse was dangerous, but *ought*, with the exercise of proper care, *to have known*.[130] The jury in *White* had found that the defendant ought to have known, if proper care had been taken, that the horse was not safe. Mr White had hired a horse and cart for an afternoon drive, but the horse had shied upon encountering motor vehicles and caused injury also to Mrs White. The central problem before Lush J was Mrs White's claim; her husband had a straightforward claim on the contract of hire, but Mrs White was not a party to that contract.[131] Unsurprisingly, it was argued for the defendant that the defendant owed no duty to her. This was the question left to Lush J to decide.[132] Lush J found that Mrs White was indeed owed a duty in this case. He explained that Mrs White was one of a class of persons whom the defendant must have contemplated might use the carriage. The carriage was provided for her use, as well as that of her husband.[133] He found that the duty of a person letting out a horse with a 'vicious propensity' was the same as

> that which any person is under who allows others to use or come in contact with an animal or chattel that is dangerous in itself, i.e., of a dangerous character as distinguished (as regards a chattel) from a danger only arising from defective manufacture or repair.[134]

He went on:

> He is under a duty to warn not only the person who hires it, but any person who he knows or contemplates or ought to contemplate will use it. The duty is not dependent on and is not created by the contract. It exists independently of contract. That which creates it is not the contract, but the supplying of a dangerous animal or chattel for the use of another person.[135]

Lush J cited *Clarke* as a case in which this duty was recognised.[136] The principal complication with respect to Mrs White's claim was said to be the defendant's knowledge. If the defendant had known of the horse's vicious propensity, then 'it [was] clear that Mrs White could have recovered'.[137] However, Lush J rejected the notion that the defendant, through his own carelessness, could be in a better position because he did not use 'the means of knowledge at his disposal'.[138] He suggested that one who keeps an animal for hire cannot hide behind his own want

[129] *White* (n 113) 343.
[130] ibid.
[131] ibid 346.
[132] ibid.
[133] ibid 347.
[134] ibid.
[135] ibid.
[136] ibid 348.
[137] ibid.
[138] ibid.

of knowledge, if that lack of knowledge arises from indifference or carelessness. If he has the means of acquiring knowledge and deliberately 'shuts his eyes', he will not diminish his duty towards those to whom he supplies that animal.[139] He noted that Mathew LJ in *Clarke* spoke of 'the means of knowledge as being identical with knowledge'.[140] That Lord Dunedin in *Dominion Natural Gas* had cited *Thomas* as good law, was also noted by Lush J: in that case, he said, it had been held that a person who sent out a dangerous compound, the dangerous character of which he did not know, but would have known if he had used reasonable care, was as liable to third persons as if he had known.[141] Finally, Lush J turned to *George*, and said the following:

> In my view the decision in the much discussed case of *George* ... would, as I suggested in my judgment in *Blacker* ... have been in accordance with the authorities if it had been put on this ground. It has been disapproved, as the Court held in that case, in so far as it lays down or appears to lay down the principle that negligence in manufacturing an article gives a cause of action to a person who is not a party to the contract, but that is all. As I have pointed out, a duty to warn those who a manufacturer knows or contemplates will use a chattel which is dangerous in fact does not arise from contract.[142]

For these reasons, he said, Mrs White was entitled to judgment in this case. There was also said to be an alternative ground upon which judgment for Mrs White might be justified, based on control of the carriage and the defendant having invited or permitted Mrs White to use the carriage.[143]

White is thus at odds with *Bates*. What is clear is that Lush J equated actual knowledge with negligent failure to find out. Horridge J in *Bates* appears to have been trying to find a way to suggest that Lush J had not elided deliberate deception and negligent ignorance. This reasoning was not open to Lush J; it would amount to an overruling of *Winterbottom*. As noted above, this lack of clarity as to the precise knowledge requirement continued until 1932: Lord Macmillan referred in his speech in *Donoghue* to the apparent inconsistency between comments in *Bates* and in *White*, quoting Lush J's comments that a person who has the *means* of knowledge and avoids acquiring such knowledge is as liable as a person who has actual knowledge.[144] Lord Macmillan was in 1932 able to comment that in his view 'in a true case of negligence, knowledge of the existence of the defect causing damage is not an essential element at all'.[145] That Lush J took such an expansive view almost 20 years earlier is surprising.

Nevertheless, the argumentative strategy or alternative route to potential success for injured consumers was established. Ideally, it would be argued that the product was a thing 'dangerous in itself', following Lush J's description of the

[139] ibid.
[140] ibid. See *Clarke* (n 24) 168.
[141] *White* (n 113) 349.
[142] ibid.
[143] See discussion in *White* (n 113) 348–49 and authorities there cited.
[144] *Donoghue* (n 111) 616.
[145] ibid 617.

hair-wash in *George* as such an item in *Blacker*. If that were not possible, there may still have been scope for suggesting that an item was dangerous because of a defect about which the defendant knew or *ought to have known* (though this latter argument was on more shaky ground). Indeed, it was an argument that was pursued, albeit unsuccessfully, in *Mullen*: the pursuers' case, the assertion of a 'third exception' to the general rule that no duty existed between manufacturer and ultimate consumer, was based on the argument that it had been 'recognised that [*George*] could be supported on the ground that a person who sent out a dangerous compound, the dangerous character of which he did not know but would have known if he had used reasonable care, was in the same position as if he had known'.[146] For this proposition, *White* was cited. Even if there was lack of success in *Mullen*, it will be suggested later in this chapter that, before some courts at least, it appears to have been successful.

The major treatises on tort at this time were amended to include consideration of *Blacker*, *Batey* and *White*.[147] However, the numerous references to this 'supply of dangerous things' principle in the *Solicitors' Journal* are perhaps the most persuasive evidence of the notion that, certainly post-*Blacker*, it was part of common legal knowledge and recognised broadly as a pathway to success, across the legal community. This is a journal that was being read at the coal face of legal practice. These were principles and ideas that would have reached most of the legal community, and therefore are likely to have had an effect on the way claims were framed.

An early discussion of the matter appears in the December 1879 issue of the *Solicitors' Journal*.[148] It is consistent with the understanding that the 'supply of dangerous things' principle seems not to have been widely recognised as applicable to the sale and supply of goods before the twentieth century. The article, entitled 'Liabilities for negligence not arising out of contractual obligations', begins by introducing the recently decided *Parry*,[149] in which the defendant gasfitter was held liable for injuries caused to an employee of the party with whom he had contracted. After considering *Langridge* and *Longmeid*, discussion turns to the case of *George*. The authors note that, in that case, the court extended the doctrine in *Langridge* to a situation in which there had not been fraud but merely negligence.[150] They add, however, that they could not 'help thinking that the analogy between this case and *Langridge*, which the Court of Exchequer [in *George*] insisted on, is misleading'.[151] The authors suggest that *Langridge* turned on the defendant's false representation to the plaintiff, whereas *George* 'must turn … on

[146] *Mullen v Barr* 1929 SC 461, 465.
[147] See, eg, F Pollock, *The Law of Torts*, 10th edn (Stevens and Sons, 1916) 529; JW Salmond, *The Law of Torts*, 4th edn (Stevens and Haynes, 1916) 423–24.
[148] 'Liabilities for negligence not arising out of contractual obligations' (1879) 24 *Solicitors' Journal and Reporter* 101.
[149] Considered in ch 2.
[150] 'Liabilities for negligence not arising out of contractual obligations' (n 148) 103–05.
[151] ibid 104.

the principle that a person is responsible in damages for his negligence to any person whom he knew that his negligence might injure'.[152] In support of this argument, they observe that it would seem absurd that if a man purchased a bottle of hair-wash, and told the seller that it was for his wife, his wife could recover but that if she were not mentioned to the seller, she could not do so. They note, though, that, if *George* were as broad as they suggest, this may lead to some 'rather sweeping and startling consequences'.[153] Given their wider formulation, it does not seem that the authors of this article understand *George* to be a case falling within the class concerning the supply of dangerous goods.

By 1913, however, there appears to have been more confidence in the availability of damages for non-contracting parties, provided certain features were present. An article published in a June 1913 issue of the *Solicitors' Journal* identifies three classes of case where a remedy in tort is available 'to new parties in addition to those who can claim in contract'.[154] The first type of case is said to be where a railway company accepts, as passengers, a master and servant; while the master alone is the contracting party, both master and servant may sue if injured during transit by the negligence of the railway company's employees.[155] The second is where a surgeon operates on one party at another's request, the example given being where a surgeon attends to a child but contracts with the parent. If the child is injured by the negligence of the surgeon, the parent can recover for breach of contract, but the child can also recover in tort for 'the surgeon's performance of a dangerous act in an unskilful way'.[156] Finally, it is said that where a 'dangerous gun or a poisonous hair-wash is supplied by a dealer … (who warrants it harmless)',[157] a member of the contracting party's family who uses the item and is injured in the process can recover in tort. The reason for liability is said to be that the sale of such articles 'is a fraud'.[158] *Langridge* and *George* are both cited for this proposition. It does appear as if the outcome in *George* is, once again, being understood as based on fraud. However, later in the article it is noted that the outcome in *Earl*, where the injured passenger of a poorly repaired wheel was unsuccessful, may have been different if 'the wheel had been a dangerous thing, *or* had any element of fraud entered in' (emphasis added).[159] Then, it is said, *Langridge* would have applied and a duty would be owed.[160] In any event, what is evident here is that there is, by this time, a pathway to a remedy seen as being available to plaintiffs. This is particularly evident in the

[152] ibid.
[153] ibid.
[154] 'Tortious Breach of Contract' (1913) 57 *Solicitors' Journal and Weekly Reporter* 571, 575–76.
[155] For this, *Marshall v The York, Newcastle & Berwick Railway Company* (1851) 11 CB 655, 138 ER 632, is cited.
[156] 'Tortious Breach of Contract' (n 154) 575.
[157] ibid 575.
[158] ibid.
[159] ibid.
[160] ibid.

final part of this 1913 article, which discussed the recently decided case of *White*. It is explained that, in order to recover in tort,

> the wife had to shew an independent duty owed to her on the part of the carriage-owners apart altogether from the contract. In other words, she had to bring her case within the class of which *Levy v. Langridge* (supra) is typical, and not the class of which *Cavalier v. Pope* is the most familiar example.[161]

Fortunately for Mrs White, she had been able to bring her case within the class: the horse was vicious, and the defendants ought to have known about it. The authors final comment is that Lush J's judgment in *White* avoided 'such an awkward result as that which followed in *Cavalier*'.[162] The availability of the 'supply of dangerous things' argument was evidently seen by these authors as a welcome development.

In a July issue of the same year, the principle is articulated from the outset of the article, which is entitled 'Dangerous Things':

> In *Bates* .... Horridge, J., had to consider the question whether or not a ginger-beer bottle is an inherently dangerous thing so as to saddle with liability, for damage to any person injured by the bursting thereof, the original manufacturer or wholesale vendor of the bottle.[163]

Having cited cases including *Langridge*, *George* and *White*, the article explains that, in cases such as these, a 'stranger … both as regards privity in contract and immediacy in tort', recovers, because the supplier of a dangerous thing is guilty of 'a nuisance' if the thing does harm.[164] The word 'nuisance' appears to be used in a loose sense here. The understanding of *George* as a case concerning the supply of a dangerous item is clear; it is said that in *George*, the 'dangerous chattel was a "hair-wash"':

> But it is otherwise if the article supplied is not inherently dangerous, but only becomes so because of some latent defect; then the supplier is only liable if he knew of the latent defect or otherwise by his negligence caused it (*per* Parke B in *Longmeid*).[165]

The inclusion of 'or otherwise by his negligence caused it' is surprising but adds to the picture created by the decision in *White* that there was some flexibility in the application of this principle. In any event to the list of such articles not inherently dangerous but potentially so 'must now [following *Bates*] be added bottles which contain ginger-beer', said the authors.[166]

The issue of the *Solicitors' Journal* of 6 May 1922 contains a short piece commenting on a decision of Rowlatt J, *Macrorie v Smith*.[167] This case,

[161] ibid 576.
[162] ibid.
[163] 'Dangerous Things' (1913) 57 *Solicitors' Journal and Weekly Reporter* 639, 641.
[164] ibid.
[165] ibid.
[166] ibid.
[167] 'Hair-Dyes as a Dangerous Chattel' (1922) 66 *Solicitors' Journal and Weekly Reporter* 467, 467.

reported in *The Times*, concerned a married woman who was a customer of the defendant hairdresser. She alleged that she had been to have her hair dyed by him in the past with no resulting harm, and that he had told her then that the dye was 'in some sense poisonous but not dangerous for use'.[168] However, on the occasion in question, she had become very unwell after this service was performed. She claimed that the defendant hairdresser had been told of her propensity for attacks of psoriasis and that she would only have her hair dyed if it was safe to do so. He had said to her that he would put on a little of the dye and finish the treatment the following week. However, after this first treatment she became very ill with acute dermatitis – her head 'had become one running blister, and … [h]er body was also covered with spots and her nails became black'.[169]

Various witness testimonies are reported in two articles in *The Times*.[170] The doctor called as witness for the plaintiff is reported to have said under cross-examination that the dye, 'the analysis of which he knew', might be used by most people whose skin was in good condition, and in 'favourable circumstances it might be applied to a head afflicted with psoriasis, which was a complaint liable to sudden outbreak'.[171] It appears that in this case, the manufacturer of the dye had been called as a witness but was not a defendant. His evidence was that he had never known of any ill effects from the use of the dye, called 'Remido', and that on numerous occasions it had been applied to persons suffering from skin disease. He claimed that if given the opportunity, he could 'prove by direct evidence before the Court … that "Remido" did not hurt a person who was suffering from skin disease'.[172]

The defendant hairdresser denied that he had ever had a conversation with the plaintiff about whether or not 'Remido' was dangerous. Reference was made to the spate of cases concerning the 'Inecto' hair dye, considered in detail in chapter four. Mr Shakespeare, counsel for the defendant, referred to an earlier 'Inecto' case[173] in which the manufacturer (rather than the hairdresser) had been held liable, and said that 'the defendant [in the present case] would never have been such a fool as to defend the action if he had not honestly believed himself to be in no way to blame'.[174] Counsel for the plaintiff had replied that it made no difference whether or not it was 'Remido' that was used; whatever the preparation used, the

[168] See 'Hair Dyes: A Woman's Claim to Damages' *The Times* (29 April 1922); 'Hair Dyes: Woman's Claim against a Barber' *The Times* (2 May 1922).

[169] ibid.

[170] See 'Hair Dyes: A Woman's Claim to Damages' (n 168); 'Hair Dyes: Woman's Claim against a Barber' (n 168).

[171] 'Hair Dyes: A Woman's Claim to Damages' (n 168).

[172] 'Hair Dyes: Woman's Claim against a Barber' (n 168).

[173] See 'Injury Caused by a Hair Dye: Rivette v. Inecto, Ltd' *The Times* (28 February 1922).

[174] 'Hair Dyes: Woman's Claim against a Barber' (n 168).

defendant was guilty of negligence, as it was clear that the preparation had caused the injuries.[175]

Rowlatt J delivered judgment in favour of the plaintiff, awarding £60 in damages. He is reported to have said that, in this, and all similar cases, the basis of the claim must be negligence, and it could not be founded on breach of warranty.[176] The (somewhat confusing) reason given for this assertion is that, when a woman goes to a hairdresser, she cannot know what was in the composition being used but puts her trust in her hairdresser – it is for him to show that what he had used was harmless. There might also be cases, he noted, where the hairdresser would warrant that the preparation was harmless. By the 1950s it had been held that, in a contract between hairdresser and customer involving the application of dye, there was an implied term in the contract, analogous to the corresponding term for the sale of goods, of fitness for purpose. However, it is not clear that this was the position before the 1930s.[177] In any event, Rowlatt J relied upon the ground of negligence. He was convinced that the dye had caused the injuries, but noted that the evidence of negligence was not strong and he was not convinced that 'Remido' was actually used.[178] 'Remido' contained cobalt, and no trace of cobalt was found in the hair sample analysis. However, '[o]n the whole he was satisfied that the illnesses from which this unhappy woman suffered … were the results of the hair dye' and he gave judgment for the plaintiff.[179]

Several things are noteworthy about this case, as well as the report of it in the *Solicitors' Journal*. The case itself suggests that plaintiffs injured by a defective product enjoyed a strong chance of success. The judge here notes that there was not strong evidence of negligence, apparently in the provision of treatment, on the part of the hairdresser, yet the plaintiff is still successful. Of course, the product was clearly defective and, in the absence of alternative explanations, it would often not be an unreasonable conclusion that it was the defendant's fault. However, here the defendant was not the maker of the product. The comments by counsel for the defendant as to the choice to defend at all suggest that successful claims following this sort of event were relatively common.

In the corresponding article in the *Solicitors' Journal*,[180] the author notes that the judge appeared to see two possible bases for the plaintiff's claim: it was either in 'negligence' or in 'warranty'. The author explains further: 'either the defendant had warranted that the hair-dye could be applied to the scalp without danger, or

[175] ibid.
[176] ibid.
[177] See *GH Myers v Brent Cross Service Company* [1934] KB 46; *Ingham v Emes* [1955] 2 QB 366.
[178] 'Hair Dyes: Woman's Claim against a Barber' (n 168).
[179] ibid.
[180] 'Hair-Dyes as a Dangerous Chattel' (n 167) 467.

else he had been guilty of ignorance or carelessness as an expert, in [the] treatment of the hair'.[181] The author of the article suggests that there is, in fact, a third possibility,

> namely, that anyone who supplies a dangerous article in the course of trade, or practices an art entailing concealed dangers, must be held to do so at his peril! Indeed, in *George* ... it was held that a 'hair-wash' is a 'dangerous chattel' to which the principle of *Langridge* ... applies.[182]

This suggests a loosening of what might be considered sufficiently 'dangerous' to give rise to a duty of care, and therefore to suppliers' liability. It also provides another example of *George*'s being recharacterised, or confirmed, as a case concerning the supply of a dangerous chattel. This recharacterisation of *George*, as well as the accompanying loosening of the boundaries of what might be a sufficiently dangerous chattel, opened up a viable legal pathway for would-be litigants. Anything that causes harm is, by definition, 'dangerous'; the exception has the potential to contain every case.

As to the knowledge requirement, a short question and answer in the 'Points in Practice' section of the 18 October 1930 issue of the *Solicitors' Journal* gives some insight as to what might create 'actual knowledge', though little detail is provided. A question was sent in by a subscriber seeking advice on the action available where '[a] coat with a fur collar was sold ... at a very low price, and the wearer of the fur contracted dermatitis and seeks to saddle the firm with damages for the resulting consequence ... [and] no warranty [was] given'.[183] The reply given is that an action would be maintainable under the Sale of Goods Act 1893, though there could be an issue of proving that the dermatitis was caused by the collar. This is unsurprising; of greater interest is the further comment provided towards the end of the answer: 'if there is any evidence of previous complaints, an action will also lie for negligence'.[184] A bevy of complaints could mean that an item might be deemed dangerous in itself, or, at least, would saddle the manufacturer with 'actual knowledge' sufficient for a negligence claim based on the supply of a defective, dangerous item. It is likely that it was this notion underpinning the numerous successful claims against hair dye manufacturers (and potentially also suppliers of fur coats) outlined in chapter four.

B. Hair Dye: A 'Dangerous Thing'

The vast majority of reports of the actions considered in chapter four, whether with respect to furs, dye or foodstuffs, contain little information as to the precise

[181] ibid.
[182] ibid.
[183] 'Points in Practice: Q: 2034' (1930) 74 *Solicitors' Journal* 687, 687.
[184] ibid.

grounds upon which the claim was based. This makes analysis of their argumentative strategy speculative. Occasionally, though, a more detailed glimpse is provided. More informative reports appeared in *The Times* during the 1920s relating to injuries sustained through the application of hair dye. It seems that, certainly for injuries caused by hair dye, the claims were framed as arising out of the supply of a dangerous thing. A significant loosening of what might be considered 'dangerous' is evident. Privity was, therefore, no problem for parties seeking redress.

The clearest indication that this is the strategy used by litigants comes from a report in *The Times* of an action by Miss Rivette against Inecto Limited, as she had sustained injuries after using a hair dye manufactured by Inecto.[185] Inecto was, as seen in chapter four, sued several times during the 1920s, and was said to have gained notoriety following the Rivette action – before being wound up.[186] This was not a case of a married woman's bringing an action: Miss Rivette was, in all likelihood, straightforwardly a party to the contract of service with the hairdresser. However, in her action she was suing, in addition to the hairdresser, the manufacturer Inecto as principal defendant. There was no contractual relationship with Inecto. The report describes the case for defendant:

> In opening the case for Inecto, Limited Mr. Giveen said he would call no evidence, but would submit that there was no contractual liability between the plaintiff and his clients. The plaintiff had to show that the company sent out, without adequate warning, a substance which was dangerous. It could not be said that this dye came within the category of dangerous things, as it had been used in thousands of cases without ill effects. He cited Blacker and Lake v. Elliot … in support of his contention.[187]

Mr Beazley, for the other defendant (the hairdresser, Mr Lauper), submitted that there was no negligence, and that he had no knowledge that the hair dye preparation was dangerous.[188] He cited, in support, *Clarke*.

Bailhache J gave judgment for the plaintiff in the action against Inecto, and she was awarded £200 in damages. The warning sent out by the company had been insufficient.[189] The action against Mr Lauper was, however, dismissed without costs. The report goes on:

> Bailhache J … [held] that he was not negligent in the circumstances, but he (his Lordship) thought that a letter of complaint from Lauper to Inecto, Limited, that four customers had complained of erysipelas after the use of the dye – although largely untrue – ought to have put him on his guard, but he must distinctly understand that after this warning he could not hope to be absolved again if he continued to use this preparation.[190]

[185] 'Injury Caused by a Hair Dye: Rivette v. Inecto, Limited' (n 173).
[186] See 'Compulsory Winding-up of Hair-Dye Company' *The Times* (5 July 1922).
[187] 'Injury Caused by a Hair Dye: Rivette v. Inecto, Limited' (n 173).
[188] ibid.
[189] ibid. See also 'Hair-dye Injury' *Chemist and Druggist* (4 March 1922).
[190] 'Injury Caused by a Hair Dye: Rivette v. Inecto, Limited' (n 173).

Inecto was also sued by Mrs Lillie Pendry in the King's Bench, and settled the claim, in January 1922.[191] Again, the argument as reported in *The Times* seems to have been that Inecto had supplied a dangerous article:

> Mr White, opening the case, said that the allegation was that the defendants were guilty of breach of warranty and negligence in supplying the plaintiff with the compound, which was known as 'Inecto Rapid', a hair colouring dye, which was poisonous and likely to give anyone who used it eczema.

It is reported that the plaintiff's evidence was that she was not told that the dye was dangerous. Medical evidence was also given to the effect that the dye was not safe to use in certain cases and could produce a rash in 'predisposed cases'.[192] The strength of this line of argument appears to be confirmed by the fact that Inecto apparently chose not to defend the claim and settled after the first day of evidence.

Another Inecto case was reported in the *The Times* in October of the same year, though this time it was a case before the Westminster County Court.[193] The report is short, but it is noted that Mrs Ellen Williams was awarded £100 in damages in her claim against the manager of Inecto for the injuries she had sustained. Counsel for the plaintiff is reported to have claimed that she proceeded to have the treatment done 'on the assurance of the defendant that the process was harmless'.[194] The defence put forward for Inecto appears to have been based on causation grounds, rather than taking issue with the duty point: 'Mr Hilbury, for the defence, contended that the defendant was not liable, and called medical evidence to dispute the plaintiff's case that her injuries were the result of the dye applications'.[195] Judge Tobin was said to have found that the defendant had represented to the plaintiff that the process was harmless, 'although at the time he must have known that eczema might be produced'.[196] Again, the known dangerous nature of the preparation is the basis for the successful claim.

The 1926 case brought by Mrs Esme Gozney was considered in chapter four. Mrs Gozney's claim was also against Inecto as manufacturer. The additional detail provided in *The Times* report of this case suggests that it was indeed another instance of the successful use of the 'supply of dangerous things' argument.[197] The report describes the action as one in which Mrs Gozney 'sought to recover from Rapidol, Limited … the proprietors of the hair-dye "Inecto Rapid" damages for alleged negligence, and breach of duty and warranty of the *sale of dangerous goods*' (emphasis added).[198] Evidence was given by several witnesses of numerous

[191] 'A woman's hair dye' *The Times* (12 January 1922).
[192] ibid.
[193] 'Eczema from Hair Dye' *The Times* (31 October 1922).
[194] ibid.
[195] ibid.
[196] ibid.
[197] 'The "Inecto" action: £500 damages' *The Times* (19 May 1926).
[198] ibid.

complaints about the preparation; the company certainly knew of the risks posed by their hair dye. The jury in this case returned a verdict for the plaintiff, and she was awarded the sum of £544 in damages.

There is another aspect of this case that deserves attention. A report of proceedings in the *Bucks Herald* highlights a further detail:[199] evidence was given that 407,000 sets of two bottles had been sold each year in the last three years, yet only three actions had resulted.[200] This does suggest a rather more liberal understanding of something that might be 'dangerous' than we might expect from comments in earlier case law. Similarly, a report in the *Leeds Mercury* notes that a Dr Footner, who appears to have been called as witness, had said that in the past 16 months, he had seen 16 cases of complaints about Inecto but that they were not serious cases.[201] Certainly, the defendant company knew of the risk of dermatitis from the use of their product; there had been several actions. However, here (as in other similar cases) that risk, known but small, and perhaps only rarely serious, is being treated as taking the product into the category of a 'dangerous thing'. Interestingly, the product clearly came with some instructions, in an accompanying pamphlet, to conduct a test before application, which had not been followed by Mrs Gozney.[202] This did not, however, change the result. Evidence of the rarity of illness, as well as the accompanying instructions, was also given in Mrs Akerman's successful suit against the vendors of the product, which was considered in chapter four. The defendants said that they took care not to recommend Inecto, knowing that it was not suitable for everyone, and took care that when they did sell Inecto they also provided the instructions.[203]

Beyond *The Times*, there is the occasional glimpse of the utilisation of this legal pathway in other newspapers as well. It will be recalled that Permanol Limited was successfully sued in the King's Bench in 1924 by Mrs Louise Barber.[204] In that case, Permanol 'denied negligence or warranty, or that Permanol was *a noxious and dangerous preparation*'.[205] In 1928, a report of yet another hair dye case, this time from Scotland, clearly shows that the claim was argued on the grounds that hair dye was a 'dangerous thing'.[206] Mrs Macrossan was successful in her claim in the Court of Session against Mary London, a hairdresser, and was awarded £450 by the jury. It is expressly noted in the report that Mrs Macrossan 'averred that [the defender's manager] used a hair dye that was of a dangerous character and that, if applied to some persons, acted as an irritant poison and produced dermatitis and

[199] 'Lady's Injuries from a Hair Dye' *Bucks Herald* (22 May 1926).

[200] ibid.

[201] 'Hair Dye Poison' *Leeds Mercury* (19 May 1926).

[202] See, eg, '£544 Damages: Woman's Action against Hair Dye Company' *Sheffield Daily Telegraph*, 19 May 1926.

[203] See, eg, 'Hair Dye in a Court Case' *Pall Mall Gazette* (17 October 1923).

[204] 'Women's Use of Hair Dye' *Westminster Gazette* (29 March 1924).

[205] ibid.

[206] 'Danger in Hair Dye' *The Scotsman* (23 June 1928).

other diseases of the skin'.[207] Of course, she alleged that, had she been aware of the particular dye that was to be used, she would not have permitted the application. The defender claimed to have warned of the risks, but apparently did not convince the jury.

C. Application to Other Kinds of Goods

How, then, does this assist us to understand the prevalence of successful cases against suppliers and manufacturers of all kinds of defective goods during the 1910s and 1920s, which was the subject of chapter four? While a few reports of hair dye claims make explicit reference to the 'supply of dangerous things' principle, most cases considered in chapter four do not. Nevertheless, the hypothesis that this principle was the basis for most of these claims provides a plausible explanation as to why these cases are causing no kind of legal 'splash'. The defendants, or rather, their lawyers, were not raising the lack of privity as a bar to the plaintiff's claim because it was not a bar to a claim concerning the supply of a dangerous article.

Would we not, then, expect the lawyers to object that the items were scarcely *dangerous* in themselves? A loaded gun is very different from some hair dye. Alternatively, perhaps an objection that the defendant did not *know* of the defect or danger?

We turn first to the numerous claims during the 1920s involving dermatitis caused by hair dye. Already in the first decade of the twentieth century, and certainly by the 1920s, hair-wash (as in *George*) was identified as a dangerous article, to which a duty of care might attach if sufficient care were not taken in its supply. This would have required some considerable loosening in what might be considered 'dangerous'; previously, successful claims involved things like guns or deadly poisons – more obviously dangerous things. A pathway to a successful claim was thus open to women who had contracted dermatitis and suffered after the application of the defective hair dye, but who were not parties to the contract of sale. This would neatly explain why these cases appeared to have been moved with ease through the courts, sometimes resulting in settlement, and often resulting in significant awards of damages in favour of the injured women. There would be no need even to enquire into their ability to sue: as parties injured through the receipt of a dangerous article, or an article dangerous if defective, the contract need not supply the obligation: they were owed a duty outside the contract. The courts involved did not have to address the tension between the strict application of the privity rule and the desire to provide compensation: the 'supply of dangerous things' exception provided the mechanism for resolving any tension in the hands of a sympathetic court. Of course, there may have been

[207] ibid. See also 'Hairdresser to pay £450 damages' *Dundee Courier and Advertiser* (23 June 1928).

unsympathetic courts which refused to engage in any loosening, and defendants providing a serious legal argument for the court to address. The cases considered in chapter four are not a representative sample; we are not necessarily seeing the cases where the claim has failed. Nevertheless, an answer must be sought for the trend described.

The same legal mechanism would have been open to the women affected by cheap, dermatitis-inducing fur garments. Again, as considered in chapter four, there is no discussion of the problem privity might pose for these claims: defendants seem generally to have relied upon arguments of fact and causation. A reason for this might be that the point of law could not sensibly be contested: the 'danger' posed by treated furs of acute dermatitis was so well-known that defendants simply accepted these articles as dangerous items carrying a duty of care beyond the contract. The method of defending such claims would then fall to arguments of fact, suggesting that there was insufficient evidence that the fur contained the requisite harmful chemicals or caused the dermatitis.

The claims involving exploding ginger beer bottles were unsuccessful. After several such incidents received publicity in the newspapers, it is perhaps surprising that defendants could still escape liability, as in *Bates*, by claiming lack of knowledge. On the other hand, it may be unsurprising that the manufacturer could escape liability when the vendor, too, would have known of the danger. However, as in the case of the seven-year-old Camelo, where a bottle contained some surprise item (there, a mouse) that led to illness upon consumption, this might indeed ground a successful claim – at least before a single judge of the King's Bench, if not before the Scottish Court of Session in *Mullen*.[208] It is difficult to suggest that the contents of a beverage bottle might be *inherently* dangerous, unless the same were to be said of all items of food and drink, which necessarily carry some level of risk of contamination. It is more likely that it was a case of danger by defect, and that here, as in *White*, it was found that the defendant *ought to have known*. It is reported of the *Camelo* case that Salter J was satisfied that there had been negligence and was satisfied that the mouse had 'rendered [the drink] somewhat dangerous to health'.[209] It is, it must be admitted, more difficult to understand how cases of unexpected objects in items of food and drink could have met with success in the courts. Nevertheless, they seem to have succeeded, at least on some occasions. Unexpected objects in items of food and drink were also a frequent enough occurrence. Given contemporary concerns with food safety (leading, amongst other things, to the enactment several pieces of legislation concerned with safety standards) it is not unlikely that some courts might be prepared to find contaminated food to be sufficiently 'dangerous', and for knowledge requirements to be satisfied. Lord Moncrieff, who delivered the first instance decision in favour

[208] See ch 4; 'Mouse in Bottle of Lemon Squash' *Evening Telegraph* (24 June 1920); *cf Mullen* (n 146) 461.

[209] 'Mouse in Bottle of Lemon Squash' (n 208); 'Mouse in Bottle of Lemon Squash' *Leeds Mercury* (25 June 1920).

of Mrs Donoghue in her action against Stevenson,[210] appeared convinced that, if bringing a claim within the exceptional category of the 'supply of dangerous goods' were necessary for success (which he denied), then a snail in a bottle was a fitting example:

> I am unhesitatingly of the opinion that those who deal with the production of food or produce fluids for beverage purposes ought not to be heard to plead ignorance of the active danger which will be associated with their products, as a consequence of any imperfect observation of cleanliness at any stage in the course of the process of manufacture. *The danger of infection is such as is or should be known in every domestic kitchen and still room. Tainted food when offered for sale is, in my opinion, amongst the most subtly potent of 'dangerous goods', and to deal in or prepare such food is highly relevant to infer a duty. I fail to see why the fact that the danger has been introduced by an act of negligence and does not advertise itself, should release the negligent manufacturer from a duty, or afford him a supplementary defence* (emphasis added).[211]

The case of accidental strychnine poisoning is likely to have been approached as a case involving the supply of an inherently dangerous thing, as in *Thomas*.[212]

We might, therefore, understand the claims revealed in chapter four as being examples of litigants and their lawyers using a route that had been opened to them from around 1903 and the *Clarke* decision, then confirmed and widely advertised in cases, journals and textbooks of the later 1900s and 1910s. This legal mechanism was wide in scope: anything causing injury could, by reason of that very fact, potentially be described as 'dangerous'. It would provide a way of side-stepping *Winterbottom* prior to *Donoghue*, in the hands of a sufficiently sympathetic judge and jury.

D. 'Dangerous Things' in *Donoghue*

Another question remains. Why did these cases not feature more prominently before the House of Lords in *Donoghue*? Counsel for Mrs Donoghue certainly raised and acknowledged the existence of exceptions to the general principle of no duty on the manufacturer based upon the article's being dangerous per se, or being dangerous to the knowledge of the manufacturer.[213] It was submitted for

[210] Lord Moncrieff's opinion was not reproduced in the report of the House of Lords decision, but is available on the Scottish Council of Law Reporting's website: *Donoghue v Stevenson: Resources*, Scottish Council of Law Reporting, www.scottishlawreports.org.uk/resources/donoghue-v-stevenson/appeal-papers/index-of-appendix-opinion/.

[211] Opinion of Lord Moncrieff, 27 June 1930, ibid, 6.

[212] See, with respect to the supply of poison, Stallybrass (n 40) 379.

[213] *Donoghue* (n 111) 564.

Mrs Donoghue that the duty was not, in fact, so limited.[214] However, the claims and trends outlined in chapter four do not feature expressly in the opinions of the Law Lords.

It has already been noted that Lord Macmillan acknowledged the need for injured consumers, if they were to succeed, to fit their claims within the 'supply of dangerous things' line of authorities. All speeches in *Donoghue* do, in fact, acknowledge and discuss, in varying detail, the 'supply of dangerous things' exception to the general principle against suits by third parties. It may be that the method by which most of these claims were reported – in local newspapers – simply meant that the Law Lords did not have a comprehensive view of how many successful claims had been brought.

Lord Buckmaster, part of the dissenting minority in *Donoghue*, said that 'no-one [could] suggest that ginger-beer was an article dangerous in itself'.[215] As to *George*, Lord Buckmaster did not appear to understand it as a 'supply of dangerous things' case but, rather, saw it as a case turning on fraudulent misrepresentation. Commenting on Cleasby B's substitution of 'negligence' for 'fraud', he said, witheringly, that it was 'unnecessary to point out too emphatically that such a substitution cannot possibly be made … [n]o action based on fraud can be supported by mere proof of negligence'.[216] So far as it involved an attempt to lay down a wider principle, namely that the manufacturer of an article owed a duty in the law of negligence to the final consumer, it was in conflict with *Winterbottom* and could not be supported. He preferred that it be 'buried so securely that [its] perturbed spirit[] shall no longer vex the law'.[217] He characterised *Thomas* as a case involving the supply of an article dangerous in itself: 'It seems to me that the decision might well rest on the principle that he, in fact, sold a drug dangerous in itself, none the less so because he was asked to sell something else, and on this view the case does not advance the matter'.[218] Indeed, Lord Buckmaster's comments fit the notion that the only route to success for plaintiffs would be by arguing that their claim involved the supply of a dangerous thing, though there is no indication that he was aware of the cases discussed in the previous chapter:

> [W]ith the exception of *George* … no case directly involving the principle has ever succeeded in the Courts, and, were it well known and accepted, much of the discussion of the earlier cases would have been waste of time, and the distinction as to

[214] ibid.
[215] ibid 569.
[216] ibid 570.
[217] ibid 576.
[218] ibid 577.

> articles dangerous in themselves or known to be dangerous to the vendor would be meaningless.[219]

Lord Tomlin's speech is brief and largely in agreement with Lord Buckmaster.

In the majority, Lord Atkin's speech appears far more concerned with tackling *Winterbottom* directly. Rather than considering at length the 'supply of dangerous things' exception, he attempted to formulate a general principle, which, with appropriate qualifications, would make restrictive rules and specific exceptions unnecessary.[220] Lord Atkin argued that *George* was based on an 'ordinary duty to take care',[221] and not on fraud (or, presumably, since it is not mentioned, the supply of a dangerous article).[222] As to the 'supply of dangerous things' category, Lord Atkin said:

> I do not find it necessary to discuss at length the cases dealing with duties where the thing is dangerous, or, in the narrower category, belongs to a class of things which are dangerous in themselves. I regard the distinction as an unnatural one so far as it is used to serve as a logical differentiation by which to distinguish the existence or non-existence of a legal right.
>
> . . .
>
> The nature of the thing may very well call for different degrees of care, and the person dealing with it may well contemplate persons as being within the sphere of his duty to take care who would not be sufficiently proximate with less dangerous goods; so that not only the degree of care but the range of persons to whom a duty is owed may be extended. *But they all illustrate the general principle* (emphasis added).[223]

Lord Thankerton, also part of the majority, was dismissive of any suggestion that Mrs Donoghue's case might be a case concerning the supply of a dangerous article, which, he said, would give rise to a special duty of protection or adequate warning on the person using or distributing it.[224]

Lord Macmillan, of course, acknowledged that the 'supply of dangerous things' exception had, until this point, been one of the few potential routes for injured consumers seeking damages – they were 'driven to bring [their claims] within … the exceptional cases'.[225] It might be objected here, against the argument advanced in this book, that one would not find oneself 'driven to' an obviously successful strategy. However, even if it provided a route to success for a good number of claims pre-*Donoghue*, there was, of course, always the possibility that a particular court would not be amenable to any 'loose' arguments about danger (or knowledge). The appellant in the case before the House, Lord

[219] ibid 578.
[220] See, eg, *Donoghue* (n 111) 580–82.
[221] ibid 584.
[222] See also *Donoghue* (n 111) 591.
[223] ibid 596.
[224] ibid 603.
[225] ibid 611.

Macmillan noted, was not attempting to invoke the cases making up the 'special instance of negligence' concerning dangerous things. She did not 'require' to do so, he said.

III. Conclusions: A Solution within the Orthodox Law

This chapter has suggested that the trend observed in chapter four (namely, the success of claims that ought, on their face, to have failed) may plausibly be explained, at least in part, by a legal pathway opened to litigants at the beginning of the twentieth century and based on the supply of dangerous articles. While this line of argument is explicitly identified in certain reports of the 1920s claims concerning harm-inducing hair dye, it is obscured by the brief reporting of many other actions. Nevertheless, it explains why these successful claims, many against manufacturers, seemed to be causing no legal 'splash' (and would not immediately be overturned on appeal): the argument was available in the orthodox law – in the hands of a sufficiently sympathetic court. The 'supply of dangerous things' exception provided a mechanism whereby courts were able to provide compensation where they perceived justice demanded it. It provided a way of resolving a tension that might otherwise exist between doctrine – the privity rule, which was to be strictly applied – and the results perceived to be just. In many of the cases discussed in chapter four, the doctrinal argument would have been rather feeble. However, it is plausible that courts were sufficiently sympathetic to those injured by defective products that they sometimes ignored the doctrinal difficulty – and even, on occasion, appeared to have stopped the defendant from raising it.

There were limits to the 'supply of dangerous things' argument. It could be defeated where there were insufficient grounds for knowledge of the danger – whichever view is taken of the knowledge requirement. There would also have been cases where it would clearly be stretching the argument to its limits to suggest that there was indeed a truly 'dangerous' article being supplied. Lord Macmillan's opinion contains a glimmer of discontent with the practice, necessitated by the perceived gap in the law, of litigants' squeezing their claims into the 'supply of a dangerous thing' category. This seems to have been influential in his acceptance of Mrs Donoghue's arguments for a duty in the supply of goods outside this category.

Nevertheless, it seems to have succeeded on numerous occasions. The trend observed in chapter four could be seen as undermining, or at least side-stepping the effect of, the privity rule. The more widespread such a practice becomes, the greater the pressure brought to bear upon the formal rules to avoid the incongruity. This is not something happening tucked away in the countryside; many of the decisions reported come from the King's Bench. We are dealing with higher court decisions, not merely county court matters. As early as 1920, there seems to have been a King's Bench doppelgänger, in facts but also outcome, of *Donoghue* (albeit with a mouse and a lemonade bottle in the lead roles).

That the argument based on the 'supply of dangerous things' was rejected in *Mullen* in 1929 is likely to have brought matters to a head. With that line of argument shut down by a court at that level, the need for reconsideration of the restrictive rules was more urgent than ever. The time was ripe for a snail in a bottle to precipitate a change to the formal rules.

Conclusion: *Donoghue v Stevenson* in Legal History

Donoghue did not remake the law of negligence in 1932. It acquired its near-folkloric status much later. At the time, it was understood in narrow terms: *Donoghue* had recognised another relationship potentially giving rise to a duty of care, and ultimate consumers were thereafter able to bring actions in negligence against manufacturers of products, though only in circumstances where there was no opportunity for inspection of the product and therefore detection of its defect.[1] Lord Atkin's rejection of the analysis of negligence based on many duties of care, and his preference for a general principle requiring reasonable care to avoid foreseeable injuries,[2] was not the approach that was followed in the aftermath of the decision. Instead, many contemporary commentators and courts continued to see as correct an approach to negligence based on numerous categories of recognised duty situations, albeit with the possibility of new categories' being recognised.[3]

However, for consumers who had suffered loss through manufacturers' carelessness, the case was a significant, and welcome, step. This book has sought to understand better the ousting of the privity rule from the law of negligence in 1932. It has been suggested here that several strands of development, both within and outside the law, may be identified which, taken together, created a climate where one further problem became the tipping point for legal change. Mrs Donoghue's case, the tipping point, was brought at a time when the economic, social and legal circumstances were markedly different from those present in 1842, when *Winterbottom* was decided.

There were several conditions creating pressure for change by the 1930s. Consumerism, aided by technological developments of the industrial age, had reached all parts of British society. Producers of goods were increasingly distant from final consumers, which meant greater consumer vulnerability, as there might

[1] See, eg, *Dransfield v British Insulated Cables* [1937] 4 All ER 382, (1936–38) 54 TLR 11; *Otto v Bolton and Norris* [1936] 2 KB 46; 1 All ER 960; *Grant v Australian Knitting Mills* [1936] AC 85, 102–05. See also D Ibbetson, *A Historical Introduction to the Law of Obligations* (Oxford University Press, 1999) 190–; P Mitchell, *A History of Tort Law, 1900–1950* (Cambridge University Press, 2015) 5; RFV Heuston, '*Donoghue v Stevenson* in Retrospect' (1957) 20 *Modern Law Review* 1, 6–9.

[2] He was not, however, suggesting an unlimited approach: he emphasised the need for proximity, and a negligent manufacturer would avoid liability if there had been a reasonable opportunity of inspection before receipt by the consumer: see D Ibbetson, 'The tort of negligence in England' in N Jansen (ed), *The Development and Making of Legal Doctrine* (Cambridge University Press, 2010) 65.

[3] Ibbetson, *Historical Introduction to the Law of Obligations* (n 1) 190–91.

be no direct relationship between the two parties on which to rely if anything were to happen. Production of goods was also occurring on a much larger scale, and often in the hands of large enterprises more capable of spreading losses than their nineteenth-century predecessors. Related to this, liability insurance was, by the 1920s, readily available to protect manufacturers and vendors from the dangers posed by recognition of liability in negligence: the losses would not fall upon an individual party but could be spread amongst all who turned to insurance for protection. This meant that the *Winterbottom* court's concerns about the burden of increased litigation and liability, caused in part by the inability of many commercial parties to spread their losses, no longer held the same persuasive force. It has been argued elsewhere that a change in loss-spreading practices and the development of liability insurance might lie behind the outcome in *Donoghue*. This book confirms that the timing of its development supports this theory. However, a mono-causal understanding is not realistic. It is clear that the development of liability insurance meant that the economic context in 1932 was very different from that in 1842. Nevertheless, it is just one part of a complex picture with several strands, which, all taken together, created pressure for a change in the law.

The changes to retail practices and rise of consumer culture also exacerbated the continuing difficulties with respect to married women's contracts. Women's status in society had changed from the 1840s to the 1930s; they could and did seek employment in almost all sectors. Women occupied a central role in the new consumer society of the early twentieth century, yet married women might still face the obstacles of privity, consideration and agency if injured by a consumer product. A legal rule restricting the ability of married women to bring an action for an injury caused by a defective product would have appeared out of step with modern society.

It has been demonstrated that parties were finding a way around the restrictive privity rule. In the cases uncovered in this book, reported principally in regional newspapers, married women, and occasionally children (who faced similar obstacles), were successfully suing suppliers and manufacturers when injured by the use of defective products. It is argued that the most likely explanation for this is that a legal pathway was opened to litigants at the beginning of the twentieth century, based on the law concerning the supply of dangerous articles. Using this, it was possible to assert that a duty might be owed to a third-party consumer, irrespective of contract, and unrestricted by the privity rule.

This argument is advanced principally in relation to English law. Of the cases uncovered, there are few from Scottish courts. Unsuccessful cases are, of course, less likely to be newsworthy, and claims doomed to fail will be unlikely to progress even as far as the preliminary stages. If cases such as these were not succeeding in Scotland, they would not be present in the newspapers. We are thus left with the hypothesis that courts in Scotland might have been less sympathetic to plaintiffs, or more pro-defendant, in a way that English courts were not. However, that must be a question for future consideration.

There was, however, uncertainty in the way the 'supply of dangerous things' mechanism worked. There was a lack of clarity as to when a product might be a thing dangerous *per se* or dangerous because of a defect. The language being used was unstable. There was also inconsistency in the authorities as to the requisite level of knowledge needed – did the defendant have to have actual knowledge of the defect (meaning that the argument was based on misrepresentation as to safety), or was it sufficient that the defendant had failed to take reasonable care to discover the danger? In 1927, an article published in the *Solicitors' Journal* considered the lack of clarity and declared that a 'decision of the Court of Appeal is urgently required on the … subject'.[4]

Despite these uncertainties, it seems that, at least in English law, the 'supply of dangerous things' exception did indeed provide a mechanism whereby courts were able to reach the results perceived to be just, without having to confront the legal obstacle posed by the doctrine of privity. If there was a perception that the rule was outdated and no longer productive of just outcomes, this alternative mechanism allowed courts to resolve this tension using the orthodox law and without altering the formal rules. However, this was an unsatisfactory state of affairs: that the outcome in *Donoghue* could be reached without a formal change to the rules undermined the strength of the rule and added to the pressure for change. The decision in *Mullen* that, in 1929, the privity rule would still prevent an injured consumer's successful claim against a beverage manufacturer was the final piece of the puzzle: a change to the law was required.

With the decision in *Donoghue*, the husk of the old restrictions, by that point weakened by circumvention, fell away. It seems very likely that *Donoghue* was set up to achieve this outcome. The question to be answered by the House of Lords was narrow; Mrs Donoghue did not attempt to argue that her case fell within the 'supply of dangerous things' line. After *Donoghue*, it was no longer necessary for litigants to bring their cases within that exceptional category involving dangerous things; they could bring the claim straightforwardly on the basis that a duty was owed by manufacturers where the consumers had no chance of examining the product. Where there was no chance of casting the exchange as the supply of a dangerous product, this was no longer a barrier to compensation.

The story advanced in this book provides an extraordinary example of the potential for difference between the formal 'law in the books' and the 'law in practice'. The formal law – that is, as stated in treatises and appellate cases – appeared to be settled and stable in the 20 years before *Donoghue*. The law in practice – the outcomes reached in county courts and before single judges of the King's Bench Divisional Court – was more dynamic. The formal law changed *after* the law in practice, as litigants' lawyers pushed the boundaries of the formal rules

[4] 'Our County Court Letter: Manufacturer's Liability for a Defective Article' (1927) 71 *Solicitors' Journal and Weekly Reporter* 941.

and found ways to evade doctrinal obstacles. Perhaps as a result of incomplete law reporting, much of this development seems not to have been addressed by the highest courts.

How are we, then, to understand the significance of *Donoghue*? *Donoghue* remains an important case. Most obviously, the arguments advanced in this book do not detract from the importance of Lord Atkin's neighbourhood principle to the development of the modern tort of negligence and new approaches to the duty of care concept in the 1960s and 1970s. However, we ought now to reject a narrative which paints the outcome in *Donoghue* as a sudden shift brought about by the heroics of a bold majority in the House of Lords – the forces were already at work before *Donoghue*. *Donoghue* was indeed important, though principally, in its immediate aftermath, in restoring coherence and certainty to an area of law made murky through subtle evasion.

BIBLIOGRAPHY

Books and Articles

Abraham, D, 'Liberty and Property: Lord Bramwell and the Political Economy of Liberal Jurisprudence Individualism, Freedom, and Utility (1994) 38 *American Journal of Legal History* 288.

Abraham, KS, 'The Rise and Fall of Commercial Liability Insurance' (2001) 87 *Virginia Law Review* 85.

Adburgham, A, *Shops and Shopping 1800–1914* (Unwin Brothers, 1981).

Addison, CG, *Treatise on the Law of Contracts and Liabilities ex Contractu* (W Benning & Co, 1847).

—— *Wrongs and their Remedies*, 2nd edn (Stevens, Sons, and Haynes, 1864).

—— *Wrongs and their Remedies*, 4th edn (Stevens and Sons, 1873).

—— *Wrongs and their Remedies*, 5th edn (Stevens and Sons, 1879).

—— *A Treatise on the Law of Torts*, 7th edn (Stevens and Sons, 1893).

—— *A Treatise on the Law of* Torts, 8th edn (Stevens and Sons, 1906).

Alexander, S, 'Becoming a woman in London in the 1920s and 1930s' in D Feldman and G Stedman Jones (eds), *Metropolis: London* (Routledge, 1989) 245–71.

Anton, AE, 'Effect of Marriage on Property in Scots Law' (1956) 19 *Modern Law Review* 658.

Anson, WR, *Principles of the English Law of Contract* (Macmillan and Co, 1879).

Ashton-Cross, D, 'Donoghue v Stevenson' (1955) 71 *Law Quarterly Review* 472.

Atiyah, PS, *The Rise and Fall of Freedom of Contract* (Oxford University Press, 1979).

Austin, J, *Lectures on Jurisprudence*, Vol 2 (J Murray, 1863).

Baker, J, *Introduction to English Legal History*, 5th edn (Oxford University Press, 2019).

Baker, JH, 'New Light on *Slade's Case*' (1971) 29 *Cambridge Law Journal* 213.

—— 'Reviews: The Rise and Fall of Freedom of Contract. By P.S. Atiyah' (1980) 43 *Modern Law Review* 467.

Baker Welford, AW *The Law Relating to Accident Insurance*, 2nd edn (Butterworth & Company, 1923).

Barlow, ACH, 'Gifts and other Transfers Inter Vivos and the Matrimonial Home' in RH Graveson and FR Crane, *A Century of Family Law, 1857–1957* (Sweet & Maxwell, 1957) 197–226.

Barton, JL, 'The Enforcement of Hard Bargains' (1987) 103 *Law Quarterly Review* 118.

—— 'Liability for Things in the Nineteenth Century' in JA Guy and HG Beale (eds), *Law and Social Change in British History* (Royal Historical Society, 1984) 145–55.

Bartrip, P, 'The impact of institutions and professions on compensation for occupational injury in England' in P Mitchell (ed), *The Impact of Institutions and Professions on Legal Development* (Cambridge University Press, 2012) 36–58.

Bartrip, PWJ, 'Pedestrians, Motorists, and No-Fault Compensation for Road Accidents in 1930s Britain' (2010) 21 *Journal of Legal History* 45.

Beever, A, *Rediscovering the Law of Negligence* (Hart Publishing, 2007).

Bell, J and Ibbetson, D, *European Level Development: The Case of Tort* (Cambridge University Press, 2012).

Benjamin, JP, *A Treatise on the Law of Sale of Personal Property* (H Sweet, 1868).

Benjamin, JP et al, *A Treatise on the Law of Sale of Personal Property*, 5th edn (Sweet & Maxwell, 1906).

Bentham, J, *Introduction to the Principles of Morals and Legislation* (Clarendon Press, 1879).

Berg, M and Hudson, P, 'Rehabilitating the Industrial Revolution' (1992) 45 *Economic History Review* 24.

Beven, T, *Principles of the Law of Negligence* (Stevens and Haynes, 1889).

——*Negligence in Law*, 2nd edn (Stevens and Haynes, 1895).
——*Negligence in Law*, 3rd edn (Stevens and Haynes, 1908).
——*Negligence in Law*, 4th edn (Sweet & Maxwell, 1928).
Blackman, J, 'The Development of the Retail Grocery Trade in the Nineteenth Century' (1967) 9 *Business History* 110.
Bohlen, F, 'Liability of manufacturers to persons other than their immediate vendees' (1929) 45 *Law Quarterly Review* 343.
Bohlen, FH, 'The Basis of Affirmative Obligations in the Law of Tort' (1905) 53 *American Law Register* 273.
Bowstead, W, *A Digest of the Law of Agency*, 7th edn (Sweet & Maxwell, 1924).
Brenner, JF, 'Nuisance Law and the Industrial Revolution' (1974) 3 *Journal of Legal Studies* 403.
Brown, B, 'Legislation' (1936) 14 *Canadian Bar Review* 265.
Brown, J, 'The Mouse and the Snail: Reappraising the Significance of *Donoghue v Stevenson*: Part One – A Case Worth Celebrating?' (2022) 35 *Scots Law Times* 229
Burns, CB, 'Are we forever to be behind Scotland?' (1978) 12 *Law Teacher* 76.
Bynum, B, 'Discarded diagnoses' (2001) 357 *The Lancet* 1050.
Chamberlain, E, 'Lord Buckmaster: The reluctant villain in *Donoghue v Stevenson*' (2013) 3 *Juridical Review* 245.
Chitty, J, *Practical Treatise on the Law of Contracts, not under Seal* (S Sweet, 1826).
Clark, JP, *The Business of Beauty: Gender and the Body in Modern London* (Bloomsbury Visual Arts, 2020).
Clerk, JF and Lindsell, WHB, *The Law of Torts* (Sweet & Maxwell, 1889).
—— *The Law of Torts*, 6th edn (Sweet & Maxwell, 1912).
Conn, J, 'Gingerlore: The Legends of Donoghue v Stevenson' (2013) 3 *Juridical Review* 265.
Cornish, W, 'Wives: The Quest for Civil Independence' in W Cornish et al (eds), *The Oxford History of the Laws of England, Vol XIII: 1820–1914 Fields of Development* (Oxford University Press, 2010) 757–66.
——'Children' in W Cornish et al (eds), *The Oxford History of the Laws of England, Vol XIII: 1820–1914 Fields of Development* (Oxford University Press, 2010) 802–22.
Cornish, W et al, *Law and Society in England, 1750–1950*, 2nd edn (Hart Publishing, 2019).
Cotterrell, R, *The Sociology of the Law: An Introduction*, 2nd edn (Oxford University Press, 1992).
Davies, M, 'The end of the affair: duty of care and liability insurance' (1989) 9 *Legal Studies* 67.
De Cruz, SP, 'Assumpsit, Consideration and Third Party Rights' (1986) 7 *Journal of Legal History* 53.
Dinsdale, WA, *History of Accident Insurance in Great Britain* (Stone & Cox, 1954).
Epstein, RA, 'For a Bramwell Revival' (1994) 38 *American Journal of Legal History* 246.
Evans, J, 'Precedent in the Nineteenth Century' in L Goldstein (ed), *Precedent in Law* (Clarendon Press, 1987) 35–72.
Finn, M, 'Working-class women and the contest for consumer control in Victorian County Courts' (1998) 161 *Past & Present* 116.
——'Women, Consumption and Coverture' (1996) 39 *The Historical Journal* 703.
Flannigan, R, 'Privity – the End of an Era (Error)' (1987) 103 *Law Quarterly Review* 564.
Fraser, P, *Treatise on Husband and Wife according to the Law of Scotland* (T and T Clark, 1876–78).
Furmston, F and Tolhurst, GJ, *Privity of Contract* (Oxford University Press, 2015).
Garnett, WHS, *Children and the Law* (J Murray, 1911).
Gloag, WM, *The Law of Contract* (W Green & Son, 1914).
Godley, A, 'Foreign Multinationals and Innovation in British Retailing 1850–1962' (2003) 45 *Business History* 80.
Gordley, J, *Philosophical Origins of Modern Contract Doctrine* (Clarendon Press, 1991).
Gurney, P, *The Making of Consumer Culture in Modern Britain* (London, Bloomsbury, 2017).
Heppell, EA, *Products Liability Insurance* (Pitman & Sons Ltd, 1967).
Heuston, RFV, '*Donoghue v Stevenson* in Retrospect' (1957) 20 *Modern Law Review* 1.
——'Judicial Prosopography' (1986) 102 *Law Quarterly Review* 90.

Holcombe, L, *Wives & Property* (Toronto, University of Toronto Press, 1983).
Holmes, OW, 'Trespass and Negligence' (1880) 14 *American Law Review* 1.
—— *The Common Law* (Little, Brown and Company, 1881).
Horwitz, MJ, *The Transformation of American Law, 1780–1860* (Oxford University Press, 1992).
Howells, RL, '*Priestley v Fowler* and the Factory Acts' (1963) 26 *Modern Law Review* 367.
Ibbetson, D, 'The tort of negligence in England' in N Jansen (ed), *The Development and Making of Legal Doctrine* (Cambridge University Press, 2010) 46–72.
Ibbetson, DJ, 'Sixteenth Century Contract Law: *Slade's Case* in Context' (1984) 4 *Oxford Journal of Legal Studies* 295.
—— *A Historical Introduction to the Law of Obligations* (Oxford University Press, 1999).
—— 'Comparative legal history: A methodology' in A Musson and C Stebbings (eds), *Making Legal History* (Cambridge University Press, 2012) 131–45.
—— 'English Law before 1900' in J Hallebeek and H Dondorp (eds), *Contracts For a Third-Party Beneficiary: A Historical and Comparative Account* (Brill, 2008) 93–114.
—— 'George v Skivington (1869)' in C Mitchell and P Mitchell (eds), *Landmark Cases in the Law of Tort* (Hart Publishing, 2010) 69–94.
—— '"The Law of Business Rome": Foundations of the Anglo-American Tort of Negligence' (1999) 52 *Current Legal Problems* 74.
—— 'The Tort of Negligence in the Common Law in the Nineteenth and Twentieth Centuries' in E Schrage (ed), *Negligence: The Comparative Legal History of the Law of Torts* (Duncker & Humblot, 2001) 220–71.
Ibbetson, DJ and Schrage, EJH, 'Ius quaesitum tertio: A Comparative and Historical Introduction to the Concept of Third Party Contracts' in EJH Schrage (ed), *Ius Quaesitum Tertio* (Duncker & Humblot, 2008) 1–34.
Ibbetson, DJ and Swain, W, 'Third Party Beneficiaries in English Law: From *Dutton v Poole* to *Tweddle v Atkinson*' in EJH Schrage (ed), *Ius Quaesitum Tertio* (Duncker & Humblot, 2008) 190–213.
Ipp, DA, 'Policy and the swing of the negligence pendulum' (2003) 77 *Australian Law Journal* 732.
Jackson, RV, 'Rates of industrial growth during the industrial revolution' (1992) 45 *Economic History Review* 1.
Jacob, JIH, *The Reform of Civil Procedural Law* (Sweet & Maxwell, 1982).
James, F, 'Accident Liability Reconsidered: The Impact of Liability Insurance' (1948) 57 *Yale Law Journal* 549.
Kent, S, *Making Peace: The Reconstruction of Gender in Interwar Britain* (Princeton University Press, 1993).
Kostal, RW, *Law and English Railway Capitalism 1825–1875* (Clarendon Press, 1994).
Labatt, CB, 'Negligence in Relation to Privity of Contract' (1900) 16 *Law Quarterly Review* 168.
Lancaster, B, *The Department Store: A Social History* (Leicester University Press, 1998).
Law Revision Committee, *Fourth Interim Report* (Cmd 4770, December 1934).
Leake, SM, *The Elements of the Law of Contracts* (Stevens and Sons, 1867).
Lewis, G, *Lord Atkin* (Butterworths, 1983).
Lewis, J, *Women in England, 1870–1950* (Wheatsheaf Books Ltd, 1984).
Lobban, M, 'Contractual Fraud in Law and Equity c1750–c1850' (1997) 17 *Oxford Journal of Legal Studies* 441.
—— 'Consideration' in WR Cornish et al (eds), *The Oxford History of the Laws of England, Vol XII: 1820–1914 Private Law* (Oxford University Press, 2010) 358–99.
—— 'Contractual Terms and their Performance' in WR Cornish et al (eds), *The Oxford History of the Laws of England, Vol XII: 1820–1914 Private Law* (Oxford University Press, 2010) 473–521.
—— 'The Development of Tort Law' in WR Cornish et al (eds), *The Oxford History of the Laws of England, Vol XII: 1820–1914 Private Law* (Oxford University Press, 2010) 879–902.
—— 'Introduction' in WR Cornish et al (eds), *The Oxford History of the Laws of England, Vol XII: 1820–1914 Private Law* (Oxford University Press, 2010) 297–328.
—— 'The Law of Insurance' in WR Cornish et al (eds), *The Oxford History of the Laws of England, Vol XII: 1820–1914 Private Law* (Oxford University Press, 2010) 674–727.

—— 'Negligence' in WR Cornish et al (eds), *The Oxford History of the Laws of England, Vol XII: 1820–1914 Private Law* (Oxford University Press, 2010) 903–57.
—— 'Nuisance' in WR Cornish et al (eds), *The Oxford History of the Laws of England, Vol XII: 1820–1914 Private Law* (Oxford University Press, 2010) 1068–1111.
—— 'Personal Injuries' in WR Cornish et al (eds), *The Oxford History of the Laws of England, Vol XII: 1820–1914 Private Law* (Oxford University Press, 2010) 958–1000.
—— 'Workplace Injuries' in WR Cornish et al (eds), *The Oxford History of the Laws of England, Vol XII: 1820–1914 Private Law* (Oxford University Press, 2010) 1001–32.
MacGillivray, EJ, *Insurance Law relating to All Risks other than Marine: including Life, Fire, Accident, Guarantee, Burglary, Third Party Risks, and Employers' Liability* (Sweet & Maxwell, 1912).
MacQueen, HL, 'Third Party Rights in Contract: Jus Quaesitum Tertio' in K Reid and R Zimmermann (eds), *A History of Private Law in Scotland: Volume Two: Obligations* (Oxford University Press, 2000) 220–51.
MacQueen, HL and Sellar, WDH, 'Negligence' in K Reid and R Zimmermann (eds), *A History of Private Law in Scotland: Volume Two: Obligations* (Oxford University Press, 2000) 517–47.
—— 'Scots Law: Ius quaesitum tertio, Promise and Irrevocability' in EJH Schrage (ed), *Ius Quaesitum Tertio* (Duncker & Humblot, 2008) 357–83.
MacQueen, HL and Thomson, J, *Contract Law in Scotland*, 4th edn (Bloomsbury, 2016).
Manchester, AH, *Modern Legal History* (Butterworths, 1980).
McBryde, WW, 'Donoghue v Stevenson: The Story of the 'Snail in the Bottle' Case' in AJ Gamble (ed), *Obligations in Context: Essays in Honour of Professor DM Walker* (Edinburgh W Green, 1990) 13–32.
Millner, MA, 'Ius quaesitum tertio: comparison and synthesis' (1967) 16 *International and Comparative Law Quarterly* 446.
Milsom, SFC, *A Natural History of the Common Law* (Columbia University Press, 2003).
—— *Historical Foundations of the Common Law*, 2nd edn (Oxford University Press, 2009)
Ministry of Health Report on Public Health and Medical Subjects (No 27, 1924).
Mitchell, P, 'The development of quality obligations in sale of goods' (2001) 117 *Law Quarterly Review* 645.
—— 'The impact of institutions and professions on fault liability in England' in P Mitchell (ed), *The Impact of Institutions and Professions on Legal Development* (Cambridge University Press, 2012) 14–35.
—— *A History of Tort Law, 1900–1950* (Cambridge University Press, 2015).
Morgan, J, 'Liability for independent contractors in contract and tort: duties to ensure that care is taken' (2015) 74 *Cambridge Law Journal* 109.
Morrell, CF, *Insurance: A Manual of Practical Law* (Adam and Charles Black, 1892).
Murphy, K, 'A Marriage Bar of Convenience? The BBC and Married Women's Work 1923–1939' (2014) 25 *Twentieth Century British History* 533.
O'Brien, PK, 'Introduction: Modern Conceptions of the Industrial Revolution' in P O'Brien and R Quinault (eds), *The Industrial Revolution and British Society* (Cambridge University Press, 1993) 1–26.
Odgers, WB, *Bullen and Leake's Precedents of Pleadings*, 7th edn (Stevens and Sons, 1915).
Oldham, J, 'The Law of Negligence as Reported in *The Times*, 1785–1820' (2018) 36 *Law and History Review* 383.
Oliphant, K, 'Tort Law, Risk, and Technological Innovation in England' (2014) 59 *McGill Law Journal* 819.
Orwell, G, *The Road to Wigan Pier* (Penguin, 2020).
Palmer, VV, 'Why Privity Entered Tort – An Historical Re-Examination of Winterbottom v Wright' (1983) 27 *American Journal of Legal History* 85.
—— 'The History of Privity: The Formative Period (1500–1680)' (1989) 33 *American Journal of Legal History* 3.
—— *The Paths to Privity: A History of Third Party Beneficiary Contracts at English Law* (Austin & Winfield, 1994).
Phillips, J and French, M, 'Adulteration and Food Law, 1899–1939' (1998) 9 *Twentieth Century British History* 350.

Plunkett, J, *The Duty of Care in Negligence* (Hart Publishing, 2018).
Plucknett, TFT, *A Concise History of the Common Law*, 5th edn (Butterworth & Company, 1956).
Polden, P, *A History of the County Court, 1846–1971* (Cambridge University Press, 1999).
—— 'The Judicial Roles of the House of Lords and Privy Council, 1820–1914' in WR Cornish et al (eds), *The Oxford History of the Laws of England, Vol XI: 1820–1914 English Legal System* (Oxford University Press, 2010) 528–68.
Pollock, F, *Principles of Contract at Law and in Equity* (Stevens and Sons, 1876).
—— *The Law of Torts* (London, Stevens and Sons, 1887).
—— *The Law of Torts*, 6th edn (Stevens and Sons, 1901).
—— *The Law of Torts*, 7th edn (Stevens and Sons, 1904).
—— *The Law of Torts*, 8th edn (Stevens and Sons, 1908).
—— *The Law of* Torts, 10th edn (Stevens and Sons, 1916).
—— 'The Snail in the Bottle, And Thereafter' (1933) 49 *Law Quarterly Review* 22.
—— 'August 31, 1893' in M De Wolfe Howe (ed), *Holmes–Pollock Letters: The Correspondence of Mr Justice Holmes and Sir Frederick Pollock 1874–1932, Vol I* (Harvard University Press, 1942).
—— 'February 10, 1880' in M De Wolfe Howe (ed), *Holmes–Pollock Letters: The Correspondence of Mr Justice Holmes and Sir Frederick Pollock 1874–1932, Vol I* (Harvard University Press, 1942).
Porter, JB, *The Laws of Insurance: Fire, Life, Accident and* Guarantee, 6th edn (Gilbert Stone, 1921).
Powell, JJ, *Essay upon the Law of Contracts and Agreements* (1790).
Prichard, MJ, 'Scott v Shepherd (1773) and the Emergence of the Tort of Negligence' in *The Selden Society Lectures, 1952–2001* (Hein, 2003).
Pugsley, D, 'London Tramways (1898)' (1996) 2 *Journal of Legal History* 172.
Randall, AE, *Leake's The Law of Contracts*, 6th edn (Stevens & Sons, 1912).
Rappaport, ED, '"The Halls of Temptation": Gender, Politics, and the Construction of the Department Store in Late Victorian London' (1996) 35 *Journal of British Studies* 58.
—— *Shopping for Pleasure: Women in the Making of London's West End* (Princeton University Press, 2001).
Raynes, HE, *A History of British Insurance*, 2nd edn (Pitman & Sons Ltd, 1964).
Rodger, A, 'Lord Macmillan's speech in Donoghue v Stevenson' (1992) 108 *Law Quarterly Review* 236.
Salmond, JW, *The Law of Torts* (Stevens and Haynes, 1907).
—— *The Law of Torts*, 2nd edn (Stevens and Haynes, 1910).
—— *The Law of* Torts, 4th edn (Stevens and Haynes, 1916).
—— *The Law of Torts*, 7th edn (Sweet & Maxwell, 1928).
Samuels, G, 'Contracts for the Benefit of Third Parties' (1967–68) 8 *University of Western Australia Law Review* 378.
Stallybrass, WTS, 'Dangerous Things and Non-Natural User of Land' (1929) 3 *Cambridge Law Journal* 376.
Scottish Law Commission, *Family Law: Report on Outdated Rules in the Law of Husband and Wife* (Scot Law Com No 76, 1983).
Shanley, ML, *Feminism, Marriage and the Law* (Princeton University Press, 1989).
Shannon, B, 'ReFashioning Men: Fashion, Masculinity, and the Cultivation of the Male Consumer in Britain, 1860–1914' (2004) 46 *Victorian Studies* 597.
Simpson, AH, *A Treatise on the Law and Practice relating to Infants*, 3rd edn (Stevens and Haynes, 1909).
Simpson, AWB, 'The Horwitz Thesis and the History of Contracts' (1979) 46 *University of Chicago Law Review* 533.
—— *Legal Theory and Legal History* (The Hambledon Press, 1987).
—— *Leading Cases on the Common Law* (Oxford University Press, 1996).
Smith, TB, 'Jus Quaesitum Tertio: Remedies of the "Tertius" in Scottish Law' (1956) *Juridical Review* 172.
Stapleton, J, 'Duty of care and economic loss: a wider agenda' (1991) 107 *Law Quarterly Review* 249.
—— *Product Liability* (Butterworths, 1994).
—— 'Tort, Insurance and Ideology' (1995) 58 *Modern Law Review* 820.
—— 'Duty of Care Factors: A Selection from the Judicial Menu' in P Cane and J Stapleton (eds), *The Law of Obligations: Essays in Celebration of John Fleming* (Clarendon Press, 1998) 59–95.

Stein, MA, Guzelian, CP and Guzelian, KM, 'Expert Testimony in Nineteenth Century Malapraxis Actions' (2015) 55 *American Journal of Legal History* 194.
Stetson, DM, *A Woman's Issue: The Politics of Family Law Reform in England* (Greenwood Press, 1982).
Stevenson, J, 'Social Aspects of the Industrial Revolution' in P O'Brien and R Quinault (eds), *The Industrial Revolution and British Society* (Cambridge University Press, 1993) 229–51.
Swain, W, *The Law of Contract 1670–1870* (Cambridge University Press, 2015).
Syverud, KD, 'On the Demand for Liability Insurance' (1994) 72 *Texas Law Review* 1629.
Taylor, AS and Smith, FJ, *The Principles and Practice of Medical Jurisprudence* (J & A Churchill, 1905).
'Third Party Liability: Interesting Examples' *The Policy-Holder: An Insurance Journal* (25 January 1933).
'Third Party Insurance: Development of Third Party Insurance' *The Policy-Holder: An Insurance Journal* (25 August 1937).
Todd, S, *Young Women, Work and Family in England 1918–1950* (Oxford University Press, 2005).
Tosh, J, *A Man's Place: Masculinity and the Middle-Class Home in Victorian England* (Yale University Press, 1999).
Trotter, WF, *The Law of Contract in Scotland* (William Hodge and Company, 1913).
Tucker, RB and Kuhn, JC, 'The Decline of the Privity Rule in Tort Liability' (1950) 11 *University of Pittsburgh Law Review* 236.
Underhill, A, *The Law Reform (Married Women and Tortfeasors) Act 1935* (Butterworth & Company, 1936).
Vincent, S, *Hair: An Illustrated History* (Bloomsbury, 2018).
Weinrib, EJ, *Corrective Justice* (Oxford University Press, 2012).
Wentworth, J, *A Complete System of Pleading* (vol 8, 1799).
Wharton, JJS, *An Exposition of the Laws Relating to the Women of England; Showing their Rights, Remedies, and Responsibilities, in Every Position of Life* (London, 1853).
Whitlock, TC, *Crime, Gender and Consumer Culture in Nineteenth-Century England* (Taylor & Francis, 2005).
Whittaker, S, *The Development of Product Liability* (Cambridge University Press, 2010).
Wildman, C, *Urban Redevelopment and Modernity in Liverpool and Manchester, 1918–1939* (Bloomsbury, 2016).
Williams, GL, 'The Legal Unity of Husband and Wife' (1947) 10 *Modern Law Review* 16.
Winfield, PH, 'The History of Negligence in the Law of Torts' (1926) 42 *Law Quarterly Review* 184.
—— *The Province of the Law of Tort* (Cambridge University Press, 1931).
—— 'Duty in Tortious Negligence' (1934) 34 *Columbia Law Review* 41.
'Women in Industry' (1930) 30 *Monthly Labour Review* 71.

Solicitors' Journal Articles (by volume/publication date)

'The Solicitors' Journal' (1857) 1 *Solicitors' Journal and Reporter* 1.
'Right of Action – Privity – Negligence: George and Wife v Skivington' (1870) 14 *Solicitors' Journal and Reporter* 309.
'Liabilities for negligence not arising out of contractual obligations' (1879) 24 *Solicitors' Journal and Reporter* 101.
'Damage to a third person caused by a defective article' (1882) 26 *Solicitors' Journal and Reporter* 665.
'Privileges of Infancy' (1911) 56 *Solicitors Journal and Weekly Reporter* 81.
'Tortious Breach of Contract' (1913) 57 *Solicitors' Journal and Weekly Reporter* 571.
'Dangerous Things' (1913) 57 Solicitors' Journal and Weekly Reporter 639.
'Hair-Dyes as a Dangerous Chattel' (1922) 66 *Solicitors' Journal and Weekly Reporter* 467.
'Our County Court Letter: Manufacturer's Liability for a Defective Article' (1927) 71 *Solicitors' Journal and Weekly Reporter* 941.
'The Married Woman as Fraudulent Debtor' (1930) 74 *Solicitors' Journal* 427.
'Points in Practice: Q: 2034' (1930) 74 *Solicitors' Journal* 687.

Newspapers and Other Periodicals (by publication date)

'Dreadful Railroad Accident Near Paris: Immense Loss of Life' *The Times* (11 May 1842).
'The Late Railroad Accident Near Paris' *The Times* (12 May 1842).
'Court of Exchequer, Monday, June 6' *The Times* (7 June 1842)
'The Accident on the Versailles Railway' *The Times* (9 December 1842).
'Court of Exchequer, Nov. 15' *The Times* (16 November 1869).
'Insurance Companies' *The Times* (13 September 1898).
'The Poisoning Cases' *Daily Derby Telegraph* (16 September 1902).
'The Ptomaine Poisoning Case' *West Sussex Journal* (30 September 1902).
'Stone in a Bun' *Derby Daily Telegraph* (28 June 1905).
'Law Report, Jan 17' *The Times* (18 January 1908).
'Pork Pie Perils', *The Standard* (4 June 1908).
'Wealdstone Wedding Sequel' *Harrow Gazette* (2 October 1908).
'Wedding guests ill: allegations of ptomaine poisoning' *Shipley Times and Express* (2 October 1908).
'Poison at a wedding' *Weekly Times & Echo* (4 October 1908).
'A wedding breakfast: alleged poisoning' *Harrow Observer* (16 October 1908).
'Litigation after a wedding breakfast' *West Herts and Watford Observer* (17 October 1908).
'Wedding Party Sequel: Action against caterer for alleged poisoning' *Cheltenham Chronicle and Gloucester Graphic* (17 October 1908).
'Insurance Notes' *Daily Telegraph* (2 July 1910).
'Ptomaine Victims' *Nottingham Evening News* (17 August 1910).
'Glass in Mincemeat' *Daily News* (11 July 1911).
'Damages for Meat Poisoning' *Whitby Gazette* (3 November 1911).
'Mr Blacker's Accident: Appeal Case' *Harrow Observer* (9 February 1912).
'Special Articles' *The Times* (2 May 1912).
Advertisement, *The Times* (17 January 1913).
'About a Mouse' *Drogheda Independent* (24 May 1913).
'Injury Through the Bursting of a Bottle' *The Times* (26 June 1913).
'The Co-op Tea: Interesting Denaby Case at the County Court' *South Yorkshire Times* (8 November 1913)
'A Stone in a Bath-Bun' *Newcastle Daily Chronicle* (29 June 1915).
Advertisement *The Times* (22 December 1915).
'Situations Vacant' *Essex Newsman* (8 July 1916).
'Had Mice Been Tasting the Marmalade?' *Aberdeen Weekly Journal* (1 December 1916).
Untitled, *Forward* (9 December 1916).
'The Marmalade Not Guilty' *Daily Record and Mail* (19 May 1917).
'Free Insurance' *Edinburgh Evening News* (28 February 1919).
'Dead Mouse in Lemon Squash' *Edinburgh Evening News* (24 June 1920).
'Dead Mouse in Lemon Squash: Bottled Shock for Thirsty Boy' *The Globe* (24 June 1920).
'Mouse in Bottle of Lemon Squash' *Dundee Evening Telegraph* (24 June 1920).
'Mouse in Bottle of Lemon Squash' *Evening Telegraph* (24 June 1920).
'Mouse in Bottle of Lemon Squash' *Leeds Mercury* (25 June 1920).
'Mouse in a Beer Bottle' *Belfast Telegraph* (6 September 1921).
'Illness that Followed a Restaurant Meal' *Yorkshire Evening Post* (28 October 1921).
'A Bad Dinner' *Nottingham Journal* (29 October 1921).
'A Dinner at Frascati's' *Leeds Mercury* (29 October 1921).
'Kidneys and Bacon to Blame' *Gloucester Citizen* (29 October 1921).
'Law Report, Oct. 28' *The Times* (29 October 1921).
'Rum Omelette and Kidneys' *Daily Herald* (29 October 1921).
'A woman's hair dye' *The Times* (12 January 1922).
'Effects of a Hair Dye: Lady's Painful Experience' *Yorkshire Post* (12 January 1922).

'Hair Turned Green: Effect of a Poisonous Dye' *Daily Mail* (12 January 1922).
'Woman's Hair of Many Hues' *Daily Mirror* (12 January 1922).
'Hair-dye claim' *Chemist and Druggist* (14 January 1922).
'Injury Caused by a Hair Dye: Rivette v. Inecto, Ltd' *The Times* (28 February 1922).
'Hair-dye Injury' *Chemist and Druggist* (4 March 1922).
'Aberdeen Grocers: Ptomaine Poisoning Insurance' *Aberdeen Daily Journal* (5 April 1922).
'Hair Dyes: A Woman's Claim to Damages' *The Times* (29 April 1922).
'Hair Dyes: Woman's Claim against a Barber' *The Times* (2 May 1922).
'Strychnine in Cough Cure' *Pall Mall Gazette* (18 May 1922).
'Old-Fashioned Cold Cure' *Halifax Daily Courier* (18 May 1922).
'Chemist's Sale of Strychnine by Mistake' *The Times* (19 May 1922).
'Chemist Sued' *Chemist and Druggist* (27 May 1922).
'Compulsory Winding-Up of Hair-Dye Company' *The Times* (5 July 1922).
'Eczema from Hair Dye' *The Times* (31 October 1922).
'Cheap Furs Danger: Skin Eruption Caused by Chemicals' *Sunderland Daily Echo* (9 February 1923).
'Fur Poison: Doctor Thinks It Due to Arsenic' *Nottingham Evening Post* (16 March 1923).
'Skin Trouble from Fur' *The Scotsman* (18 July 1923). CORRECT THIS
'Collar Gives Disease: Many Cases of Skin Complaint Set Up by Cheap Furs' *Leeds Mercury* (18 July 1923).
'Hair Dye in a Court Case' *Pall Mall Gazette* (17 October 1923).
'Hair Dye Illness' *Daily Mirror* (18 October 1923).
'Judge and Woman's Glory' *Nottingham Evening Post* (18 October 1923).
'Judge on Grey Hair' *Leeds Mercury* (18 October 1923).
'Judge on Women's Hair: Charm of a Little Grey' *Northern Daily Mail* (18 October 1923).
'The Charm of the Grey Hair' *Westminster Gazette* (18 October 1923).
'Hair-dye Damages' *Chemist and Druggist* (20 October 1923).
'Another Hair-Dye Case' *The Times* (28 March 1924).
'Hair Dye Action: Woman's Claim for Damages' *The Scotsman* (28 March 1924).
'Danger of Hair Dyeing: £300 Damages' *The Times* (29 March 1924).
'Women's Use of Hair Dye' *Westminster Gazette* (29 March 1924).
'Another "Inecto" Hair Dye Case' *The Times* (28 May 1924).
'The "Inecto" Hair Dye Case Result' *The Times* (29 May 1924).
'Injurious Dye in a Fur Collar' *The Scotsman* (8 July 1924).
'Court of Appeal: A Hair Dye Case' *The Times* (26 July 1924).
'Fur Dermatitis' *Western Daily Press* (4 September 1924).
'Skin Disease and Furs: Cheapness and Danger' *The Scotsman* (4 September 1924).
'Appeal Dismissed: Aftermath of Dyed Hair' *The Scotsman* (27 November 1924).
'Court of Appeal: "Inecto" Hair Dye' *The Times* (27 November 1924).
'Insurance that Shields!' *Northern Whig and Belfast Post* (29 November 1924).
'Glass in a Mince Pie' *The Times* (4 December 1924).
'Mince Pie and Glass' *Liverpool Echo* (4 December 1924).
'Mince Pie Law Suit: Was There Glass in It?' *Lancashire Daily Post* (4 December 1924).
'Glass in Mince Pie' *Daily Herald* (5 December 1924).
'Glass in a Mince Pie' *The Times* (5 December 1924).
'Glass in Mince Pie' *Sheffield Daily Telegraph* (5 December 1924).
'Glass in Mince-Pie' *Western Daily Mail* (5 December 1924).
'Company Meetings: Ocean Accident and Guarantee Corporation' *The Times* (29 April 1925).
'Danger of Cheap Dyed Fur' *Evening Telegraph* (14 May 1925).
'Outer House: A Dyed Fur Danger' *The Scotsman* (15 May 1925).
'Risk of Cheap Furs' *The Herald* (22 May 1925).
'Action against Broxburn Draper: Risk of Cheap Furs' *Linlithgowshire Gazette* (22 May 1925).

'Skin Disease from Fur Collar: Leeds Furrier's Views' *Yorkshire Post* (27 June 1925).
'"Too Hasty": Northampton Woman, Firm that Compensated Fail in County Court' *Northampton Mercury* (3 July 1925).
'Women's Chat' *Thanet Advertiser* (24 October 1925).
'Skin Disease From Fur Collar: Woman Artist Awarded Damages' *Nottingham Evening Post* (24 March 1926).
'Engineering Risks: Main Classes of Policies' *The Times* (28 April 1926).
Gask, RC, 'Public Liability' *The Times* (28 April 1926).
'Poisoned by Hair Dye' *Evening Telegraph* (18 May 1926).
'Woman's Hair Dye Ordeal' *Daily Mirror* (18 May 1926)
'Hair Dye Poison' *Leeds Mercury* (19 May 1926).
'The "Inecto" action: £500 damages' *The Times* (19 May 1926).
'Hair Dye that Hurt' *Dundee Advertiser and Courier* (19 May 1926).
'£544 Damages: Woman's Action against Hair Dye Company' *Sheffield Daily Telegraph* (19 May 1926).
'Hair Dye Case: Woman Awarded £544 Damages in Action' *Aberdeen Press and Journal* (20 May 1926).
'Hair-Dye Case' *Chemist and Druggist* (22 May 1926).
'Lady's Injuries from Hair Dye' *Bucks Herald* (22 May 1926).
Untitled, The Cornishman and Cornish Telegraph (26 May 1926).
Advertisement, *Ripley and Heanor News* (4 June 1926).
'Disease caused by a fur collar' *Liverpool Echo* (21 July 1926).
'Dermatitis From Fur: £100 Damages Against a Shopkeeper' *Northern Daily Mail* (22 July 1926).
'Dangerous Fur Dyes: Jury Awards £100 Damages' *The Scotsman* (22 July 1926).
'Skin Rash from Fur' *Liverpool Post and Mercury* (22 July 1926).
'Fur Dermatitis: Important Development in Broxburn Case' *Linlithgowshire Gazette* (24 June 1927).
'My Lady's Hair' *Derby Daily Telegraph* (10 November 1927).
'Danger in Hair Dye', *The Scotsman* (23 June 1928).
'Hairdresser to pay £450 damages' *Dundee Courier and Advertiser* (23 June 1928).
'The Bainbridge Hairdressing and Beauty Salons' *Journal and North Star* (29 November 1928).
Advertising, *Journal and North Star* (29 November 1928).
'Fur Coat Bought at a Sale: Allegations of Skin Disease Infection' *Western Daily Press* (13 February 1929).
'The Bristol Fur Case' *Western Daily Press* (14 February 1929).
'Story of a Fur Coat: Dermatitis Alleged in County Court Case' *Norwood News* (21 June 1929).
'Disease from Furs: Risks Run by Women' *Thanet Advertiser* (8 November 1929).
'Life on £3 a week' *Hull Daily Mail* (24 April 1930).
'Fur Collar: Sheffield Purchaser Awarded £50 Damages' *Yorkshire Post* (16 July 1931).
'Skin disease from fur collar' *Sheffield Daily Independent* (16 July 1931).
'Snail said to be in Ginger-Beer' *Sheffield Independent* (11 December 1931).
'Reflections on Public Liability Insurance' *Post Magazine and Insurance Monitor* (19 August 1939).
'Third Party Insurance' *Post Magazine and Insurance Monitor* (3 February 1940).

Miscellaneous

Donoghue v Stevenson: Resources, Scottish Council of Law Reporting: www.scottishlawreports.org.uk/resources/donoghue-v-stevenson/.
'Donoghue v Stevenson – The Immortal Snail – 90th Anniversary Conference Papers' (The Continuing Legal Education Society of British Columbia, Vancouver, 2022).
British Newspaper Archive, British Library: www.britishnewspaperarchive.co.uk/ *The Times Digital Archive*, 1785–2014, Gale Cengage.

James Edelman, 'Fundamental Errors in Donoghue v Stevenson?', Speech to the Friends of University of Western Australia, London, July 2014: www.supremecourt.wa.gov.au/_files/Fundamental%20Errors%20in%20Donoghue%20v%20Stevenson%20by%20Edelman%20J%20July%202014.pdf.

General Accident Fire & Life Assurance Corporation Ltd, Specimen and completed proposal documents, Aviva Group Archive (Norwich), GA863

MR Taylor, 'Mrs Donoghue's Journey', *Donoghue v Stevenson: Resources*, Scottish Council of Law Reporting: www.scottishlawreports.org.uk/resources/dvs/mrs-donoghue-journey.html.

INDEX

www.ingramcontent.com/pod-product-compliance
Ingram Content Group UK Ltd.
Pitfield, Milton Keynes, MK11 3LW, UK
UKHW020818290926
15470UKWH00003B/1241

9 781509 987641